THE GREAT COMPASSION MANTRA

OF NATURAL WISDOM:

A GUIDE FOR THE PERPLEXED

Described as
INFINITE, WORTHY, PERFECT, COMPLETE,
and UNIMPEDED, being the GROWTH of WISDOM
and LIBERATION from SUFFERING and STRESS

A SVABHAVADIN PSYCHOLOGICAL COMMENTARY

WISDOM IS CLOSE TO THE GRASP OF AN ALERT AND OPEN MIND
WHICH HAS PAINFULLY AND CAUTIOUSLY REACHED INWARD
SEEKING ITSELF AND HAS THEREFORE EARNED A CHANCE
TO LISTEN TO THE NOBLE AND NATURAL TRUTH AVAILABLE

Shanjian Dashi

Website: www.mahabodhisunyata.us

First edition: December 2013

ISBN-13: 978-1493582631

TABLE OF CONTENTS

PART FIVE:
THE FOURTH PHASE OF THE GREAT MANTRA OF COMPASSION

PREFACE

The present text is the first in a series of three volumes comprising the complete commentary on the Great Compassion Mantra (known as *Mahakaruna Dharani* in Sanskrit and *Da Bei Zhou* in Chinese) by Dharma master Shanjian Dashi.

Until now, this precious commentary had survived precariously in a single typewritten copy. We are very glad to see it published at last and thus hopefully salvaged from oblivion. May it be for the benefit of all sentient beings!

In revising the text, we have kept master Shanjian Dashi's use of capital letters for emphasis while making minor adjustments in the language in order to bring it in line with the teachings he gave during the last years of his life. For those who wish to be really precise in chanting the Mantra, the Sanskrit original is offered in the Appendix along with the Chinese characters and their pinyin transcription.

We hope to complete the series shortly by publishing the remaining two volumes of the commentary, entitled respectively *The Path of Benevolence and Wisdom Within the Great Compassion Mantra: A Practical Guide to Liberation and Happiness*, which deals with the forty-two Hand and Eye practices presented in the Mantra, and *The Path of Serenity and Understanding Within the Great Compassion Mantra: A Practical Guide to Love and Equanimity*, which explains the Ten Heart Attributes of the Buddha Nature.

San Lorenzo de El Escorial, Spain
December 2013

PART ONE:

FOCUS ON THE PROBLEM

THE LEGEND

The figure of Sahasrabhuja Lokeshvara presented here represents BENEVOLENT LOVE, COMPASSION, and GLADNESS and, as such, symbolizes the spirit of the GREAT COMPASSION MANTRA of NATURAL WISDOM, which is a powerful Mantra developed by Mahayana Buddhists. This Mantra is said to have the power to liberate all sentient creatures from the HELL of SUFFERING, delivering them from IGNORANCE.

The world has always been filled with the torment of those who suffer and yet cling to that suffering, but there arises occasionally someone who is so gentle and caring that they are moved by all the suffering of Mankind. Sahasrabhuja was one of these, and because of his VIRTUE he did not exist in this living HELL. He saw all the SUFFERING of the WORLD. Moved by this, he selflessly vowed to give up his own salvation until all sentient creatures were free from torment.

Sahasrabhuja opened his mind and heart and went down into this HELL of SUFFERING to help those who were plagued by the DEMONS of DELUSION, the HUNGRY GHOSTS of GREED, and the RAGING BEASTS of HOSTILITY. He walked through this HELL and, listening to the cries of those in torment, to the sounds of the world, he was so stricken with grief that his head shattered into eleven pieces. His spiritual master, Amitabha, on seeing this, out of COMPASSION for Sahasrabhuja and for all those in torment, created a new head out of each of the eleven pieces and set them upon the Bodhisattva's strong shoulders to replace his shattered head. Amitabha placed nine heads in three tiers so that Sahasrabhuja could perceive the past, the present, and the future, and each member of the trio in a different direction so that he could perceive the world of desires, the world of living forms, and the formless world. On top of these he placed a head with a fierce aspect to ward off DEMONS, GHOSTS, and SAVAGE BEASTS and finally, on top of this head, a replica of his own, giving the protection of WISDOM.

With one thousand uniting and holding arms, Sahasrabhuja is said to sustain all the torment of those in the HELL of SUFFERING and to offer assistance to all who wish to deliver themselves. Each of his hands represents a BENEVOLENT ACTION and in the center of each is an eye which represents the available WISDOM of ATTITUDE. Eight hands stretch outward, six holding objects which are symbols of special Hand and Eye practices which can be developed. The two remaining hands are placed together in devotion, symbolizing COMPASSIONATE REFUGE.

The figure, seen often in Northern Asia, is a constant reminder of the availability of the release from SUFFERING through one's own volition, the guidance of wise masters, and the use of the GREAT COMPASSION MANTRA of NATURAL WISDOM.

THE MANTRA

The GREAT COMPASSION MANTRA is a verbal form of *DHARANA*, a SUTRA which uses syllables to transmit a powerful and effective transcendental message, creating a special state of consciousness. The transcendental message and the special state of consciousness set the conditions necessary for major changes in ATTITUDES, INTENTIONS, and ACTIONS. They awaken BENEVOLENT LOVE, COMPASSION, and GLADNESS, engender the LIBERATION of WISDOM, and facilitate the elimination of SUFFERING and STRESS.

The MANTRA and the COMMENTARY provide then the knowledge which leads to personal growth and the firm establishment of WISDOM, and can therefore be used to completely change the focus of one's own life or the lives of others who are open and receptive to what we can call COSMIC CONSCIOUSNESS.

Do not make the mistake of believing that this COSMIC CONSCIOUSNESS is some single POWER which exists within all universes above and beyond the human creature and can somehow be contacted, bringing some divine inspiration or revelation. It is not a consciousness which exists independent of the human mind.

What then is this COSMIC CONSCIOUSNESS? It is, in fact, nothing more complex than an expanded human consciousness which embraces both the world of the senses, which can be perceived, and the infinite world beyond the senses, which cannot be perceived.

Now, this makes it appear as if there are two different worlds in existence, but this is not the case at all. Actually, there is ONE real phenomenon, consisting of timeless and infinite ever-changing universes of energy. This is the known ONTOLOGICAL world. Let it be fully understood that we cannot under any circumstances know this world beyond the senses in any absolute way. We can, however, understand its existence, just as we can know the presence of a stick by its shadow when it is cast upon the ground.

The impression which this ONTOLOGICAL world makes upon our senses is called the PHENOMENOLOGICAL world. The former is REAL, while the latter is pure ILLUSION created by consciousness. Those who possess a COSMIC CONSCIOUSNESS can see the ILLUSION clearly and clearly sense the presence, but not the reality, of the REAL. Now, that makes these fortunate people extremely special, because they are not deceived by the ILLUSIONS of the world. These people are masters who can share their WISDOM.

Many men and women can see that difference INTELLECTUALLY, but that does not mean that they have really touched this COSMIC CONSCIOUSNESS in any way. There must exist an internalization of the TRUTH about ILLUSION and an UNDERSTANDING of the subtlety of the ILLUSIONS created by the mind below the level of conscious intellect, so that it penetrates the human creature and becomes a rare ILLUMINATION.

We have said that the GREAT COMPASSION MANTRA is a verbal form of *DHARANA*. The term *DHARANA* is linked with what Occidental teachers and scholars call "meditation." Actually, it is the fixing of ATTENTION upon either a subjective or objective target. This ATTENTION is ONE-POINTED, that is to say, uninterrupted and completely unmoving, so that there arises an enriched perception in relation to that object instead of a mundane perception or set of thoughts created by CONSCIOUS INTELLECT.

DHARANA is a PREPARATION for union with the object of attention. This final union is called DHYANA or concentration, which is a higher level of consciousness. The GREAT MANTRA is then a verbal form of PREPARATION for union with the object of attention, which is COMPASSION, an experience which accompanies the process of CORRECT INTENTIONS when they arise. These CORRECT INTENTIONS are built from CORRECT ATTITUDES, which are accompanied by GLADNESS, and precede CORRECT ACTIONS, which are accompanied by BENEVOLENT LOVE.

Fig. 1 The Path of Mantra Meditation

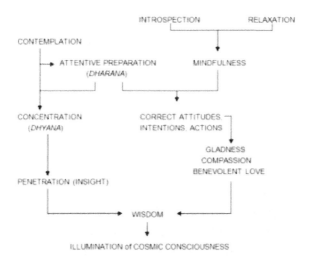

You can see from the diagram that DHARANA is central to the MEDITATIVE PATH. You can also see that while both INTROSPECTION and RELAXATION can lead to MINDFULNESS, it requires the development of DHARANA to lead to the CORRECT ATTITUDES, INTENTIONS, and ACTIONS which release GLADNESS, COMPASSION, and BENEVOLENT LOVE. Note too that both MINDFULNESS and CONTEMPLATION are prerequisites for DHARANA. Neither need be fully developed before you begin, for once you begin DHARANA, the intensity of both your MINDFULNESS and CONTEMPLATION will increase. The three are completely mutually supportive and you will find that once the cycle of progress begins and your confidence increases you will experience MINDFULNESS and CONTEMPLATION in a way which is both gratifying and inspiring.

The first tentative steps towards the FULL release of WISDOM from bondage will require, in addition to the development of CORRECT ATTITUDES, INTENTIONS, and ACTIONS through *DHARANA*, the accompaniment of either CONCENTRATION or PENETRATION. The Mantra then, as *DHARANA*, is also an efficient and important way to achieve unswerving access to CONCENTRATION or PENETRATION. It is of particular utility for those who have difficulty in attaining access to these higher mental states in more conventional ways, or for those whose SUFFERING seems like an insurmountable barrier to liberation.

The Great Compassion Mantra of Natural Wisdom

The GREAT MANTRA of COMPASSION is said to be "of NATURAL WISDOM" because COMPASSION is one of the three important experiences which have their roots in the natural process which is known as the BUDDHA NATURE, the WISE NATURE which exists subconsciously within each sentient creature. It is here, within the BUDDHA NATURE, that three distinct forms of WISDOM reside. They are the WISDOM OF NOBLE JUDGMENT, the WISDOM OF CAUSE AND EFFECT, and the WISDOM OF ILLUMINATION. It is the release of these various forms of WISDOM that forms a cycle of mutual growth with CORRECT ATTITUDES, CORRECT INTENTIONS, and CORRECT ACTIONS.

The experience of COMPASSION, which is the principal theme of the GREAT MANTRA, is of great importance. Be sure that you remember that it is experienced with the development of CORRECT INTENTIONS. Remember also that the two other equally important experiences of GLADNESS and BENEVOLENT LOVE accompany CORRECT ATTITUDES and CORRECT ACTIONS respectively. The cultivation of these three experiences forms a powerful internal liberating force which leads to the nurture of the cycle and the fruitful development and perfection of WISDOM.

Fig. 2 The Cycle of Wisdom

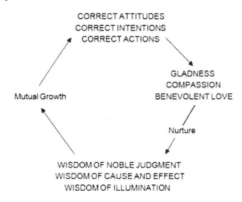

There are few who would reject this WISDOM if it were offered as a gift, but it is surprising how many reject that WISDOM when they have to give up the FOLLY which they cling to every day. Promise WISDOM and no toil and there will be masses waiting to receive. Promise WISDOM without sacrifice and the crowds will multiply. There is a price, however. To receive one you must give up the other, and folly appears to give such enticing rewards that this often becomes too difficult.

One of the problems with FOLLY is that it doesn't allow you to know what WISDOM is all about. For most people it appears only to be something that it would be nice to have. WISDOM is more than that. It is an internal knowledge which tells you exactly how to live in HARMONY with all things without SUFFERING or STRESS. It is an internal knowledge which brings true comfort, true security, and a true sense of belonging. It is an internal knowledge which allows you to lead a correct, happy, and healthy life. It is a knowledge that is accompanied by the liberation of BENEVOLENT LOVE, COMPASSION, and GLADNESS. It is your birthright, which most have sold for a few glittering baubles, believing that they would bring comfort, security, and a true sense of belonging. Instead, those who have embroiled themselves in the tangles of this life have purchased false comfort, false security, and false belonging.

If you are one of these who have sold your birthright, inside you a smothered voice may occasionally cry out for deliverance. You sense, perhaps, that there is something wrong with the life that you are leading. Most of the time you do not listen. You are too busy enjoying the false and very seductive delights of this world.

Listen to this voice which protests within you. The growth of WISDOM will bring the ILLUMINATION which will allow you to enjoy the fruits of real knowledge in a manner which will make all false delights appear insignificant. Listen and be aware that the GREAT COMPASSION MANTRA can be your key to a CORRECT and NATURAL LIFE.

The wonderful thing about this WISDOM is the fact that, although its voice has been blanketed by the "noise" in your memory, in consciousness, and in your subconscious processes, it has not been completely silenced. This "noise" has been set in place by all the FOLLY that you have accepted as TRUTH. No one else is to blame for this. You yourself chose that FOLLY, and every day you continue to build up more and more. Your major task is not to receive WISDOM, but just to begin to cast out this FOLLY so that WISDOM can be heard.

Great seers and masters have described this GREAT MANTRA, which can bring about the natural growth of WISDOM and the liberation of BENEVOLENT LOVE, COMPASSION, and GLADNESS, as INFINITE, WORTHY, PERFECT, COMPLETE, and UNIMPEDED.

They have called it INFINITE because it has no fixed beginning and no end and is said to reach into the UNKNOWN INFINITY of the ten directions.

They have called it WORTHY because it deserves the respect and recognition of all human creatures.

They have called it PERFECT because it is without flaws, and they have called it COMPLETE because nothing is superfluous and nothing need be added to make it effective.

They have called it UNIMPEDED because if care is taken in its recitation and presentation, and if there is correct readiness, then all its objectives will be attained.

To many it would appear rather absurd that a Mantra could achieve so much, and this is understandable considering the fact that Mantras are often used with folly as a panacea for personal social problems or for other selfish reasons by those with little understanding. Used in this way, Mantras are quite ineffective, although they continue to be plied by misguided masters, rather like the spells of wizards of legend. Although quite impotent when mishandled in this manner, their use nonetheless calls legions of believers to the side of these masters.

It is, however, because Mantras can work if they are used correctly that so many ineffective Mantras have been presented by apparently wise men and are clung to by those who want easy answers. This abuse has led to the common belief that Mantras are magical, and this has urged many who refute superstition and have their feet firmly planted in this world to shy away from an important psychological tool which aids growth and development.

The Substance of Mantras

One could, in explanation of effective Mantras, create a cloud of esoteric words and ideas which might be convincing proof of their power. Indeed this has often been done, and the sad result is the further abuse of Mantras and unfortunate misunderstanding of their real great utility and force. It is necessary, therefore, that we should take a correct course and explain, without esoteric flim-flam, the details which will make the use of a Mantra both more productive and understandable, for many Mantras can be effective and really do work if all the correct conditions of their use are met.

A Mantra is a series of sounds or syllables (you may call them words if you wish) used alone or in a simple line or phrase, as *DHARANA*. Each Mantra line has a certain esoteric but not complex significance which is said to be both SECRET and MYSTICAL. It may be said that if a Mantra is chanted or recited correctly, then it will certainly have a positive effect upon both the reciter and the listener. Sometimes a Mantra may be the carrier of a known concept. Sometimes it may be a sound in its own right, without cognitive meaning, with an independent resonance which, when heard, produces a particular desired effect. The variety of effects of any Mantra depend upon the contents of the Mantra, the way it is chanted or spoken, and the preparedness of the reciter or listener who is receptive to the resonance.

We have said that Mantras are considered by many to be SECRET, but the word SECRET suggests that the knowledge of a Mantra is prohibited. This is a complete misconception. A Mantra's sounds or phonemes have a significance which CAN be understood. That significance is not specific and is therefore sometimes DIFFICULT to comprehend. What this non-specific significance does is prevent the sounds from eliciting a variety of SENSATIONS, EMOTIONS, and THOUGHTS from MEMORY, so that they are not perceived in CONSCIOUS INTELLECT. These perceptions are wholly antagonistic to Mantras and their use.

A Mantra consists of a single or series of binary sounds, each without specific significance. To be effective, this series of sounds must not create a fixed significance when those elements are chained together. If a group of phonemes within the group *HĒ LÁ DÁ NÀ DUŌ LÁ YÈ YĒ*, for example, were to become, through repetition, the equivalent of a cognitive phrase or concept embraced by intellect, then nothing would be achieved by using nonsense syllables. We would actually only have constructed a new language, creating a situation which would encourage a clinging to the meaning, instead of allowing the concept to rest unhindered quietly in consciousness.

Each Mantra line is related to a broad concept which has many shades of meaning, and to concepts which can only be really understood by a deeper internalization below the level of normal consciousness. Mantras are designed to be DYNAMIC and the apparent significance of individual sounds and series of sounds is designed to change, depending upon the context in which they are placed. We can say then that a well-conceived Mantra is DYNAMIC, rather than SECRET, evading the allocation of PERMANENT MEANING sought after by CONSCIOUS INTELLECT.

MYSTICAL? This is the other word often used in explanations of Mantras. This word is equally misleading. We might say that the ultimate TRUTH of a Mantra is incomprehensible to conscious intellect, and while this may be true with regard to its esoteric details, it is certainly not true when we look at any Mantra as a WHOLE ACTIVE PROCESS which brings about an apparent result which is physically and psychologically correct and beneficial.

Furthermore, we can see that this claim of MYSTERY is invalid, for we are able to VOLUNTARILY initiate the ACTIVE PROCESS with an apparent OBJECTIVE TARGET and PROCESS in mind. Calling a Mantra mysterious is rather like calling a chair mysterious even though we well know where, when, and how to use it. True, we may not know how to build one or know actually what it is made of, but that hardly makes it mysterious.

What is served by calling a Mantra secret and mystical? It does appear to give it a certain aura of spiritual worth. To do this, however, is to camouflage the wonderful truth. Mantras have immeasurable PRACTICAL VALUE, which allows the user to make contact with his or her own TRUE NATURE, which is submerged below learned ATTITUDES, INTENTIONS, and ACTIONS which are not in the best interest of any sentient being.

That this great value cannot be seen immediately does not demean that value. A Mantra does not require an aura of mystical spiritualism, attracting transcendental seekers like moths to a flame. A Mantra is a magnificent tool in its own right and it does not need to be colored with rainbow hues to make it appear wonderful.

Liberating Mantras from their present association with superstition and magical practice allows them to be understood and used as a practical tool in the everyday world of the senses. This makes them available for the elimination of SUFFERING and STRESS for everyone. It also prevents Mantras from being a sought-after HOLY GRAIL for those who search for things spiritual as a life raft, denying themselves by this attitude a real understanding of their own true nature.

The Mantra: A Nucleus of Energy

We have said that *DHARANA* is a PREPARATION for union with the object of attention and that this final union is called *DHYANA* or concentration. Since the Mantra is a verbal form of *DHARANA*, it will help to understand how a Mantra really works.

We can think of a Mantra as a nucleus of energy. This nucleus of energy is not vague and indefinable, nor is it mysterious. A Mantra is chanted by the human voice and requires a concentration of energy on the part of the chanter when making the specific sounds. It also requires a corresponding concentration of energy on the part of a listener who is attending to those sounds. It is these sounds and their transcendental significance, understood by both the chanter and listener, which become the FOCUS of attention. This focusing of attention, many will realize, is the base for any form of access meditation which is to provide an altered state of consciousness.

You will note that the MANTRIC process can be divided into two parts, the PRODUCTION and the RECEPTION. The energy of Mantra production is transmitted naturally into the environment upon chanting in the form of specific vibrations. Each single Mantra sound or set of Mantra sounds then has its own specific resonance in space.

The correct creation of this resonance is an essential prerequisite for access concentration. You will notice that the Mantra syllables are designed so that the endings are not "hard." One variety of Mantra provides a vibration at the end of the binary syllables, which aids in the focusing of attention if the final letter is held for a moment. Try this with the Mantra "*OM*," which is often used as a focus for relaxation and access meditation, and you will note the vibrant quality.

A second variety ends with a soft vowel sound, which provides an easy and natural flow of sound into the following syllable when there is a whole series. Try this with the series "*HĒ LÁ DÁ NÀ DUŌ LÁ YÈ YĒ*." Notice also that the vowel sounds allow emphasis to be placed upon the consonants so that a pleasant rhythm is produced which aids chanting.

In the second variety, which is used in the GREAT MANTRA of COMPASSION, intonation is important and requires practice, for chanting is plagued by two distinct temptations: first, the temptation to create an even pulse which smooths over binary differences and second, the temptation to modulate the phrasing. One must allow an ebb and flow between these two, which provides a harmony. This delivery of the Mantra is called *hǎicháo*, the ebb and flow of the tide.

The Mantra is designed so that one can create with human speech a specific target for CONCENTRATION. You will remember, however, that each Mantra line may also have a general significance which may be related to both abstract and tangible concepts. Contemplation upon these concepts during the chanting helps to prevent artificiality and over-emphasis on the produced sounds and creates a more correct "ONE-POINTEDNESS" in preparation. This is a very important secondary function of the significance which should not be overlooked, for you will see when you begin that it is very easy to become so entranced with your verbal chanting that internal tension develops. This internal tension is completely antagonistic to the natural tranquility which is required.

The Mantra can be chanted while various percussion instruments (drums, bells, cymbals, and gongs) are used to punctuate phrases, and while they sometimes aid in the chanting, they are not essential. You will probably also have heard of the YANTRA. The YANTRA is the visual equivalent of a Mantra and is used as the nucleus for visual attention. It too functions efficiently if it is used correctly. MANTRAS and YANTRAS complement each other and may be used together after a Mantra has been understood and practiced for some time.

Now that we have discussed the construction of the Mantra target, which is the PRODUCTION, let us consider the ATTENTION directed at that target. If further energy is used to create a second perceptual "ONE-POINTEDNESS" simultaneously focused upon the unique sound or sounds which have been produced, then we have an ideal situation for access concentration. We have a one-pointedness in PRODUCTION and a one-pointedness in RECEPTION. We are all very sensitive to vibrations and to changes of body energy. During the period of this compound concentration, the energy used in the RECEPTION of the MANTRA SOUNDS acts as a carrier of the CONCEPT which is received during the chanting of the Mantra.

Because the Mantra is performed as an act of access concentration, the concept is not fed back to normal consciousness, which will have been suspended. Instead, the concept becomes a powerful stimulus in its own right, which is internalized subliminally instead of being scrutinized and contaminated by conscious intellect in the normal way. What we effectively accomplish with the Mantra chanting is the changing of the CONCEPT, which is contaminated by intellect during PRODUCTION, into a "PURE CONCEPT," which becomes subliminally available to the system and can be lodged in memory in its pure form.

Let's examine for a moment in greater detail the way that this functions. When you chant the MANTRIC SOUND accompanied by the CONCEPT, that concept is adulterated by all sorts of sensations, emotions, and thoughts which are associated with that concept in your memory. This "noise" enters into consciousness and activates all sorts of chains of thought. Normally you listen and attend to all that noise as well as the basic concepts, and this interferes with your normal decision-making and functioning. It also reinforces all the error-filled ATTITUDES and concepts which you hold in memory.

When you concentrate with ONE-POINTEDNESS, the noise falls out of consciousness, leaving only the correct unadulterated concept. Continued one-pointedness then establishes this purified concept in memory. These new subliminal traces thus displace all contaminated ideas and concepts and gradually change the pattern of our daily ATTITUDES, INTENTIONS, and ACTIONS. Look at the diagram and you will perhaps more easily understand the process which is taking place during Mantra chanting.

Fig. 3 Concept Purification by Mantra Chanting

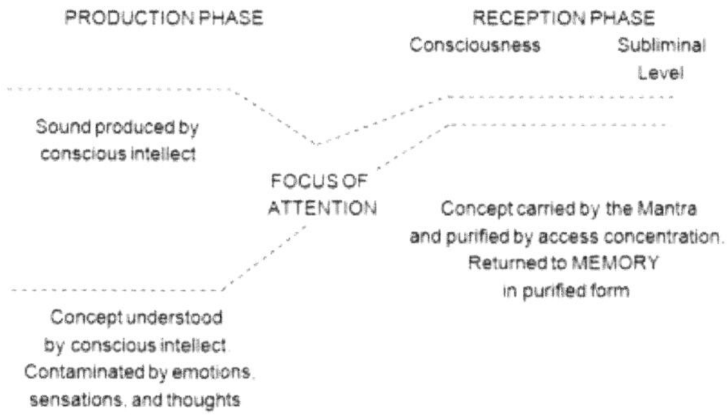

If the chanter, during ACCESS concentration, can pass into the higher state of consciousness, which is pure CONCENTRATION, then all the effects will, of course, be magnified. This is, however, not an essential prerequisite for normal effective Mantra chanting. For this, ACCESS is sufficient.

The Mantra resonance can be received by others in normal transmission or by oneself as feedback. If correctly chanted, it is a powerful tool which narrows the debilitating learned disparity between each person's distorted personality and their true nature, which has the task of monitoring CORRECT ATTITUDES, CORRECT INTENTIONS, and CORRECT ACTIONS.

Because of this powerful effect of the Mantra, some authorities like to call a Mantra a form of concentrated cosmic power. It is preferable, however, to think of a Mantra as a focus for the natural concentration of energy. This energy is not interfered with by the chanted Mantra syllables because they are not imbued with cognitive meaning and are natural sounds more akin to music than language. Since they are not directly connected with conscious intellect, the syllables are unassociated with internal recall and become accepted as a part of the natural system, being completely non-antagonistic. This idea can be made more esoterically palatable for those who prefer such language by saying that a Mantra evokes the common structure of man and the cosmos.

Mantras can, of course, be chanted silently. The concentration of energy is identical, but the vibrations and manner of reception are quite different and much more subtle. The most effective target in silent chanting is, therefore, one's apparent self.

The Mantra, correctly used as a meditative vehicle, therefore requires the same pre-preparation as any other act of access to concentration or penetration, namely a suitable space free from distraction and preferably, if the chanter is inexperienced, a united community of chanters. The more correct the concentration is, the more one can extend access concentration towards a state of higher consciousness which facilitates stronger internalization.

A Mantra consisting of a single syllable can be used to concentrate energy more intensely. The Mantra "*OM,*" with which most people are familiar, summons up energy which certainly creates a resonance which aids concentration meditation, while the Mantra "*HRIM*" is believed to effectively stimulate the BUDDHA NATURE. The Mantra "*KLIM,*" another well-known Mantra, is said to function as a condenser of energy in sensual union. In all cases the user must beware of self-deception, for it is very easy to use a Mantra like a placebo, convincing oneself that the Mantra has had some specific effect when in fact it has not. This is one of the effects of EGO attachment.

The Danger of Ego Attachment

We know that a Mantra can be used to benefit oneself, but it is very clear that if there is any vestige of EGOISM inherent in this action, then the internalization will be drastically reduced or may not occur at all. In most cases, the Mantra recitation will only serve to inflate the EGO and reinforce whatever contamination there is in memory regarding the concept generated. A Mantra cannot be effective if the reciter has conscious EXPECTATIONS of gaining something from the recitation. The Mantra will only be effective if there is an open-minded acceptance that is not SELF-related. In fact, for anyone using a Mantra for the first time, it is essential that the Mantra be other-directed.

The way in which we can eliminate this danger altogether is to forget personal benefit entirely and sincerely direct the Mantra recitation to the sentient world in its totality, to a group, or to an individual. When a Mantra is sincerely recited for the benefit of others, it has an important apparent secondary effect: it actually does benefit the reciter. However, it is no use at all building a mask of pretense. One has to begin to develop SELFLESS CORRECT ATTITUDES and SELFLESS CORRECT INTENTIONS first.

This is not as easy as it might seem, for both must be developed without the contamination from conscious intellect. At first, of course, there will be little to work with except one's conscious intellect. That is all right. It is the place to start, as long as one does not become deceived and believe that the ATTITUDES and INTENTIONS which one elicits in the beginning are actually uncontaminated.

When one is practiced in Mantra recitation, one can indeed direct the Mantra towards one's own development and growth, but it requires complete freedom from IDENTITY attachment. Do not expect too much when you begin. You must have patience. There is no way that you will be able to completely dismiss an EGO which has been developed over a lifetime. All that you can do in the beginning is set it aside for the duration of the Mantra session. With the use of energy, effort, and resolution, EGO will weaken and success will be assured.

When a Mantra is repeated hundreds or thousands of times consecutively, then there is a torrent of vibrations which become extremely powerful. This constant repetition is called *JAPA*. Perhaps you can see how important the repetition is in both the production stage and the reception stage. Certainly, at a subliminal level, the more strongly the concepts are reinforced, the more they will counteract the intense forces of IDENTITY ATTACHMENT which act against every individual's personal growth and destroy the formation of CORRECT ATTITUDES, INTENTIONS, and ACTIONS.

Complete Attention

Now another point must be made. Chanting the Mantra without complete attention upon the target which is the concept, upon the resonance production, and upon the reception of the objective target, which is the resonance produced, will bring few results except fatigue and perhaps a false feeling of having accomplished something. Correct attention requires the setting aside of all other stimuli. Loose unattached thoughts, sensations, and emotions must be allowed to fall away. If you cling to these, you will get nowhere at all. This is not easy, and many people will require the initial assistance of a DHAMMA master, although others can proceed with chanting while practicing constant vigilance.

When we speak of paying ATTENTION, we normally mean that MOST of our sensory system is directed at capturing information about a stimulus at which we are supposed to direct this attention. This is not really paying ATTENTION at all. It is more akin to randomly casting a hook and line with bait attached into a pool, in the hope of catching something. This is clearly an error if you really are a serious fisherman. What the wise fisherman does is, first, select the area into which he wishes to cast his line, and second, select a specific point precisely where he wants his baited hook to land. Then he cleanly and precisely casts his line exactly on that spot using all the concentration he can muster. If he has chosen the correct rod, the correct hook, and the correct bait, then perhaps he will get his fish.

Paying ATTENTION to the target concept, the resonance production, and the reception of the resonance produced requires the same procedure. First, a general UNIVERSAL attention is required. This must be followed by two PARTICULAR phases of ATTENTION, called SELECTION and CONCENTRATION.

This operation is not as easy as it seems, for one's mind appears to slip away, exactly as the fish slips away from the first-time fisherman when he casts his line. In fact, the fishing analogy is right on the mark. Any expert fisherman will tell you exactly what true ATTENTION is, for correct ATTENTION continues long after the bait has settled to the desired level. At that point you must watch the tip of the line and hold your rod, waiting for the first tremor that signals that you have a nibble. You cannot be tense; you must completely relax and let the correct sequence "just happen."

You will know, of course, that we receive all our information about the apparent internal and external worlds through various senses. We call these senses the SENSE DOORS. It is apparent also that we are conscious of the constant presence of these senses and, when we wish, are also conscious of the information which is available through their functioning. We call this consciousness the SENSE DOOR CONSCIOUSNESS. This process of CONSCIOUSNESS detects the presence of the SENSE DOORS (which are the sensors of vision, audition, touch, olfaction, and taste) and the MIND DOOR of perception, and reads all the sensations of these receptors on the screen of CONSCIOUSNESS. When we direct the SENSE DOOR CONSCIOUSNESS in a manner which is efficient, then we say that we are using COMPLETE ATTENTION.

In psychological terms, we can divide CORRECT ATTENTION into three parts, which we have previously discussed. They are called *MANASIKARA, ADHIMOKKA,* and *EKAGGATA.* The relationship of the three phases of SENSE DOOR CONSCIOUSNESS is shown below and it is these which you will hone as you proceed with the Mantra.

Fig. 4 Correct Attention

	SENSE DOOR OPERATION (five sense organs)	
UNIVERSAL	*MANASIKARA* ATTENTION Turning towards objects and yoking higher states	
PARTICULAR	*ADHIMOKKA* SELECTION Electing the particular target	SENSE DOOR CONSCIOUSNESS
PARTICULAR	*EKAGGATA* CONCENTRATION One-pointedness upon the target Alerting and yoking the Mind Door	
	To the process of SENSATION and the SCREEN of CONSCIOUSNESS	

The Target Concept

Two things about the concept are important. First, you must really understand the concept well. Now, exactly what does this mean? It means that it isn't enough to simply understand the words. When we speak, for example, of EQUANIMITY, you must really understand all the implications of that idea. It isn't a word that has only an intellectual definition. It is a concept which has attached to it ATTITUDES, INTENTIONS, and ACTIONS. It is a concept which must be considered and investigated with an open and energetic mind. In other words, what we are saying is that you must carefully examine every concept and not allow that concept to simply flow through consciousness because you think that you understand it.

This means that you cannot hurry. Understand each idea and concept thoroughly before you pass on to another. Go back frequently to check or clarify a point. The whole process which must take place in Mantra chanting is one of learning at a deeper level of consciousness. You do not require academic discipline. You do require a calm alertness without any internal pressure to either get to the actual chanting, or to finish the Mantra altogether. Read for UNDERSTANDING. That is what is required. Perfection is not essential, but taking a correct posture towards understanding the Mantra and the Commentary is.

Second, you must achieve the difficult task of allowing the Mantra during chanting to stand for the concept, without bringing ANY detail of that concept to mind which may permit the mind to flow off into a chain of distracting conscious thoughts. You actually must allow the Mantra syllables to subtly REPRESENT the concept so that it seems to float around the syllables like a cloud, supporting the Mantra syllables without distracting from them.

This is best achieved by being constantly aware of the activity of CONSCIOUS INTELLECT. If you are aware of chains of thought, then you are still too attached to the realm of consciousness. If at an unconscious level all is understood, there is no need for ponderous intellectual thought. If, for example, you understand what EQUANIMITY is, then you have no need to bring any details to mind. You need only lightly touch the concept of EQUANIMITY, perhaps only with a single word, and you will be tuned as a communicative human creature to perceive EQUANIMITY in whatever form it may present itself.

On the other hand, if you do not really understand EQUANIMITY at a subliminal level, conscious intellect will attempt to define it, interpret it, call examples to mind, call out sensations and emotions from memory, and fill consciousness with a stream of thought which will be completely disruptive. That is what we must avoid and that is why you will need to do more than simply repeat the Mantra syllables.

The first and second points therefore meld together. You must internalize and understand the concepts and comprehend so that internally, at a subconscious level, when a concept is lightly touched, then the subliminal network of valid facts that you have learned related to that concept will be primed, but not relayed to your consciousness.

Valid facts will conflict with old invalid concepts and ideas. Don't concern yourself with that, for it is one of the prime functions of the Mantra to put your internal ATTITUDES in order. It really is much more automatic than you can now imagine. You must invest a little faith in your own internal integrity and the natural systems which are there for your internal use and protection.

The key is relaxation. Never force the mind to focus upon anything at all. Allow it to focus gently and naturally. There is a considerable difference between the two ways. You often see students, brows furrowed, poring over their books, trying to force information into resisting minds with hammer-like blows and ponderous thought. This never works. The mind is always perceptive and ready to accept information. It is always curious if you do not close off that natural curiosity out of custom or subliminal anxiety. The mind knows what to do.

Many teachers have declared the MIND to be an enemy. They tell their pupils to "leave their MIND outside the door." This is an error, for neither the MIND nor CONSCIOUS INTELLECT is the enemy. The enemy is the attachment which most people have to the DATA of MIND.

When you see a common old tabby cat hunting a mouse, its eyes piercing, don't believe for one moment that its mind is teeming with activity. Its physical body may be active, but its mind is quiet and alert.

That is the natural state which it is best to develop within human consciousness during most of the waking day. Your consciousness does not have to be a boiling cauldron of mental activity just because you are doing something. All that you have to do is select a correct ambience, turn towards the target with complete relaxation, calmly select what you wish to attend to, and then, with one-pointedness, open your mind while allowing the noise to fall away. It is not easy at first. The secret is to see and observe all that noise and then let it fall away. Don't force the unwelcome sensations, emotions, and thoughts away, just let them go. They are there only because you are, in folly, clinging to them.

Benevolent Love and Gladness

There are three great EXPERIENCES which can be developed by a person on the correct path to personal LIBERATION. They are BENEVOLENT LOVE, GLADNESS, and COMPASSION, and we cannot in this GREAT MANTRA OF COMPASSION isolate either of the first two from COMPASSION, because they all play an integral part in the transmission of the Mantra.

When BENEVOLENT LOVE (traditionally called LOVING KINDNESS) is active as a PROCESS, then you direct your own LOVE and JOY towards someone or a group as pure ENERGY or as a BENEVOLENT ACTION, wishing them to be eternally HAPPY.

When GLADNESS is active as a PROCESS, then you develop your own ATTITUDE of HAPPINESS and JOY, yoking yourself to someone or a group, being GLAD when they are GLAD.

It is important in both these cases that you do not in any way create any SUFFERING within yourself. If you do, there will be an over-awareness of the SELF and we say then that a SELFISH IDENTITY is present.

These two definitions of BENEVOLENT LOVE and GLADNESS are quite specific, so you may intuit that there exists another LOVE which is not BENEVOLENT at all. This is FALSE LOVE. Accompanying the apparent pleasant sensation of this FALSE LOVE, there may be EGO experiences of POSSESSIVENESS, JEALOUSY, DEPENDENCE, FEAR, and a hundred or more other subtle states of SUFFERING.

The surprising thing is that this FALSE LOVE plays an important part in most people's lives. That is because it is a very strong experience and we have been conditioned to the idea that this type of love is important.

Indeed, true BENEVOLENT LOVE is important, but no one has ever bothered to teach us in our lives what real love is all about. That is one of the great things about the GREAT MANTRA. It permits you to experience true love by DIRECT EXPERIENCE and to set aside the INDIRECT ANTAGONIST of BENEVOLENT LOVE, which is actually AFFECTION. The condition of FALSE LOVE is a complex meld of this AFFECTION and other IDENTITY attributes.

If asked about the LOVE which appears to exist between parents and children, between partners, friends, and perhaps between a person and nature, it would be tempting to think of these as different. In fact they are not. All are related to BENEVOLENT LOVE when they are generated and experienced, and when there is the presence of WISDOM.

Moreover, there is not just one apparent IDENTITY which resides within each person's subconscious MIND; there are four. When these four IDENTITIES interfere with the mental states of parental love, partner love, and loving friendship, these forms of love appear extremely different from BENEVOLENT LOVE, because of the different selfish demands and expectations imposed by each of the IDENTITIES. These differences really lie only in the way in which your own mind perceives the demands of these IDENTITIES and the way in which the DEMANDS are interpreted.

You will learn a great deal about the IDENTITIES as you proceed with the commentary, but it is useful now to understand a little about their nature. First of all, there is a VISCERAL IDENTITY which we call ID. This IDENTITY has as its objective the full satiation of its VISCERAL NEEDS, which, as you will see, are corruptions of the NATURAL requirements of the human creature. Next, there is the IDENTITY called EGO. We have all heard a great deal about EGO, for this term is used in everyday conversation to describe a particular IDENTITY state. It stands for SELFISHNESS, actually GREED. The EGO IDENTITY, like ID, seeks satiation; in this case, in order to attain the SECURITY which it requires. The third major IDENTITY is SUPER

EGO. Basically it is a social IDENTITY. It too seeks the satisfaction of its demands, which take the form of DOMINATION and HOSTILITY.

Each of these IDENTITIES influences ATTITUDES, INTENTIONS, and ACTIONS. Fundamentally, however, the IDENTITY which most influences ATTITUDES is the ID IDENTITY, INTENTIONS are most influenced by the EGO IDENTITY, and all our human ACTIONS are influenced by the SUPER EGO. In matters which rule important behavior in each person, one of the IDENTITIES, decided by inherited factors, is actually the GOVERNOR.

Needless to say, with so many different IDENTITIES present, nothing is decided easily and thus ATTITUDES, INTENTIONS, and ACTIONS become a potpourri of errors. To complicate matters, there is a fourth IDENTITY, which is each person's IDEAL IDENTITY's view of how he or she wishes to be seen by others. This IDENTITY also keeps the witches' cauldron of internal bickering bubbling.

Why are all these different IDENTITIES present? We shall see later they are in the human subconscious, having grown from NATURAL roots. However, they are now a corrupting influence which we could well do without. It is part of the task of the Mantra to eliminate these IDENTITIES and the DEMANDS which they control.

Where does that leave the human creature if they are eliminated? Will he be in a limbo without an IDENTITY? No, for he will possess a liberated BUDDHA NATURE, which is a sort of IDENTITY without a SELF. This seems like a paradox, but everything will become clear as you progress.

Because society has a strong influence on the four IDENTITIES, the true potential loving behavior of each person for others has been distorted. In fact, it is so distorted in human creatures that it cannot be considered as genuine LOVE at all.

TRUE LOVE, which is derived from BENEVOLENT LOVE, is a recognition of complete UNION both physically and mentally. That LOVE is transmitted and experienced as a product of that UNION. FALSE LOVE, on the other hand, is created by the mind and it forces a FALSE UNION. The impetus for that FALSE UNION is the SUPER EGO. This FALSE UNION also melds VISCERAL and EGO selfishness with a NATURAL DRIVE to belong or be united with others. The roots of this drive are quite natural, but selfishness has destroyed all the natural components and now selfishness dictates our behavior and creates SUFFERING.

Fig. 5 Genesis of True Love

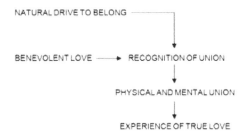

Fig. 6 Genesis of False Love

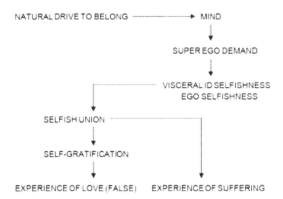

Most who read this will immediately protest and say, "I love my children, I love my friends, I love my partner." Do you really? Examine yourself and your behavior closely. Is your love totally benevolent and selfless? Are you truly in UNION, reserving nothing selfishly for yourself? Do you give this love unconditionally? Is your love that which Jesus Christ, Buddha, and other great masters talk about, or is it different? Clearly, every human creature has this BENEVOLENT LOVE available. Is what you express that BENEVOLENT LOVE or something else?

While it may be accepted easily that human LOVE is distorted mainly by the ACTIVITY of SUPER EGO, it is not as easy to see that most of our GLADNESS is also tainted. We seem to experience GLADNESS often for other people, do we not? It seems free of taints.

When others receive a gift, are we not happy? It appears so, but there is a very subtle form of FALSE GLADNESS which often slips into our minds. It is an infectious vicarious enjoyment which declares, "That's the way I would feel if I received that," "I am pleased that they enjoy the gift I gave," or "I am happy because this is creating a very pleasant and happy environment." There is a very subtle IDENTITY attachment in this false GLADNESS. Philosophically it is called hedonism.

While the hedonist philosophy says that this selfish IDENTITY called ID is ALWAYS present, we say that it is MOST OFTEN present. True GLADNESS exists, the problem is that it can only be released if there is a growth of WISDOM and if there is a mindfulness which detects the presence of INCORRECT ATTITUDES and can sense the contamination of the IDENTITIES.

Compassion and Suffering

Now that we know in a general way what BENEVOLENT LOVE and GLADNESS are, we can examine COMPASSION, which is a central theme of the GREAT COMPASSION MANTRA. So let us place the definition of COMPASSION alongside those of BENEVOLENT LOVE and GLADNESS.

When BENEVOLENT LOVE or LOVING KINDNESS is active as a PROCESS, then you direct your own LOVE and JOY towards someone or a group as pure ENERGY or as a BENEVOLENT ACTION, wishing them to be eternally HAPPY.

When GLADNESS is active as a PROCESS, then you develop your own ATTITUDE of HAPPINESS and JOY, yoking yourself to someone or a group, being prepared to be GLAD when they are GLAD.

When COMPASSION is active as a PROCESS, then you develop your WILL or CORRECT INTENTIONS, wishing someone or a group of persons to be FREE from SUFFERING.

Do you see the apparent natural progression in the sentiments? COMPASSION wishes others not to SUFFER. GLADNESS enjoys their present HAPPINESS. BENEVOLENT LOVE wishes them more HAPPINESS. Each is a completely selfless sentiment and each is completely natural, although most people unfortunately have never ever experienced them.

How can you tell when you are experiencing real BENEVOLENT LOVE, GLADNESS, and COMPASSION? It is not easy, but the PROCESSES of BENEVOLENT LOVE, GLADNESS, and COMPASSION generate an experience of calm WELL-BEING within oneself which is devoid of the illusion of SELF. With patience one can detect that WELL-BEING and can tell the difference between that experience and SELF-SATISFACTION.

The difference is very subtle, so do not allow yourself to be misled. If you can sense that difference and have the volition to return to a natural and correct path, then the use of the GREAT COMPASSION MANTRA will release that WISDOM.

Just as there exist FALSE LOVE and FALSE GLADNESS, there exists FALSE COMPASSION, which is PITY and EMPATHY. Can you see that neither of these are TRUE COMPASSION, which must be SELFLESS? In both pity and empathy the EGO IDENTITY is present. This EGO IDENTITY places itself selfishly at the center of your thoughts. The IDENTITIES are all enemies of BENEVOLENT LOVE, GLADNESS, and COMPASSION and are great destroyers of all your truly natural behavior. Fortunately, the use of the MANTRA of COMPASSION will lead to the destruction of these IDENTITIES.

Fig. 7 Interference of the Identities

BENEVOLENT LOVE	SUPER EGO	FALSE LOVE
GLADNESS	ID	FALSE GLADNESS
COMPASSION	EGO	FALSE COMPASSION

What of the IDEAL IDENTITY? Does it play a part in this drama of selfishness and deception? Yes it does. It is true that the IDEAL IDENTITY is not selfish, but it plays its part in covering up the INCORRECT BEHAVIOR generated by the other IDENTITIES. While ID, EGO, and SUPER EGO create all sorts of psychological havoc beneath the surface and dictate behavior, the IDEAL IDENTITY puts a SOCIAL MASK over the external behavior so that others cannot see what is really going on. This IDEAL IDENTITY, you see, wants everyone to think that things are idyllic and perfect between interacting persons. What a terrible comedy of errors all this is.

Bearing all this in mind, let us proceed with an examination of the concept of COMPASSION. This Mantra is called the GREAT MANTRA of COMPASSION. Do you believe that you know what COMPASSION is? We have said that it is not "feeling sorry for someone," nor is it "having empathy." These are called the INDIRECT ANTAGONISTS of COMPASSION. Even if you have understood this, do you really understand what COMPASSION is?

You cannot understand COMPASSION fully if you do not understand what SUFFERING is. Everyone at some time or other has suffered, so it would appear that SUFFERING would need no definition. Actually, that is not so. Because almost everyone has suffered, and because that SUFFERING is generally intense and often unbearable, people define SUFFERING in terms of the extreme unpleasant experiences which they have. Most people do not understand SUFFERING in depth because they have not allowed themselves the luxury of true introspection, which looks at all the SUFFERING which exists within them. They are much more aware of the STRESS which accompanies SUFFERING.

SUFFERING

1. Common Mental Suffering and Mental Stress

The first form of SUFFERING is evident. We call it COMMON MENTAL SUFFERING. When you are ANXIOUS or WORRY about something, that is MENTAL SUFFERING. When you feel GUILTY, that is MENTAL SUFFERING. Indeed MENTAL SUFFERING has thousands of facets. The sad thing is that this suffering surrounds us every day. It is always avoidable. Its base is IGNORANCE and its presence can be traced to the existence of various MENTAL states of AFFECTION, CLINGING TO COMFORT, CONFUSION, and INERTIA; WANT, CLINGING TO SECURITY, PUZZLEMENT, and AVOIDANCE; and AGITATION, BAFFLEMENT, and AGGRESSION.

Actually, SUFFERING is so common a phenomenon that most of the time people are unaware of its existence unless it is quite extreme. Look at the hundreds of times each day when a slight unpleasant feeling emerges at work or in your everyday life. When you misplace something and become angry, that is SUFFERING. Do you want something that you cannot obtain? That is SUFFERING. Do you feel disappointed when your expectations are not met? That is SUFFERING. This SUFFERING is a direct result of that great enemy of the human creature: UNNATURAL MENTAL STRESS.

You may wonder why we call this STRESS unnatural. Is there, in fact, a NATURAL STRESS? Indeed there is, and this phenomenon arises when anything at all NEW happens to the system. Whenever something unexpected or new occurs, the human system responds in a very sensible way. It immediately tries to deduce or find out if this novel situation is going to be a threat to its true COMFORT, SECURITY, or its BELONGING.

The physiological system has to be ready to respond to any possible threat which may be found to exist, so the body can prepare for ACTION. It must ready itself physically and mentally. All sorts of internal physical changes take place and the mind is prepared by alerting the SENSE DOOR CONSCIOUSNESS. You will remember that this is *MANASIKARA*, turning towards the threat and yoking higher states; *ADHIMOKKA*, selecting the particular threatening problem; and *EKAGGATA*, concentrating upon the threat and alerting and yoking the Mind Door of Perception. This is to find out if the THREAT is real or not.

What the system feels when this is going on is a NATURAL STRESS, which we call "EUSTRESS," and NATURAL MUSCULAR TENSION, a physiological preparedness for ACTION. We call this STRESS and TENSION a NATURAL state of EXCITATION. In other words, there is an EXCITEMENT of the whole system. If the threat is seen to be REAL, then the body automatically takes specific programmed ACTIONS. It is the MIND and the INHERITED PERSONALITY of the person under potential threat which dictate the nature of these responses. The more extreme the THREAT, the more extreme the ACTIONS, and naturally, the more extreme the EXPERIENCES which accompany those ACTIONS. A person walking towards you with a scowl on his face is likely to be received in a different manner than one running towards you foaming at the mouth while brandishing an axe.

If the MIND functions correctly in a NATURAL way, with WISDOM, then both ACTIONS and the STRESS and TENSION will be perfectly

NATURAL and CORRECT, for it is clearly in the best interest of each person to be prepared for any eventuality. If the person is WISE, then CORRECT ATTITUDES will engender CORRECT INTENTIONS. These CORRECT INTENTIONS will, in turn, result in CORRECT ACTIONS. The human system, when it is working correctly, is a marvelous thing to behold.

If the MIND, however, due to faulty ATTITUDES and PERCEPTIONS, does not work correctly, then the INCORRECT ATTITUDES of the MIND will set in place UNNATURAL DEMANDS which are not in the best interest of the human system. It is the URGENCY for satiation of these DEMANDS that sets UNNATURAL STRESS, which we call DISTRESS, in motion. Instead, therefore, of trying to deduce or find out if this novel situation is going to be a threat to its true COMFORT, SECURITY, or its BELONGING, the system goes into a RED ALERT even when no real threat exists. The system then sets up STRESS and TENSION, the preparedness for ACTION, to defend its UNNATURAL DEMANDS.

For example, if you are operating in a healthy manner, and a person whom you have never seen before arrives at a party, there will be an immediate and automatic EXCITATION. Your experience may be of displeasure or pleasure, depending on the threat which may appear to exist. The basic EXCITATION, measured physiologically, would be exactly the same. Experiences of LOVE and HATE, for example, are physiologically identical. It is the MIND which decides which it is to be. They feel different, but they are not.

In the above situation, if your correct perceptions had told you that the person was a threat, then your responses may have been as mild as a casual turning away, watchfulness, or a disdainful look. If, on the other hand, the threat had been correctly seen by perception not to be real, then there may have been an open-hearted welcoming, a gentle smile of approval, or an expressive embrace. If the former had occurred, the experiences would have been perceived as displeasure in one form or another; if the latter, then pleasure in one of its various forms.

The natural system sees correctly, but it is probable, in the example mentioned, that you would have completely misjudged the situation. In fact, your DEMANDS in that party environment, a novel situation, would have created an URGENCY of responses, an UNNATURAL

CONDITION, and the system, based upon DEMANDS for a specific outcome and the EXPECTATIONS about that outcome, would have acted irrationally.

The DEMANDS would also have initiated a specific MENTAL STATE and there would have been UNNATURAL STRESS. It would have been your ATTITUDES which were responsible for setting the TYPE, LEVEL, and PATTERN of behavior to be followed, and if the DEMANDS had dominated, then it would have been DELUSION, GREED, and HOSTILITY which would have determined whether a threat existed or not.

It is clear that there is very seldom a real threat to the human creature, so most of the time, for a healthy human creature, there would be a quiet calmness without any mental agitation. Remember that it is equally inappropriate if there is UNNATURAL STRESS, even if the consequences of finding that there is no threat is apparent pleasure. It follows that if you hold INCORRECT ATTITUDES impregnated with irrelevant past memories of sensations, emotions, and conscious thoughts, then every response may be inappropriate.

Not only then do INCORRECT ATTITUDES result in INCORRECT ACTION, but also in UNNATURAL STRESS. The difference between this UNNATURAL STRESS and NATURAL STRESS lies in the presence of these internal forces, which we called DEMANDS. It is the strength and the prolongation of the DEMAND or DEMANDS, which are alien to natural function, and the resulting EXPECTATIONS which increase the PRESSURE to encounter a solution. This, in turn, elevates the levels of the UNNATURAL STRESS and TENSION.

Fig. 8 The Evolution of a Natural Response

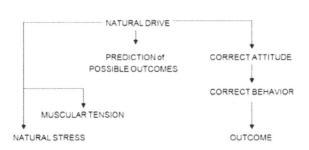

Fig. 9 The Evolution of an Unnatural Demand

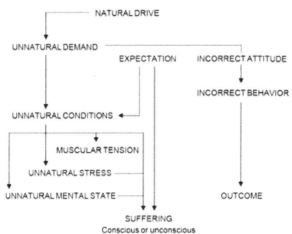

There are three of these UNNATURAL DEMANDS and they are:

1) The DEMAND for VISCERAL SATISFACTION
2) The DEMAND for EGO SATISFACTION
3) The DEMAND for SUPER EGO DOMINATION

You can see from the above diagrams that these DEMANDS and the EXPECTATIONS which arise from them create the UNNATURAL CONDITIONS which result in UNNATURAL STRESS, MUSCULAR TENSION, UNNATURAL MENTAL STATES, and the UNNATURAL EXPERIENCES which we call SUFFERING.

Below the level of consciousness, what the system does in the INCORRECT condition is define and interpret the STATE of the MIND on the basis of the nature of the initiated DEMAND and, grounded on INCORRECT ATTITUDES, form EXPECTATIONS. The MIND-STATE then is caused in part by the UNNATURAL DEMANDS and in part by EXPECTATIONS.

Fig. 10 The Mind State

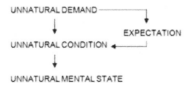

Now, the often debilitating EXPERIENCES of SUFFERING are direct MIND-STATE interpretations of STRESS, based on the nature of the DEMAND and EXPECTATIONS on the one hand, and the relationship between EXPECTATIONS and the real OUTCOME on the other.

Fig. 11 Suffering

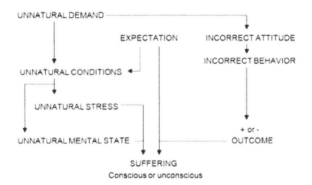

It is interesting that UNNATURAL STRESS and SUFFERING, which is the interpretation of UNNATURAL STRESS, can be experienced together. However, both STRESS and SUFFERING are perceived in error to be the cause of the MENTAL STATES. This error occurs because MENTAL STATES, STRESS, and the resulting SUFFERING, occur so contiguously in time that they cannot be perceptually separated. When the conscious intellect tries to make logical sense out of the situation in the absence of conscious information about the existence of UNNATURAL DEMANDS, it makes a mistake.

This may be confusing if you are not used to looking into intricate details, but read everything very slowly and carefully. It is important to really understand that STRESS and SUFFERING issue from the UNNATURAL DEMANDS of the SYSTEM. If you understand this, then you will see that if the DEMANDS are set aside and are allowed to fall away, there will be a release from UNNATURAL MENTAL STATES, SUFFERING, and all UNNATURAL STRESS.

Now, getting rid of these DEMANDS is not an easy task at all, but fortunately the models draw attention to a very interesting point. Do you see the central role EXPECTATIONS play in the development of SUFFERING? First, they combine, once formed, with the DEMANDS which generated them. This augments the UNNATURAL CONDITIONS which lead to SUFFERING. Second, EXPECTATIONS are contrasted with the OUTCOME, and this directly augments SUFFERING. Eliminate EXPECTATIONS and you considerably reduce SUFFERING. This is a task which is far less complicated than eliminating DEMANDS.

One additional point worthy of note is the fact that a correctly functioning system makes a variety of PREDICTIONS about POSSIBLE OUTCOMES. It has no investment at all in these predictions. The corrupted system of the DEMANDS, on the other hand, creates EXPECTATIONS which have "energy investments" in one or more expected consequences which completely satisfy the DEMAND. Anything less than satisfaction results in additional STRESS and SUFFERING.

THE PHYSIOLOGICAL EXPERIENCE OF STRESS

We have said that both NATURAL and UNNATURAL STRESS occur, and clearly, since STRESS is experienced, there must be a physiological correlate with the initiation of each form. Because NATURAL STRESS is a normal condition of the human creature, it is experienced in a rather satisfying and pleasant way. There will be a general observable innervation of the muscular system in the form of a slight TENSING. This tensing is a preparedness for ACTION in response to the STRESS signal, for if there is indeed a threat to the system, then the rapidity of the response may be a determining factor in survival. There is also a clear observable change in sensory alertness which becomes vital in threatening circumstances.

STRESS occurs in any resisting object when a force is put upon it and that best describes what the process of MENTAL STRESS actually is. In the case of NATURAL STRESS we saw that it was a subtle process to ready the system. UNNATURAL STRESS is much more feral. There is a strong TENSION of the muscles of the abdomen and a tightness in the forehead. There may often be experiences of abdominal cramp and headache if the STRESS is particularly strong. It is what one might expect when a system is overloaded, and that is exactly what occurs.

We very often in casual conversation interchange the words

STRESS and TENSION, but we use the convention here of considering STRESS to be the process in operation and reserve TENSION for an actual muscular tensing. It is these variable stressful conditions, interpreted by the MIND as SUFFERING, which result in a number of specific TENSION sites which can be used to determine the main branch of SUFFERING which is taking place both consciously and unconsciously.

Since it is TENSION, however, which is actually experienced, what we tend to do is try to relieve it. There are various systems which involve a RELAXATION of the muscles using massage, music, aromas, heat, mental relaxation, and many others. They indeed relieve the TENSION, but few of these systems relieve the UNNATURAL STRESS. This can only be accomplished by eliminating the conditions which cause that STRESS. There is no rapid antidote. The cause can be found in the nature of the UNNATURAL DEMANDS put upon the system and the ATTITUDES which appear to control behavior.

THE EVOLUTION OF PANIC, FEAR, AND RAGE

We have already seen that when the MIND receives messages of UNNATURAL STRESS and senses the existence of a certain DEMAND or simultaneous DEMANDS, then it tries to make sense out of the situation. It consequently establishes specific MENTAL STATES which are the grounds for interpretations. As a result of these interpretations, specific ATTITUDES give way to INTENTIONS and ACTIONS which are appropriate for the MIND-STATE.

These modern states can be placed in three groups, based upon their prehistoric conditions and roots. The first condition was the PRIMITIVE mind-state of INERTIA. This emerged from the primitive root response of FREEZING in order to be undetected by an aggressor. The second was the PRIMITIVE mind-state of EVASION. This EVASION also had its primitive counterpart, which was the root response of FLEEING from danger. The third, the PRIMITIVE mind-state of AGGRESSION, grew out of the PRIMITIVE reflexive root response of FIGHTING for survival. Each of these reflexive ACTIONS was an effective and natural response to the dire threats which faced primitive creatures.

Fig. 12 Prehistoric Evolution

PRIMITIVE ROOTS	FREEZING	FLEEING	FIGHTING
PRIMITIVE EXPERIENCES	PANIC	FEAR	RAGE
PRIMITIVE STATE	INERTIA MOVEMENT	AVERSION ATTRACTION	AGGRESSION ACCEPTANCE
EVOLVED MENTAL STATES	ID-RELATED	EGO-RELATED	SUPER EGO-RELATED

The evolved MENTAL STATES which reign over us today seem quite different from those primitive responses which existed when the brain of man and his knowledge were quite undeveloped. As the human being gradually developed as a sophisticated creature, both his responses and his PRIMITIVE MIND-STATES developed. He became aware of the existence of alternatives and evolved opposing MIND-STATES. The PRIMITIVE MIND-STATE of EVASION or AVOIDANCE was opposed by ATTRACTION, while INERTIA was opposed by MOVEMENT, and AGGRESSION by ACCEPTANCE.

The EXPERIENCES which accompanied the response roots to violent threats in prehistoric times, namely PANIC, FEAR, and RAGE, when felt in all their intensity, were probably as equally memorable and as decidedly offensive as they are when they are experienced today whenever there is a real threat to existence. Fortunately, we do not actually endure them frequently in our lives because we are seldom faced with threats of great magnitude which jeopardize our existence.

They can be experienced, however, under less extreme conditions of UNNATURAL STRESS when there appears to be some CONFLICT between the EXTREME PRESSURE to obtain satiation of a DEMAND and the perceived apparent IMPOSSIBILITY of satiation. This occurs because the human creature is never released from his DEMANDS, and so prolonged CONFLICT causes a virtually explosive tension which is diverted into an extreme, more primitive response to the situation.

The responses are psychologically almost identical in concept, but are most generally experienced in a modified form as PANIC of NON-SATISFACTION, FEAR in the face of FAILURE, and RAGE in the face of POWERLESSNESS. These modern experiences of SUFFERING are attached to UNNATURAL STRESS, however, not to NATURAL STRESS, as they were primitively.

Each of these original and primitive experiences, PANIC, FEAR, and RAGE, have also left indelible imprints which reflect their character on the less intense EXPERIENCES of SUFFERING which today accompany the evolved MENTAL STATES. The actual nature of the experiences depends upon the various evolved MENTAL STATES which now exist and the nature of both the EXPECTATIONS and OUTCOMES with respect to the DEMANDS. Because of the high number of possible combinations, interpretations of the UNNATURAL STRESS in the form of SUFFERING are quite varied. Experiences also can be divided into three groups, each having evolved from its single corresponding primitive experience.

SUFFERING and the responses which are thought will bring satiation of the DEMAND have as their apparent root cause the three DEMANDS which have been discussed. Each of these three DEMANDS can appear at different times or can simultaneously occur, causing all sorts of very complex INTERACTIONS, subconscious CONFLICTS, SUFFERING, and STRESS.

Visceral Satisfaction

The first face of SUFFERING and UNNATURAL STRESS is that which always accompanies the DEMAND for VISCERAL SATISFACTION. Whenever this VISCERAL DEMAND is present there arises an INITIAL STATE of DOUBT about possible outcomes and UNCERTAINTY about the best way to realize objectives. This DEMAND shows itself in the continually changing ATTITUDES of the afflicted person and in BEHAVIOR which appears inconsistent. Actually, there is no real change of ATTITUDE, there is a great CONFUSION about what may occur if a strong stance is taken on an issue. The personal OUTCOME is always the most important factor in decision-making. Naturally, therefore, since most OUTCOMES are unclear, the person becomes quite INDECISIVE.

You will have experienced this DEMAND quite often and it is certainly a nagging and unpleasant sensation. This system-corrupting DEMAND has as its BASIC DRIVE the NATURAL NEED to seek

COMFORT, which was, in man's primitive past, a perfectly natural need for body warmth and food.

Actually, in this life, for most people of the Western world, this drive need seldom be activated but in its adulterated state its activation is frequent as a DEMAND, resulting in all sorts of CARES and an ANXIETY which constantly nags within consciousness and appears sometimes almost impossible to eliminate. Although these cares and anxieties feel very cognitive, because they start a whole chain of cognitive thought in motion, if you are open and sensitive to your own body signals, you will detect VISCERAL TENSION in your lower abdomen. In fact, this is one way of knowing that there is a VISCERAL DEMAND present in your subconscious.

Fig. 13 The Visceral Demand: Longing, Cares, and Anxiety

How is this DEMAND which promotes such DELUSION and CONFUSION awakened in the newborn child? It almost always arises from the false understanding about COMFORT it first encounters. From the moment in the mother's womb when it becomes sensitive to its own internal environment, it is completely COMFORTABLE. Its body is warm, oxygenated, and fed. Then suddenly it is thrust into the world. It is hung upside-down and slapped. A rude awakening. Its life support system is changed.

What it really needs at this time is a natural transition. This it does not receive. Were it simply a two-hour sequence which interrupted a continuing natural flow, equilibrium could easily be restored. Normally, however, it is left alone, abandoned as soon as the mother regains her strength. All too often in modern society this is very rapid. The natural and correct behavior following the recovery of the mother would be for the child to closely accompany the mother, being allowed to cling to her while she went about her tasks. It should be allowed to discover itself, find its own equilibrium, discover its own fount of nourishment, with gentle guidance.

Instead, a complex social molding process begins. Everything is thrust or forced upon it. All decisions, if you can call them that at this stage, are made for it. If you watch any so-called "wild" animals, you will see that the new creature has great autonomy and is guided by little nudges here and there. The mother is never distant, always vigilant, always correctly protective, and always providing an environment which allows the animal a large range of responses.

Perhaps the best training any mother could have would be to live in the jungle with a group of spider monkeys. What they would see is that there is a CONTINUAL contact psychologically between the mother and infant, which is allowed to be ruptured only by the natural development of the infant's autonomy. It is as if there is a constant mental link between mother and child. This seldom occurs between the human mother and child. There is, of course, a natural "mother love," albeit completely distorted by social norms, but the human mother too often abandons her child mentally in search of her own COMFORT, SECURITY, and her wish to BELONG to something, with somebody. Thus this debility, this DEMAND, is awakened and strengthened generation after generation.

The human child is forced to develop in the way in which the parents decide. It becomes a victim of their impatience and lack of understanding. It is, paradoxically, either abandoned or over-comforted at the whim of its guardians. When it cries, according to its "owners," it is "time for changing, time for feeding, or time for burping." Hardly ever in the early stages does it have the opportunity to choose anything. Food is thrust upon it. It is pawed and cooed over.

Parents simply do not understand that the child is born with only a rudimentary sense apparatus. It has to learn things like hand-eye coordination, limb movement in space, centricity, and a thousand and one other fundamental aptitudes. Is it any wonder that the child is confused and develops a NEED for COMFORT, at least to some degree? Most children fortunately do not have a strong disposition to be confused, but if genetically such a disposition exists, you can be sure that that particular child will become a completely CONFUSED and DELUDED adult.

Two concepts are fixed together as if they were opposites in the early life of a child: they are CRITICISM and TRUE AFFECTION. Positive CRITICISM is a part of the learning process, and the child has to learn from these constant nudges. When CRITICISM is given, however, parents withdraw AFFECTION at the same time. This is because they are victims of their own IDENTITY. Their CRITICISM is generally not directed at the child's welfare, but at their own COMFORT or their own DESIRES and WANTS.

The result is that CRITICISM, for the child, means that receiving LOVE is dependent upon CORRECTNESS, or at least being perceived to be CORRECT. Can you see this problem? The child then not only begins to resent CRITICISM, it feels that it is not LOVED. It then is placed in a paradoxical position. It wants GUIDANCE, but it does not want CRITICISM. It wants LOVE, but not from a parent that doesn't LOVE it. The result is CONFUSION, and more CONFUSION. It seeks solutions both CONSCIOUSLY and at a SUBCONSCIOUS level. It starts all sorts of strategies of deception which actually aggravate the relationship. It begins to deceive and lie. It learns strategies to get the COMFORT that it wants. It's a sad, sad situation. Parents respond just to keep an external equilibrium. "Give the blasted kid something to shut it up," that is one battle cry. The other is, "Ignore it, shout at it, or slap its backside." It clearly is totally inappropriate behavior, but that is exactly what occurs much too often.

What all children then apparently learn is that this world is not COMFORTABLE, and that SUSTENANCE is not readily available. The DEMAND is then awakened. It demands COMFORT. It demands AFFECTION. That is why the subconscious MENTAL STATE related to the non-satiation of the adulterated BASIC DRIVE is called AFFECTION.

Now, it may come as a surprise that AFFECTION, which everyone thinks of as a beautiful sensation, is associated with SUFFERING. This simple and apparently loving sensation is a mental state with a thousand traps.

It can erupt into a debilitating clinging to the object of AFFECTION. We sometimes mentally exaggerate it if it is a strong physical attraction for someone, calling it LOVE. This AFFECTION, however, is very deceptive and debilitating. Victims, as adults, invariably feel "IN LOVE" or "ATTACHMENT," for this is what consciousness tells them.

What hides below consciousness is not the need to give a love which is unconditional, but to receive AFFECTION. This state of AFFECTION is ID-controlled, but it is aided and abetted by supporting EGO forces which enhance the strength and modify the nature of the combined EXPERIENCE. Any AFFECTION which is offered is invariably given on the condition that AFFECTION is received. Beware of this AFFECTION, for it is not truly LOVE. It is an adulterated need for COMFORT.

There is a TRUE AFFECTION available which can be directed towards all things, but it bears no relation to the AFFECTION which you normally feel. The real experience is called LOVING KINDNESS or BENEVOLENT LOVE. It is unrelated to any of the DEMANDS. It arises from the BUDDHA NATURE.

If you use the COMPASSION MANTRA with diligence, then you will learn to release yourself from the bonds which prevent expression of this BENEVOLENT LOVE. This will show the state of AFFECTION that arises from the DEMAND for VISCERAL SATISFACTION to be completely inferior.

Our VISCERAL DEMANDS can also create AFFECTION for an inanimate object, but do not mistake this for the DESIRE which is experienced under the force of the DEMAND for EGO SATISFACTION. Remember that AFFECTION is a CRAVING for COMFORT, not for SECURITY. You can have AFFECT for something as simple as a dish of ice-cream or a comfortable bed. It can even be abstract, like a CRAVING to be loved and physically comforted. In most cases, if you are sensitive, the demand appears viscerally strong, especially when it is prohibited or difficult to secure. As a result of AFFECTION and VISCERAL CRAVING, there is a CLINGING to any object or condition which eventually satisfies this CRAVING.

The experience of suffering related to this AFFECTION, VISCERAL CRAVING and CLINGING, is a painful LONGING which appears incessantly in consciousness, for the object or condition CRAVED is seldom always present. Indeed, the object of AFFECTION seems so marvelous in its absence that the LONGING is accepted as part of this perverse condition, and all positive qualities are enhanced. Examine your own experiences and you will no doubt recognize this situation.

The presence of this VISCERAL DEMAND after a prolonged period of non-satisfaction brings even more suffering. The MENTAL STATE will change to CONFUSION and there will be strong sensations of DISCONTENTMENT and IRRITATION, the result of the confused state in which the person doesn't know what to do to resolve the problem.

If there is constant and intense DISCONTENTMENT and IRRITATION and no relief is foreseen, then the mind defends itself against the extreme SUFFERING and STRESS by reverting to the primary state, INERTIA, a stubborn indifference towards the original demanded object which it was believed would bring COMFORT.

Fig. 14 The Visceral Demand: Panic, Discontentment, and Irritation

When a strong VISCERAL demand is thwarted again and again, then the person under the thrust of ID SATISFACTION will sulk and retreat into himself to mull over the situation, silent, moody, disturbed. This is a return to the PRIMARY state of PANIC. This PANIC, mild though it sometimes seems, arises from the fear of consequences due to a loss of COMFORT. Its roots are based in the primitive FREEZING and TERROR experienced in the face of real danger.

This first face of SUFFERING shows:

 Cares and Anxiety

 Longing

 Discontentment

 Irritation

 Panic

Each of these is directly related to the MENTAL STATES of:

 Doubt and Uncertainty

 Affection

 Craving for Comfort

 Confusion

 Inertia

Naturally, both the conscious and unconscious undefined STRESS and TENSION which accompany these are greater as the conditions become more extreme or the longer the expected solution is in arriving.

Take the time to sit down quietly and examine this SUFFERING closely; don't let their apparent weightiness confound you. You don't need to remember them, but note the frequency with which each, at least consciously, appears in your life. It is useful to see and know the part that this visceral demand plays in directing your day-to-day behavior. Remember that you are never advised to resist the flow of this SUFFERING when it occurs. It is instead best to be MINDFUL and note the arousal of the first small wave of the SUFFERING.

Name each wave only as SENSATION, EMOTION, or THOUGHT, without allowing conscious thought to grasp hold of the experiences. You will thereby avoid the stimulation of the networks of folly which exist in memory, waiting for the correct moment to burst into consciousness.

Since CARES and ANXIETIES are very common experiences, the Mantra deals specifically with these unwelcome SENSATIONS and accompanying STRESS in a special Mantra line. In a separate line it collectively deals with all the more serious debilitating SUFFERING and STRESS which arise from other SENSATIONS generated by the DEMANDS for VISCERAL SATISFACTION.

You can see then that for effectivity, the Mantra is directed at changing the basic ATTITUDES and INTENTIONS which promote UNNATURAL CONDITIONS, so that FOLLY-FILLED EXPECTATIONS cannot arise. Subsequent CORRECT ACTIONS will assure that only NATURAL TENSION will be experienced. If the Mantra is correctly used, with proper preparation, then SUFFERING, STRESS, and the disturbing MENTAL STATES of the VISCERAL DEMANDS can be set aside. Eventually, with constant repetition and practice, the DEMANDS themselves will fall away into dormancy, allowing the nurture of NATURAL SENSITIVITY. (see figure 15)

Remember that the words used here only represent SENSATIONS. Do not fall into the trap of playing word games with yourself, trying to decide whether what you actually feel is a SENSATION or not. The main information that signals the presence of the SENSATIONS is an

Fig. 15 The Pattern of Suffering Connected with Prolonged Non-satiation of the Demand for Visceral Satisfaction

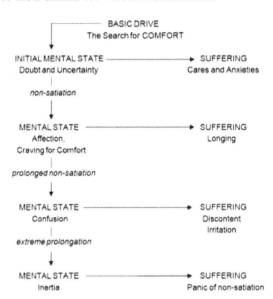

accompanying VISCERAL EXPERIENCE. It is not always easy to detect, but if you are mindful you will observe the VISCERAL SIGNALS.

The MENTAL STATES connected with DEMANDS for VISCERAL SATISFACTION, or those other DEMANDS which have been described, are not experienced as SENSATIONS. The terms simply attempt to describe the state of the MENTAL COMPLEX. With diligence, these too can be recognized, and this knowledge will help in both MANTRA recitation and preparation.

EGO SATISFACTION

Here we look in greater detail at the second face of SUFFERING, caused by the DEMAND for EGO SATISFACTION, and can begin to understand it better. The SUFFERING and STRESS connected with EGO SATISFACTION envelop you in Anguish, Desire, Disappointment, Regrets and Recriminations, Futility, Annoyance, Anger, and sometimes Fear. You can thus see that this DEMAND for EGO SATISFACTION is not simple in its manifestation, and there are further variations and fine nuances of these which exist.

The DEMAND for EGO SATISFACTION shows itself in ACQUISITIVE ATTITUDES as well as ACQUISITIVE BEHAVIOR. The subconscious objective is to build a firm base of SECURITY. This base substitutes possessions for the NATURAL NEED for a SECURE SHELTER against natural enemies and the elements. It then governs the mind and establishes a situation of INSECURITY and STRESS. The EGO IDENTITY is never satisfied and there are constant bouts of ANGUISH over the possible loss of possessions which provide an apparent security. REGRETS and RECRIMINATIONS begin to accumulate.

There abides, midst all this ANGUISH which manifests itself in many ways, an INITIAL MENTAL STATE of DISBELIEF and MISTRUST in others, which is well covered-up in social conditions. Watch for it carefully and you will see it clearly in most of your social interactions. Do you really believe and trust in people? Probably not very much.

There are many other INITIAL MENTAL STATES. Do you have a certain CONCEIT in your appearance? If the unsatiated DEMAND for EGO SATISFACTION is present, it will certainly show itself when you are in front of a mirror, or when you buy or choose things to wear. There can also arise a fierce JEALOUSY, which is usually kept hidden, and therefore a corresponding defensive POSSESSIVENESS which explodes occasionally.

There is also a constant urge to have better and more attractive things, a better car, a better house, a better lifestyle, a better job, and a better future. This ANGUISH engenders a CRAVING, and both vary in intensity and can often be hidden quite well from consciousness. Behavior gives the clues which signal the presence of this demand. The EGO here places itself at the center of all things and wants everything which is available. It is insatiable. If you wish, you can politely call the EGO-initiated behavior EGOISM or INSECURITY, but really it is the GREED which has grown from INSECURITY. (see figure 16)

Where does this INSECURITY which promotes such GREED come from? It almost always arises from the false understanding about LOVE which we first learn about. Most people are loved by their parents, are they not? Are they really? Most people would be shocked to find that the apparent great parental LOVE which they feel for their children is tainted. It is true that the basic instinct to love and care for one's children is strong within most parents, but it has been unfortunately so tainted by social conditioning that parents often do more harm than good, despite their good INTENTIONS. Is unconditional BENEVOLENT LOVE given by parents? Does the expression of LOVE often become dependent upon behavior?

Fig. 16 The Ego Demand: Desire, Anguish, Regrets and Recriminations

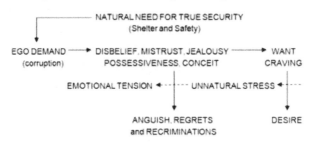

Most children quickly become possessions, shown off to others with apparent tender LOVE. They really are OBJECTS of false love and attention. The child becomes "My baby," not itself. It becomes molded by the image of the parents, society, the church, and friends. It becomes quickly and easily molded by the COVETOUS concepts which rule the world. It ceases to be itself, and this happens from the moment of its birth. It is given a name and the child becomes that name. A mantle is thrust upon it and it is forced by conditioning to take a certain role. If it rebels, it is tamed. The growth of WISDOM is smothered and instead the child is EDUCATED to fit into society, a consumer society. Where is its SECURITY?

It is perhaps given SPIRITUAL guidance, which is in a form that inhibits WISDOM but makes a healthy social balance for the ills of SOCIETY. Where is its SECURITY? It is taught that money controls the world and it sees that wealthy people appear happy. Spiritually it is informed that money cannot buy happiness. It sees powerful men and women of commerce and politics surrounded by beautiful things, being admired and respected by everyone. It is told that it must learn and be successful, but it discovers that success cannot bring love. Spiritual advice is available, but it always seems to be sought after FAILURE and SUFFERING, in order to provide consolation. Where is its SECURITY?

REAL SECURITY, if the child is not one of the millions of the world who are truly homeless, lies in knowing that it really is secure in this modern civilized life. This SECURITY, however, depends upon the development of WISDOM. Lacking this growth of WISDOM, both parents and children have become victims of this INSECURITY and the resulting GREED. It is as the Bible says, "the children will suffer the sins of the fathers." Indeed, for thousands of years, generation after generation has nurtured INSECURITY and GREED.

If there is non-satiation of your DEMANDS for EGO inflation, then a subliminal MENTAL STATE of WANT will evolve to accompany the CRAVING. Both show themselves in all-consuming SUFFERING and DESIRE.

The DEMANDS of the EGO IDENTITY are very complicated and bound up with a maze of thoughts and justifications. DESIRE, therefore, is seldom perceived in oneself. Socially this DESIRE, which results in the concept of ownership, is rewarded and is called "ambition," "getting on in the world," "being successful," and the like. It is really basic GREEDY DESIRE, nothing more. The saddest thing about this EGO DESIRE is that it separates each person from the beauty of UNITY with all things, and paradoxically it is this UNITY, and the WISDOM which accompanies it, which can create a real and abiding state of SECURITY.

The EGO DEMANDS continually create a CRAVING, just as the VISCERAL DEMANDS do, but this CRAVING is accompanied by a mass of words which sustain and amplify the state. It is these words and the creative language enabled by these words that camouflage GREED so well. "What is wrong with wanting a better house, a better car, or a better job?" the wordy and glib voice of EGO will ask. The answer is that there is nothing wrong with having these things. The problem is in WANTING these things, in CRAVING these things, and in eventually CLINGING to these things.

In the Christian Bible it is written that it is as difficult for a rich man to enter the Kingdom of Heaven as it is for a camel to pass through "the eye of a needle," which was the name given to an extremely narrow city gate in Jerusalem. This sage observation refers to the problem facing those who suffer under the pressing DEMANDS of EGO SATISFACTION. Possession of anything creates a CLINGING for that thing. The more you have, the more you cling to that SECURITY.

Any threat to that SECURITY of possession causes SUFFERING. What possessions would you give up, for example, to attain true WISDOM? Would you give up your car, your house, your job, your friends? What exactly is the price you are prepared to pay in order to gain the WISDOM which relieves you from SUFFERING and STRESS, bringing BENEVOLENT LOVE, COMPASSION, and GLADNESS? Generally not much, really.

Many people, perhaps, would take a course if it was not prolonged or too difficult. The truth is most people accept loose constructs, undefined concepts, and inexact ideas rather more easily than information that they would really have to think about deeply. They want their path to be sufficiently logical, reasonable, and scientifically based so that their EGO will not feel irrational. Unfortunately, they are then susceptible to all façades of truth. Most of all, they want to play the game of instant enlightenment without any personal risk. They are rather like those environmentalists who know that global warming is disrupting the climate, and calmly, in logical terms, address the problem at a conference to which they have driven in their car. Use critical introspection. Does this describe you in any way?

The state that actually prevents their acceptance of WISDOM is their own INSECURITY, their CRAVING. What they want is to receive the WISDOM first. Then, if they still feel insecure, they will not have to give up their security and can reject WISDOM. That is like trying to fill a full glass of bacteria-contaminated water with pure water without emptying the glass first. True, you can slowly add water and let the glass gradually overflow. Eventually it may appear that there is only pure water present, but you will actually never get all the bacteria out of the glass. The FOLLY in your mind is like that bacteria: it will multiply until the glass is once more fully contaminated.

Where can you begin if your EGO is strong? In the first place you can begin to see your DESIRE. If it makes you feel better, call it INSECURITY. It doesn't matter. Once you see that you are indeed insecure and greedy, then you will have already given up a little bit of that insecurity and greed. You will have emptied a little bit out of the glass. It doesn't take very much to begin, does it?

Whenever the DEMANDS of EGO SATISFACTION and false security are not realized after a prolonged period, the MENTAL STATE of

PUZZLEMENT evokes SUFFERING in the form of DISAPPOINTMENT, ANNOYANCE, ANGER and a feeling about the FUTILITY of everything. The responsibility for all this SUFFERING, of course, is not seen to be the SUFFERER. The EGO IDENTITY, in its own sight, is seldom to blame and it is a master of disguise, using all sorts of ideas and concepts to avoid responsibility. The more complex one's WANTS are, and the more DESIRE is experienced, the greater will be the DISAPPOINTMENT, the sense of FUTILITY, ANNOYANCE, and ANGER.

Often the DISAPPOINTMENT is so intense that it is unbearable, and although the ANNOYANCE at the situation and ANGER directed at those deemed responsible does not reach the depths of the HOSTILITY released by the DEMAND for DOMINANCE, the anger is explosive and often quite verbal. If SUFFERING persists, even greater STRESS and TENSION will develop. The mind may then take defensive action and FLEE from the scene, rejecting the person's demands and changing his perceptions of the situation, terminating the specific SECURITY-SEEKING activity. This EVASION is not the same as the behavior of the person responding to the DRIVE for VISCERAL SATISFACTION, who simply freezes.

When a strong ACQUISITIVE demand is thwarted again and again, then the person under the thrust of EGO SATISFACTION will revert to the primary state, AVERSION. This AVERSION arises as a defense against the STRESS and extreme conflict which exist. It is experienced as an illogical FEAR of never gaining the AFFECTION desired or attaining the object of DESIRE. Its primitive root is the FEAR of not securing shelter and security. In place of AVERSION, if the person was not held in unassailable esteem, there may be destructive SELF-AVERSION. Soon, however, justifications will tumble out and the whole thing will appear on the surface to have been of no real consequence. This is only on the surface. Internal strategy and tactics regarding behavior will have changed, for beneath the surface the sores and wounds will still fester. The old adage, "once bitten, twice shy" is particularly applicable to the sort of behavior demanded by EGO.

If someone is to blame for failure to achieve DEMAND satiation, then those responsible will not be forgiven or forgotten, for they have shown themselves to be betrayers. No indeed, BETRAYAL is an unforgivable sin for those who want SECURITY above all things. This too is completely unlike the behavior of those who have experienced unsatisfactory results after a VISCERAL DEMAND.

Fig. 17 The Ego Demand: Fear, Disappointment, Futility, Annoyance, and Anger

The NEED for SECURITY, driven by the EGO, soon makes itself heard again, however, and another round of SECURITY-SEEKING behavior in another direction will begin. Society is the name of the game and the person controlled by his GREEDY EGO IDENTITY plays the game very well indeed, even if he only chooses to swim in a very small pool. EGO is strong and always bounces quickly back into the fray.

In retrospect perhaps you can see how complicated the DEMANDS for EGO SATISFACTION are. The EGO uses mental agility, but its agility is not founded in either NATURAL INTELLIGENCE or WISDOM. Don't get the idea that the EGO DEMANDS force the victim to be constantly changing his mind. No, the EGO-directed person is orderly and disciplined. The quandary for the DESIRE-infested person is to cope with the endless list of changing desires which require priority decisions, and to deal with the chains of words and ideas which compound the problem by creating anguish about the possible results.

Since EGO had is birth in language, its imagination is highly creative and it normally evolves all sorts of problems in consciousness which only serve to increase the "noise." The mind is forced often into the past and that is why REGRETS and RECRIMINATIONS so often accompany the basic ANGUISH which it experiences.

Once again you are reminded not to cling to these words, which are descriptions. You will know them because they are EMOTIONS and they will often be accompanied by physical changes in heartbeat and breathing. Often when the DRIVE for VISCERAL SATISFACTION and EGO SATISFACTION are both in operation, you will experience SENSATIONS and EMOTIONS at the same time.

Fig. 18 The Pattern of Suffering Connected with Prolonged Non-satiation of the Demand for Ego Satisfaction

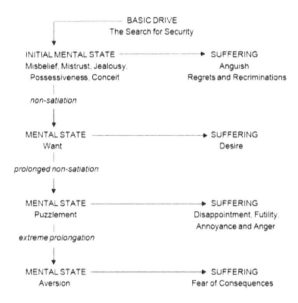

The range and variety of each EMOTION is very great, because the EMOTIONS are ruled by WORDS, not VISCERAL states. VANITY and CONCEIT, for example, are bedfellows, so do not make too much of the subtle differences. When you set aside the EGO IDENTITY which commands these EMOTIONS, the DEMANDS will gradually be destroyed and SUFFERING and STRESS will both begin to fall away.

SUPER EGO DOMINATION

The DEMANDS for DOMINATION, ruled by the third IDENTITY, called SUPER EGO, form the third face of SUFFERING and cause Frustration, Remorse, Passion, Disillusion, Hatred, and Rage. The incorrect behavior which it elicits is that which pushes the potential sufferer towards DOMINANCE of individuals or of a chosen situation, so that everything is exactly as it SHOULD be. Everyone experiences moments when they need to DOMINATE and they will have experienced not only its fruits, but the SUFFERING which this DEMAND for DOMINANCE brings in its wake.

The BASIC adulterated DRIVE which lies behind all this SUFFERING is the DRIVE to BELONG. This DEMAND shows itself in demanding and uncompromising ATTITUDES and aggressive BEHAVIOR. Unlike the two previous DEMANDS which we have discussed, this DEMAND is not awakened in early childhood. While the others are well on their way to a full but unfortunate reign by the end of the sixth year, the DEMAND for DOMINANCE awakens between the ages of six and nine and continues to develop into adolescence. That is because the DEMAND has its root in the DRIVE to BELONG, which requires a rather sophisticated basic development of the MIND with regard to relationships and the learning which is developed in the child's early relationships.

The natural and correct human being has evolved as a social creature who can grow to understand deep within his unconscious the beauty of a greater UNITY. In a real sense people really do belong, but, unfortunately, they cannot see it. They belong within nature, in harmony with all other human creatures. The problem is that they have not touched this WISDOM inside themselves which knows that all things are interdependent.

The human race has instead evolved a FALSE NEED to BELONG, which is the DEMAND. This occurs because they have divorced themselves from all things, all life. They see themselves as the center of their world, a natural but erroneous perception, and have created a dichotomy. Having evolved apart and divorced from all of nature, their subconscious need cries out for UNITY. At times they experience this need for people. Loneliness, a sense of solitude in a world filled with people, the need for someone to confide in, to talk to –all these are symptoms of the lack of TRUE BELONGING.

This sense of loneliness can be relieved by forming associations with people and by forging friendships which are generally just relationships of mutual dependency. The feelings can be reduced by continually seeking the places where people are, avoiding situations which emphasize solitude.

Most people do not experience this extreme DRIVE for DOMINANCE often, for society has evolved social strategies to avoid the problem and has created situations which give its members a sense of BELONGING to relieve the STRESS of SOLITUDE. People have also learned the tactic of being so busy that they only experience the necessity to be close to others when problems exist. Although these systems of society are false, they do satisfy the basic NEED to BELONG which does exist subliminally in most people.

Solitude, however, really only exists in your mind. It exists because you cannot "see" with WISDOM that each person does truly belong. If HARMONY is to be developed and internalized, there must be sacrifices. Most foolish human creatures, unfortunately responding to their EGO IDENTITY, are not disposed to make these sacrifices.

The REAL NEED then has become distorted, and in those who are driven by the SUPER EGO DEMAND for DOMINATION there is a failure to truly BELONG. They instead show HOSTILITY and a need for some form of DOMINATION in their life. This DOMINATION should not be confused with AMBITION, the DESIRE to be a leader, or the DESIRE to be the one who makes decisions. These are ruled by EGO. No indeed, this DOMINATION is always SUPER EGO HOSTILITY. DOMINANCE means ABSOLUTE CONTROL.

In day-to-day situations, when a DEMAND for DOMINANCE thrusts this person forward, sometimes against the commands of EGO, which sees the traps, there is failure. Then there are experiences of FRUSTRATION because things SHOULD have worked out correctly. There are also experiences of REMORSE for the ACTIONS that they SHOULD have taken.

AVARICE and ENVY are the INITIAL MIND-STATES in the SUPER EGO-dominated person. This SUPER EGO experience of AVARICE is not exactly the same as GREED, which is quite emotional. The emphasis of the SUPER EGO is not upon POSSESSION. It CRAVES for what others have because it believes that they have gained something that they SHOULD NOT have. They are perceived to be undeserving. In fact, the prevailing ATTITUDE of SUPER EGO is that few deserve the benefits which they receive. In the subconscious, the SUPER EGO believes that personal possession of something, in some obscure way, would compensate for its unjust possession by others. The SUPER

EGO at the moment of its dominion PASSIONATELY wants to deny possession to others. Do you see this perverse aspect of AVARICE?

Normally, when SUPER EGO is evoked, there is an urge to DOMINATE with a resulting MENTAL AGITATION creating a PASSION which is very strong. Passion rules and during this period the person is energized by this passion. Not always is this sense of DOMINATION exercised as an individual. Being a member of a DOMINATING group serves just as well as individual DOMINANCE, because it provides the protection and anonymity which membership in a group can bring. Fanatical and extremist groups with great passion in their rhetoric and ACTIONS are excellent havens for the satisfaction of this DOMINANCE.

Fig. 19 The Demand for Domination: Passion, Frustration, and Remorse

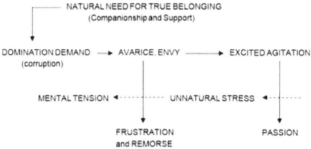

Those aroused by their SUPER EGO often become followers of the DOMINATING PERSONALITIES of this world. They often follow blindly, driven by the vicarious sensations of kinship, not with the causes which the dominant leaders stand for, but with the passions evoked or for the DOMINATING mental image created. Causes are a perfect outlet for the DEMAND for DOMINANCE, and because DOMINANCE has HATRED associated with it, the causes supported may have various degrees of violence inherent within them. Following such causes is extreme FOLLY.

Less extreme but equally folly-filled are those who compete with the DEMAND for DOMINANCE uppermost. It is often shown in the perverse joy experienced in the defeat of an adversary. It is often hidden by simultaneous aggrandizement of EGO. Watch for it and the passionate REMORSE when you lose. Remember that CORRECT

ATTITUDE in competition calls for one-pointedness ONLY on the QUALITY of your own performance.

Alas, when there is a DEMAND for DOMINANCE and things don't work out as expected, there will be a MENTAL STATE of complete BAFFLEMENT. SUPER EGO BAFFLEMENT exists because SUPER EGO can see no reason at all for perfect plans to go wrong. Sometimes the perfidy of people who were a part of the plan can be pointed to. There is BAFFLEMENT because their apparent stupidity and frailty cannot be understood. The SUPER EGO knows exactly what they SHOULD have done. SUPER EGO is bound, you see, to this concept of "SHOULD." All can become a victim of this "SHOULD." The afflicted may even condemn passionately their own stupidity or carelessness. No one is safe from SUPER EGO. Note too that the SUPER EGO accepts culpability, while the EGO resists it with vigor.

When things go wrong, the afflicted become DISILLUSIONED and HATE everyone involved and their folly. Fortunately, most people are not often under the control of this DEMAND and are therefore not frequently overcome by all these strong experiences of PASSIONATE HATRED. This HATRED, however, flares up quickly and dies down again just as quickly. When someone does, however, find himself consistently experiencing FRUSTRATION and DISILLUSIONMENT they may revert to primitive acts of AGGRESSION and REVENGE. These acts are cold, EMOTIONLESS, reasoned, justified, and calculated, although they appear spontaneous, because the PASSION behind all ACTIONS is COGNITIVE. The similar RAGE, RETALIATION, and REPRISALS of the EGO IDENTITY are, on the contrary, EMOTIONAL.

Fig. 20 The Demand for Domination: Rage, Disillusion, and Hatred

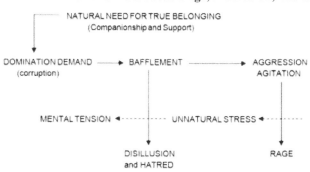

67

Can you see that this DEMAND for DOMINANCE is much more evident in your life than you might have initially thought, although it might not be too obvious or strong? The key to recognition of its presence is the PASSION, which is intellectual, and the incredible sense of INFALLIBILITY in the RIGHTNESS of all related ACTIONS. The sense of "SHOULD," which is almost God-like in its force and stance, is really quite discernible if you are mindful and watch for it.

The SUPER EGO, you see, is never wrong. It is the dispenser of TRUTH and JUSTICE. In some people its expression is quite obvious, in others very subtle, but SUFFERING and STRESS, either conscious or subconscious, is assured for all those who suffer with the expression of this DEMAND.

In particular, those who are upon a spiritual or religious path should be very vigilant, for these corrupting DEMANDS of SUPER EGO hide very well under the mantle of righteousness, being subtle manipulators of the words of wise men and holy books. Their strength under collective banners explains all national, racial, religious, and spiritual bigotry and such social disgraces as the CRUSADES, the INQUISITION, WITCH-BURNING, and a thousand and one other shameful historical events which are covered most gloriously with holy cloth. Like all DEMANDS, the DEMANDS for DOMINANCE are always unnecessary, but socially, when they become the CAUSE for all men to follow, then they generate the most contemptible human behavior.

Fortunately, when the DEMANDS become only commanders of personal FOLLY, then they can be set aside with the diligent use of the GREAT MANTRA. One of the places where they are most often seen is in verbal behavior. Somehow people feel safe in venting this DEMAND venom when it is in voiced in judgment. Here GREED and HOSTILITY seem made for each other. Actually, what occurs is that GREED can virtually bubble to the surface if it is covered by the sugar of a HOSTILE condemnation with which most people can be expected to agree: "It's a lovely dress, but she doesn't know how to wear it." Do you see the subtlety? "He's a good supervisor, but he's having problems at home." Once more the Savage Beasts are growling. Indeed you must be very careful and that is why CORRECT SPEECH as a part of the path to LIBERATION is so very important in the GREAT

MANTRA of COMPASSION. Don't gossip. Don't chatter. It is well declared that it is an empty can, when kicked, that makes the most noise, and that a wise man is most evident by the silence which most often accompanies him.

Fig. 21 The Pattern of Suffering Connected with Prolonged Non-satiation of the Super Ego Demand for Domination

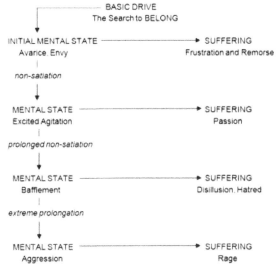

SENSATIONS, EMOTIONS, AND PASSIONS

We have used many words to describe various EXPERIENCES of SUFFERING. On inspecting all these and others which you no doubt have experienced you will wonder about some of them. What is the difference for example, between the MIND-STATES of PUZZLEMENT and BAFFLEMENT? Why is the former an EGO-initiated state and the latter a SUPER EGO state?

The experience of BAFFLEMENT is sharp, like a well-honed knife. It evokes PASSIONS which do not look at anything else except that BAFFLEMENT. It is like a cold fire that consumes itself without moving in any direction. Can you see the idea? This is in no way the same as the PUZZLEMENT of the EGO IDENTITY, which, in failure, cannot understand what exactly has gone wrong. When there is

PUZZLEMENT, the victim searches about in a consciousness filled with words for reasons and clear EMOTIONAL experiences are evoked.

Let's look at SUPER EGO FRUSTRATION for a moment. It has its EGO DEMAND counterpart in the EMOTION of FUTILITY, which is often felt after failing to satisfy a DEMAND for EGO SATISFACTION. The difference between the two is the PASSION which is attached to FRUSTRATION. This PASSION has a base which is also cognitive, but its mental states are far removed from those which rule the EMOTIONAL turmoil of FUTILITY, which is quite enmeshed with a mass of associations and a HOPELESSNESS which does not accompany FRUSTRATION.

The key to understanding the subtle differences between the EMOTIONS of EGO SATISFACTION and the MENTAL PASSION of the SUPER EGO lies in discerning the ice-like PASSION which is completely uncomplicated by chains of thought. This cold piercing PASSION is the hallmark of this DEMAND for DOMINANCE.

If you look at REMORSE, you will see the same thing. PASSIONATE REMORSE is quite different from the EMOTIONAL and wistful REGRETS and the RECRIMINATIONS manufactured by EGO. The EGO IDENTITY beats its breast and cries out its woes. In its sorrow it wants to be noticed: it wants the SECURITY which it has lost by non-satiation of the DEMAND. The SUPER EGO, on the other hand, dwells upon the more general "SHOULD not have happened" idea without dwelling on the reasons. The passionate SUPER EGO laments, but it does so silently.

ENVY too, as a condition of SUFFERING under the DEMAND for DOMINANCE, is quite different from the EMOTIONAL state of COVETOUSNESS, which is ruled by the DEMAND for EGO SATIATION. When EGO is involved there are almost always chains of thought involved, for the EGO structure has an overactive imagination prompted by ideas. The EGO mind in those moments actually searches for ways and means to secure the elusive prize.

The SUPER EGO, on the other hand, when it is in command, is simply envious of the position, influence, and power that others may have or of the way they have obtained their apparent reward. Others have it. They SHOULD NOT have it. There are no mental gyrations. There is simply injustice at work as far as SUPER EGO is concerned.

Do you see the SUPER EGO at work?

We can then separate the experiences related to the DEMAND for EGO SATISFACTION from those of the DEMAND for DOMINATION quite easily. You don't have to worry too much about the meanings of the words. If the experience of SUFFERING is EGO-dominated, there will be EMOTIONS and chains of thought running through consciousness like a train completely out of control. If the experience is that connected to a dominating SUPER EGO, then there will be a cold COGNITIVE PASSION unconnected to chains of thought.

ID-ruled behavior is easier to recognize. ID, as we have mentioned before, sends out clear VISCERAL signals which we call SENSATIONS. Sometimes SENSATIONS and EMOTIONS may be present at the same time when ID and EGO are working together with mutual DEMANDS. Watch out for them and you will detect the subtle differences.

We can also take a look at the distinction between VISCERAL DISAPPOINTMENT and COGNITIVE DISILLUSIONMENT. The latter experiences are completely different from the brooding SENSATIONS of DISAPPOINTMENT derived from ID. You can see the difference if you really are mindful, for the former is woeful and you can sense the physiological response of the body to that DISAPPOINTMENT. On the other hand, DISILLUSIONMENT is clear and concise. The MIND, COGNITIVE and PASSIONATE, can define the problem in a single strong statement. The DISILLUSIONED person may say fiercely, "You can't trust anyone," while the ID will be more concerned about its loss.

The DEMANDS we have spoken of are so evident and strong that we have referred to them as if each was ruled by an IDENTITY. Of course, these IDENTITIES do not really exist, but the power of the DEMANDS is such that it appears as if they were living internal forces that actually COMMAND. You will have seen that we call these respectively ID, EGO, and SUPER EGO. (see figure 22)

You will see from reviewing these three faces of SUFFERING that most experiences have a false mantle of insignificance placed upon them or become well hidden in your subconscious. If it were not for the presence of UNNATURAL STRESS and the resulting TENSIONS, you probably would know nothing about your subliminal SUFFERING at all. Some time in the future, if you were unfortunate, you would be shocked if you found out that this STRESS in the form of SUFFERING

Fig. 22 Different Patterns in the Development of Experiences

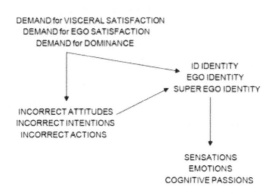

had been building up for years, causing cancer, ulcers, heart problems, or other infirmities. You might even, too late, regret your obvious FOLLY.

The greatest tragedy is, however, the fact that you are probably rejecting a full and happy life. The pleasure and happiness that you have is false. Try and understand that. Furthermore, you are trading this full, happy, and natural life for false pleasure and apparent happiness.

The human system is absolutely magnificent. It is a biological computer. You are very favored, for this computer is equipped with a failsafe device. It is a system which looks at everything going on at both cortical and subcortical levels and detects any imbalance and conflict. When there is UNNATURAL STRESS, a small non-vocal signal tells you, "Just a minute, something here is wrong." If you ignore it, then there is nothing more that the system can do for you. If you hear this signal in any form, then you will be sensible if you do something about the problem. You may be too busy, like your pleasures too much, or justify your FOLLY in a million ways. On the other hand, if you wish to do something about it, then the Mantra is available to you, as are other systems which resolve the tangle.

The GREAT MANTRA addresses both this SUFFERING and the UNNATURAL STRESS which you experience, showing you not only that these are symptoms of INCORRECT ATTITUDES, INCORRECT INTENTIONS, and INCORRECT ACTIONS, but exactly how to replace them, in chanting, with NATURAL processes.

Governing Demands

We have said that each of these DEMANDS is experienced at one time or another by all people. You have seen how complex they are and you can imagine the complications of their interaction. It is not surprising that human creatures SUFFER and feel the TENSION of STRESS in the absence of the WISDOM which can change all ATTITUDES, INTENTIONS, and ACTIONS. The surprising thing, however, is that most people don't know how much they actually SUFFER. They accept the SUFFERING so much as a part of "living" that it doesn't even seem important to them. Many have immersed themselves so much in an insane consumer society that they don't even recognize that they SUFFER at all. They accept the "PLEASURE" that they experience as compensation for any STRESS which they may feel and believe that this is a price which must be paid, declaring, "That is a part of living." They do not understand at all and do not know that they are cutting themselves off not only from correct living and their own true nature but from true joy.

That is why it has been so necessary to show the faces of SUFFERING and STRESS. Those who with diligence and an open mind examine what has been presented here may be able to see what has really been ruling their behavior. They may then be astute enough to take the steps necessary to liberate themselves, returning both their mind and body to a natural state. Those who do advance upon the correct path, having recognized the SUFFERING and STRESS within themselves, will have taken the first step to LIBERATION. They can approach the Mantra with a receptive attitude, with the certain knowledge that they can discover their true nature and liberate WISDOM.

Those who approach the Mantra without knowing their own SUFFERING will have given themselves a debilitating handicap, for the DEMANDS are exceedingly strong. In fact, it is important to realize that you cannot divorce the DEMANDS, the personified IDENTITIES, nor the UNNATURAL STRESS and TENSIONS from SUFFERING.

If you can see this, then it should be very clear that COMPASSION cannot be directed only at apparent SUFFERING, but must be offered to all those who are under the constant influence of the DEMANDS and the IDENTITIES. COMPASSION cannot be partial, although the ACTIONS taken can depend upon the circumstances. There is no such thing as MORE LOVE or LESS LOVE. BENEVOLENT LOVE is full and complete. You must, therefore, direct your COMPASSION to all people, for it should be clear now that all, including yourself, SUFFER.

THE INHERITED GIFT

It is important that you understand that the complex meld of DEMANDS which exists is dictated by past learning. Since each life is different, each person will have developed a distinctive mixture of DEMANDS. These DEMANDS, we have seen, are debilitating and unnatural. Fortunately, each person has also inherited positive DISPOSITIONS to behave in certain ways. Your behavior, therefore, is a blend of that which you have learned and that which you have inherited. The INCORRECT ATTITUDES which you have learned can be replaced by CORRECT ATTITUDES, and WISDOM can be liberated. We have then NEGATIVE DEMANDS and POSITIVE DISPOSITIONS.

If we look at what you have inherited, we find that in addition to the wonderful mind and body, the marvelous systems of organization, and the magnificent capacity to learn, each person has inherited ONE of three possible DISPOSITIONS to act. These dispositions potentially GOVERN all your behavior.

These are:
* The DISPOSITION for SENSITIVITY
* The DISPOSITION for CORRECT DISCRIMINATION
* The DISPOSITION for NATURAL INTELLIGENCE

Each human creature, without exception, has one of these dispositions potentially available. These dispositions for behavior correspond to inherited individual strengths which are correct and wise readinesses to respond to the NATURAL DRIVES. In other words, each person has within himself all the basic traits which will allow the personal growth of either SENSITIVITY, DISCRIMINATION, or NATURAL INTELLIGENCE.

The presence of these DISPOSITIONS is the good news. The bad news is the fact that the way in which man has evolved has led to a defilement of these DISPOSITIONS due to the presence of the three

74

DEMANDS. The result is that those who have a latent disposition for SENSITIVITY are actually GOVERNED by DELUSION and show a preponderance of SUFFERING due to the operation of the DEMAND for VISCERAL SATISFACTION. Similarly, those with a disposition for latent CORRECT DISCRIMINATION are GOVERNED by GREED, due to the DEMAND for EGO SATISFACTION. It will come as no surprise to anyone to discover that the disposition for NATURAL INTELLIGENCE is related to the DEMAND for DOMINANCE, and that these persons are GOVERNED by HOSTILE REVULSION.

There we have it. There are three character types: DELUDED, GREEDY, and HOSTILE. Is it any wonder that sentient beings SUFFER, and that human creatures are slowly destroying themselves and all life? Remember too that each person's GOVERNING FORCE does not have absolute sway. The two weaker NON-GOVERNING FORCES can reinforce or combat the strongest. Sometimes, depending on the circumstances, a weaker force will gain temporary strength and it will take precedence. A person with a GOVERNING EGO, for example, may consider making a certain type of response. The SUPER EGO, supported by prevailing conditions, may examine its personal list of acceptable SOCIAL behaviors which is stored in MEMORY and may decide that it is not valid. INTERNAL CONFLICT will develop and there will be additional STRESS and TENSION, causing further rounds of SUFFERING even after the power struggle has been resolved.

Under the influence of these DEMANDS each person is a victim. Do people really want to accept all this SUFFERING? Are the pleasures that they have really worth the STRESS and CONFLICT? Don't you agree that it is clearly in each person's best interest to possess WISDOM and enjoy the fruits of a strong and CORRECT DISPOSITION, supported by the two other dispositions which would never be in conflict?

THE DELUDED PERSONALITY

There are not many people who suffer with a GOVERNING state of DELUSION and have a DELUDED personality, but those that do probably don't feel deluded and would be quite insulted if they were to be called that. Many of these DELUDED people will accept the fact that they are sometimes CONFUSED, but this becomes only a game of words. The DELUDED person, you see, has a penchant for falling into the unfortunate habit of living in his or her own world.

It may well appear to be a happy world of sensitivity surrounded with charming mystique, romantic concepts, and COMPASSION. In this state of DELUSION, those who SUFFER and feel the TENSION of STRESS build this whole new world of fantasy and false ideas around themselves to provide a certain comforting environment. They do not see their own deception and accept deluded ideas as truth. The subtle hidden DEMANDS for VISCERAL SATISFACTION which form their behavior and their ATTITUDES, however, go on unabated.

They believe in SENSATIONS and, since feelings are important, they also permit themselves free expression of all the acceptable social EMOTIONS. For them to deny these sensations and emotions is to deny life. They see themselves often as being tuned to the COSMOS and they love the language which provides apparent transcendental strength.

If there are alternative physical or mental methods of healing and solving the problems of human creatures, they will find them. Faith is their way, so they may even cling to compassionate "cures" that have little worth, for they pride themselves in being intuitive. They are not analytical or scientific, so no deeper proof is necessary than the apparent success of their efforts. Experiences are important, but deeper DIRECT EXPERIENCE at a profound level demands a long dedication without the transcendental glitter which they require for apparent stability and comfort.

Subconsciously for them, it is a world that is too full of stimulation and decisions that must be made, although they do not recognize this. The ID IDENTITY, which governs the DEMAND for VISCERAL SATISFACTION, likes to see itself as the sensitive agent for greater good that both "sees" and "understands" people. It doesn't seek the limelight like EGO, for the apparent knowledge of its own humanity and humility, which is quite false, is sufficient.

Of the three GOVERNING IDENTITIES which cause such camouflaged SUFFERING and STRESS, it is this ID IDENTITY which is the most difficult to dislodge. It creates a blindness in the SUFFERER which is quite remarkable in its subtlety. We have, therefore, painted a particularly strong picture of this person who is GOVERNED by

DELUSION. It is necessary in order to break through the RESISTANCE of ID, which sees itself with such virtue and appears to speak with apparent COMPASSION. Those who have fortunately not advanced deeply upon the path of DELUSION and feel only the CONFUSION can thus be warned of future dangers, while those who are deep in DELUSION and are wise enough to see it may be shocked from their path by such a challenging alternative view of their comportment.

The vision that the DELUDED person has of himself as SENSITIVE and COMPASSIONATE is a worthy and correct vision. They do not require a mask of DELUSION. They do require a diligent application of one-pointedness and mindfulness. They are astute if they accept the label of DELUSION, difficult though it may be to do so. Then they can allow their real sensitivity and an understanding of what is spiritually correct to develop. They must not smother themselves in their own comfortable but false spiritual worthiness. With strength they can set pride aside and refuse to cling to their masks of love, sensitivity, and virtue.

If you recognize yourself in any part of the description of the DELUDED person, then relieve yourself from your burden by embracing the GREAT COMPASSION MANTRA of NATURAL WISDOM. The beauty of doing this is that you will have released yourself immediately from the strong pressing grasp of DELUSION and will be more amenable to the careful introspection which is necessary if you wish to be liberated from DELUSION altogether. Rest assured that when DELUSION is set aside, then your NATURAL GOVERNING DISPOSITION for truly beautiful SENSITIVITY will take its place. Then you will know real JOY and live with real HARMONY, having true COMPASSION for all sentient creatures.

THE GREEDY PERSONALITY

The three fine qualities of being sensitive, discriminative, and naturally intelligent have been distorted in the human creature. Sensitivity has become a thirst for VISCERAL SATISFACTION, the power to discriminate correctly has been turned to the task of GREEDY ACQUISITION, and Natural Intelligence to a shocking HOSTILITY.

Most of the world's population is GOVERNED by the DEMANDS for EGO SATISFACTION. Because, globally, GREED at all levels of government and within every stratum of society is so evident, the situation appears absurd to most people. The problem is that although they see the absurdity of the general situation and the GREED of others, they do not see this GREED in themselves. It is clear that there would be more than enough real SECURITY for every member of this planet if the world was ruled with WISDOM. Those who live in parts of the world which we call advanced certainly have real SECURITY and should easily be able to see that this is "One World." Yet almost everyone feels INSECURE, responds to their EGO IDENTITIES, and is ready to endure the consequences: SUFFERING and STRESS.

Most people are almost completely GOVERNED by their EGO IDENTITY and we say they have a GREEDY personality. The rest, although they are not governed by this IDENTITY, are greatly influenced by it. This GREEDY personality is no more the personality of anyone at birth than is the DELUDED personality.

The GREEDY person was born with the inherited DISPOSITION to be a DISCRIMINATING person. That is to say that they had the latent disposition to see all things with clarity, to be able to make correct and noble judgments, to discriminate minute differences and nuances in things, people, and conditions. Their birthright was to know the correct from the incorrect, to make correct choices and decisions about paths to be taken. They resist this label of GREEDY and that is understandable, for the person so described sounds quite despicable. They prefer to think of themselves as HOSTILE or even CONFUSED, for the GREEDY person is condemned by everyone. Strangely enough, they have no problem at all pinning this label upon others.

Try and remember that although we say that this INSECURE person has a GREEDY personality, it is really the behavior that we are talking about. This is important to remember, for behavior has nothing to with the true potential personality which lies beneath that demand-driven behavior. The GREEDY person can liberate himself and become the person whose CORRECT INTENTION is reflected in the great COMPASSION and TRUE HAPPINESS which shows externally and is really available through the GREAT COMPASSION MANTRA.

THE HOSTILE PERSONALITY

Some people, and they are not met frequently, are completely ruled by the DEMAND for DOMINANCE. We call them HOSTILE personalities, for they are basically HOSTILE to the world that does not live up to their EXPECTATIONS. They want to be on top of the heap, less as leaders, though they nourish this image of themselves, but more as dictators.

It is not success which these HOSTILE personalities CRAVE, it is the desire that everything should be exactly as they imagine it should be. They are IDEALISTS, although their ideals may be warped. They thrive on ADMIRATION and RESPECT. These are not essential, but they paradoxically loathe praise and thanks. They know that they are driven and are not filled with BENEVOLENT LOVE for individuals. They do, strangely enough, have real and great BENEVOLENT LOVE for MANKIND as a whole, providing that it shapes up. You can see that in this world of GREED they are doomed to suffer continual FRUSTRATION.

They are not perfectionists in any way, but they do expect full conformity to their own standards and rules, even in themselves. They feel that they BELONG to the world, and they actually do, perhaps more than any other type of personality, for they feel a part of the natural world with all its conflict and chaos. They revere life and respect death without consternation and fear. Their passion is intense, so they would destroy the world if they could paradoxically save it, for their respect, admiration, and love for all that is natural, except mankind, is absolute. The problem is that they belong as part of the world but they do not belong with other human creatures.

They long to BELONG as one with all people, but reject this BELONGING because the GREEDY are not worthy of union. Because the GREEDY rule the world and are perceived as the betrayers of NATURE, they reject any union at all. They have, in fact, a REVULSION for those who are filled with such FOLLY and, seeing this FOLLY, refuse to do anything about it. They are in a terrible dilemma. They love the human potential and they can forgive the confused, but the GREEDY and FOOLISH who will not listen draw their full HOSTILITY. Even if they try to BELONG socially in order to satisfy their NEED, they cannot succeed. The obstacle is that they are not like most normal people. They are on the fringe: too different to be included, too remote, too pensive, too abstract, too unemotional, too calculating, too manipulative, too demanding, and too dominating to be acceptable in an apparently social and happy-go-lucky society. That doesn't appear to bother the HOSTILE personality, at least on the surface, but inside he resents being alone with himself. It is a pity, but he accepts that with stoicism, knowing that few are worthy to be a true partner to his thoughts and passions.

In fact, the DOMINATING personality would love to be the distributor of justice or an omnipotent God, for he believes that few are as competent as he is to DOMINATE the situation. He is paradoxically torn between this lust for DOMINANCE and the idea that GREATNESS is only perceived by little minds.

Society approves of this DOMINANT personality, although it condemns that DOMINANCE if it is in excess, so he is generally rewarded well for all the success which he may have if it is in line with social norms. He is a quick learner, an abstract thinker, and highly DYNAMIC, and is as frequently loathed as he is admired for his AGGRESSIVE manner. He is a person of paradoxes and extremes and is seldom really understood. His RESULTANT STATE of DOMINANCE we call HOSTILE REVULSION, because it is weighed with such intense PASSION. He suffers STRESS more than any other personality type and is therefore prone to physiological stress-related problems.

He is clearly INTELLIGENT and knows that without smugness, but does not understand that this INTELLIGENCE is misdirected. The pity is that he seldom develops the NATURAL INTELLIGENCE which is his for the asking. Instead, his worldly intelligence is directed towards DOMINANCE which results in his HOSTILITY and REVULSION towards human creatures.

You have seen a brief outline of the three character types. Are you DELUDED, GREEDY, or HOSTILE? Some readers may say, "I'm GREEDY, but not really all that bad." The situation is similar to childbirth: one cannot be half pregnant. Similarly, others may claim, "I'm a little bit of everything." That is evading the question.

Everyone should try and see what really governs their behavior. It is foolish to evade the issue. You are either DELUDED, GREEDY,

HOSTILE, or are without SUFFERING. Look at the list of your potential for SUFFERING as a victim of the DEMANDS. Do you have any of this SUFFERING in yourself? Do you see the probability that one of these DEMANDS may actually GOVERN most of your behavior? If you can, then you will already have come a long way.

An Overview of Common Suffering

The DEMAND for VISCERAL SATISFACTION generates Cares and Anxiety, Longing, Discontent, Irritation, and occasionally Panic.

The DEMAND for EGO SATISFACTION brings Anguish, Regrets and Recriminations, Desire, Disappointment, Annoyance, a sense of Futility, Anger, and sometimes Fear.

The DEMAND for DOMINANCE causes Frustration, Remorse, Passion, Disillusion, Hatred, and Rage.

All these experiences, and hundreds of other variations of them that we have discussed, are symptoms of mankind's learned acceptance of the DEMANDS.

Would you like to relieve yourself of SUFFERING? Would you like to relieve yourself of the UNNATURAL STRESS that DEMANDS bring? Would you like to obtain a life with true joy and happiness? Do you wish to regain your birthright of SENSITIVITY, CORRECT DISCRIMINATION, and NATURAL INTELLIGENCE? Would you like to experience true GLADNESS, true COMPASSION, and true BENEVOLENT LOVE? Would you like your WISDOM to grow so that you are not GOVERNED by FOLLY?

The answers are your answers. The decisions to be made are your decisions. If you wish, you can take the CORRECT PATH to a NATURAL LIFE. Our INTENTIONS are only to make available the knowledge about the alternatives. Those who see their own SUFFERING and believe that they know what DEMANDS govern their behavior can look at the other DRIVES which have less strength within them and see how they sometimes support and sometimes resist the governing force. Sometimes the GOVERNING DRIVE will not enter into the picture at all. It is as if the commanding IDENTITY is saying to the less powerful IDENTITIES, "This is not my concern. Do what you want with the situation."

It is amazing what SUFFERING we are prepared to take in exchange for the false pleasures of this world. It is absurd that we are so blind to our own FOLLY. It is amazing that we cannot see the true beauty which is available in the NATURAL life. We needn't look at this with blindness, believing that a prosperous life must be denied. There is nothing incorrect about living in this world. There is no fault in being successful or wealthy. The problem lies in the DEMANDS which motivate the behavior which brings these things. It is the CLINGING and the CRAVING that is the error. There are ways to have, enjoy, and appreciate a fine meal without all the SUFFERING. There are ways to work and enjoy without the SUFFERING. There are ways of dancing and being merry without adulterating and destroying the human system.

It has no doubt been difficult for most readers to face this flow of concepts which point out mankind's chosen lot of SUFFERING. The serious Mantra reciter will, however, understand the necessity of analyzing the SUFFERING which is all around us every day. It is neither pessimistic nor negative to view this SUFFERING, for you cannot combat an unseen enemy. The sage person will not be burdened by the apparent seriousness of the problem. That is also FOLLY. If you feel serious yourself at this moment, let go of that seriousness. Allow happiness to flow within you. If you can do this, then you will have learned a marvelous liberating thing, that seeing the existence of your own SUFFERING is a happy event. Laugh at your past FOLLY! Enjoy the first fruits of your knowledge. You possess the keys to the door of personal LIBERATION. You can walk in the midst of the world with joy, participating and partaking in its fruits.

You can do this without CLINGING, without SUFFERING. You can be in the world without being a part of its FOLLY and madness. You can live with JOY. All that you must do is release your own NATURAL WISDOM. It is said that when the COMPASSION MANTRA is recited then the heavens quake and the earth trembles as the Mantra penetrates heaven and earth. This poetic license really does describe the power and effectivity of the Mantra.

If you don't believe with full confidence that reciting the Mantra will bring about a change, then you will have created a self-fulfilling prophecy. With sincere recitation, correct preparation and confidence, you will succeed in liberating your own natural power.

2. Quiescent Suffering

When a person wins a prize they believe that they are HAPPY. When they enjoy buying a new book they believe that they are HAPPY. When they are listening to a piece of music it is likely that they believe that they are HAPPY. Actually, in each of these cases they may be SUFFERING. That seems like a rather strange idea, doesn't it? It is, however, the truth. The problem is that they probably do not know how to really enjoy themselves and do not even recognize TRUE PLEASURE. There is nothing at all wrong with enjoying the winning of a prize, buying a new book, or listening to music if each is done in the correct way.

The problem is that most people have been taught the wrong way to enjoy things. As a result, all sorts of hidden problems are being created every day by this incorrect concept of what enjoyment is. This SUFFERING which is building itself up quietly and unobserved in everyone is the second type of SUFFERING. It is called QUIESCENT SUFFERING. It has the same base as the first, which is IGNORANCE. In this form of SUFFERING it is clear that DELUSION, GREED, and HOSTILE AVERSION are also present. The face of this SUFFERING is well hidden because it is covered with a mantle of false joy and satisfaction.

QUIESCENT SUFFERING is being laid down when someone is APPARENTLY eating and enjoying something as simple as an ice cream cone. At the actual moment of enjoyment they will not be experiencing SUFFERING, but unless they are very mindful they will probably be laying down the framework of future SUFFERING through the satiation of GREED and the creation of a state of CLINGING. This CLINGING is the SUFFERING a person experiences at the moment of the possession of an object of desire. It is based on the visceral sensations and the emotions and cognitive thoughts connected to enjoying the object.

Can you see that this type of enjoyment creates YOU, the ENJOYER; the PROCESS of ENJOYING; and IT, the OBJECT of enjoyment? In the person's mind, the IDENTITY wants to enjoy IT again. Every time that the situation of apparent enjoyment and satiation of a DEMAND occurs, the desire that YOU should have IT again in the future is reinforced.

CLINGING augments future SUFFERING by increasing the CRAVING for the object or situation. The more that possession with enjoyment occurs, the stronger the desire will be. Strangely enough, if a person doesn't always get what he wants, then this actually increases the CRAVING even more.

It is difficult to believe that this innocent experience can be so damaging. Multiply that CLINGING by hundreds of events each day and you can perhaps see the danger. Remember that every time a WANT or DESIRE is realized, then it increases the SUFFERING you will experience if that desire is not met in the future. CRAVING is like a drug. CLINGING is the latent power of that drug. The eventual reward of drug satiation is so apparently fantastic that victims are willing to take the SUFFERING of not always being rewarded. If you can see this clearly, then you will fully understand this second form of SUFFERING.

What is most important is the fact that you will have learned to see SUFFERING in its most hidden form, during the process of its reinforcement. Furthermore, you will be able to see that those who are in error in setting down their own QUIESCENT SUFFERING merit your COMPASSION as well as those who experience the other forms. Perhaps you will then also be able to see why the BUDDHA saw all as SUFFERING.

Just as there are three faces in COMMON MENTAL SUFFERING, so there are three in QUIESCENT SUFFERING.

VISCERAL SATISFACTION

In the case of the DEMAND for VISCERAL SATISFACTION, there is no benefit actually even received if the demand is satisfied. There arises a FALSE CONTENTMENT in which the person appears happy. This, unfortunately, only reinforces the DEMAND, making its foothold stronger and establishing a CLINGING which sets the stage for greater later SUFFERING.

Despite this FALSE CONTENTMENT, which allows the person under the influence of a VISCERAL DEMAND to paint a rose-colored picture of the situation governed by the DEMAND, he will be torn between the FORCE of the DRIVE and the subliminal knowledge that all is not

CORRECT. This voice is neither a social nor spiritual conscience. It is the voice of his relegated WISDOM that cries out to be heard. Naturally, being contented, he will not listen. This causes an apparently insolvable subliminal CONFLICT which must be resolved in order to maintain the system in some sort of equilibrium.

His subconscious system then solves the dilemma by creating believable justifications for the ID-controlled choice made. The believability of these false justifications is essential, for the LIFE FORCE of the human system could not tolerate the knowledge that the brain had chosen the way of self-destructive behavior. These justifications, illogical though they may be, are completely accepted as truth. This process of self-deception is psychologically called COGNITIVE DISSONANCE. This is the process which creates QUIESCENT SUFFERING.

Fig. 23 Quiescent Suffering Connected with Visceral Satisfaction

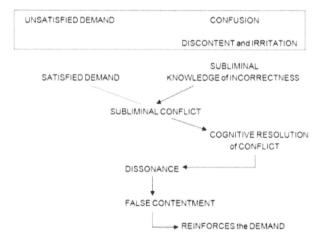

The subliminal conflict then, being eliminated, causes no STRESS or APPARENT SUFFERING. Everything appears in EQUILIBRIUM. It is, of course, a false state, for the FALSE CONTENTMENT reinforces the CLINGING to the DEMAND, which in turn ensures that there will once again be a cycle of UNSATISFIED DEMANDS with all the accompanying SUFFERING. The only way to free oneself from this cycle is to break that DISSONANCE, and that can only be achieved if there is a strong subliminal knowledge of CORRECTNESS and a solid

WISDOM of CAUSE and EFFECT operating effectively in the system. In this way, CONFLICT can be resolved in favor of the NATURAL.

EGO SATISFACTION

If a person who responds to a DEMAND for EGO SATISFACTION by great apparent sacrifice and effort is successful in achieving his desires and feels secure and happy in his FOLLY, he is not safe from SUFFERING. It is true that when EGO DEMANDS are satisfied there is great apparent joy and happiness which is hard to contain. In fact, there is nobody more apparently ecstatic and happy, ABSORBED as it were by the objects or conditions which satisfy wants, than a person GOVERNED by the EGO.

Fig. 24 Quiescent Suffering Connected with Ego Satisfaction

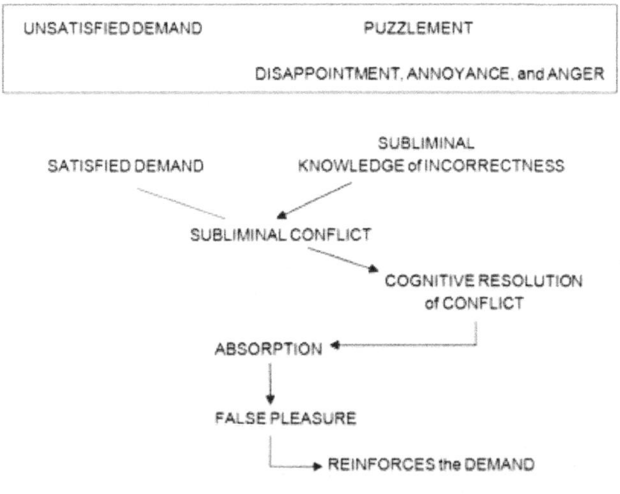

UNSATISFIED DEMAND	PUZZLEMENT
	DISAPPOINTMENT, ANNOYANCE, and ANGER

SATISFIED DEMAND   SUBLIMINAL KNOWLEDGE of INCORRECTNESS

SUBLIMINAL CONFLICT

COGNITIVE RESOLUTION of CONFLICT

ABSORPTION

FALSE PLEASURE

REINFORCES the DEMAND

This FALSE PLEASURE for both he who is GOVERNED and he who is merely responding to an EGO DEMAND really does little else except reinforce GREEDY behavior and EGO strength. Can you see that this FALSE PLEASURE is no different than the addictive drugs which most people condemn? It is a powerful drug. Almost everyone will blame money. They declare, "I haven't got much money, so I am not suffering the effects of this drug." Indeed they are, for there is a CLINGING, no matter how small it may appear in consciousness, to the possessions that they do have. Since even those who are not GOVERNED by the EGO IDENTITY succumb to the DEMANDS for EGO SATISFACTION frequently, they cannot let go of either their INSECURITY or the pleasures of the world of the senses.

SUPER EGO DOMINATION

The fruits of apparently successful behavior commanded by the DEMANDS for DOMINATION are also poisoned. He who is operating under the influence of a DEMAND for DOMINANCE experiences an apparent MENTAL STATE of SUPERIORITY at those times which is always evident by the aura created. This SUPERIORITY actually serves to override any subliminal CONFLICT which may arise between the existing SUPER EGO DEMANDS and a latent knowledge of the INCORRECTNESS of ACTIONS taken to realize the DEMANDS for DOMINANCE. Can you see that SUPERIORITY is just like the COGNITIVE DISSONANCE and ABSORPTION which we have already dealt with? Each is a mental state which is quite extreme and each is an artificial way to silence the healthy homeostatic voices of reason.

Those who don't experience this DEMAND for DOMINANCE often will find that this sense of SUPERIORITY will evaporate promptly, for their DEMANDS for VISCERAL and EGO SATISFACTION will quickly draw attention away from the SUPER EGO attachment. Nonetheless, it is a very dangerous DEMAND because of the influence it can have over others. The person GOVERNED by this DEMAND is much more extreme. He seldom sees that he has distorted his natural gift of INTELLIGENCE. It is true that his mind works quickly and imaginatively and since this SUPERIORITY needs constant demonstration, he will be generous with his time, energy, and knowledge. However, there must always be someone to receive who is worthy.

With the apparent satiation of a DEMAND for DOMINANCE in some successful project, there will also be an arousal of a mental state of SUPERIORITY and an incredible ELATION. This ELATION, when it is frequently experienced, is like an addictive drug. In occasional doses it is not so terrible, but often under the influence of clever mind-manipulators this drug of ELATION can be used to drive war machines and mass movements of hatred.

You will not see this ELATION in the SUPER EGO-DOMINATED person although those who suffer from its occasional activity will be clearly overcome by it. In the HOSTILE personality, all his ELATION and even his normal pleasures derived from the lesser DEMANDS are never demonstrated. Everything is internal, enjoyed by a SUPER EGO that savors its own superiority and worth. He floats in this aura of SUPERIORITY, which sustains him even through the SUFFERING of DISILLUSION.

In order to set the stages for this ELATION, the cognitive system has to evolve plans and expectations which are not normal. There must be some grand objective or cause to be served for the SUPER EGO to be set in motion, so the objectives cannot be insignificant. The DOMINATION-governed person, therefore, never concerns himself with that which he considers trivial or pointless.

Fig. 25 Quiescent Suffering Connected with Successful Domination

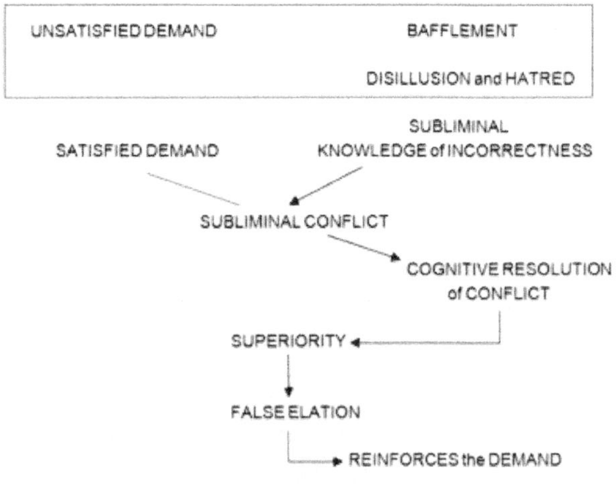

TRUE CONTENTMENT, PLEASURE, AND ELATION

If you can see that the contentment, pleasure and elation which man experiences is more often than not a FALSE state, then you will naturally wonder if there are TRUE counterparts which we have somehow discarded in our acceptance of the FALSE. Indeed there are.

Can you see that when you view a beautiful sunset you are clearly declaring, "There is the sunset and I am here seeing it"? This appears like a perfectly healthy response, but it is an INCORRECT ATTITUDE. You have created by this ATTITUDE a VIEWER who is perceiving the sunset and an OBJECT which is being perceived. The true appreciation of a sunset, and in fact anything that can be touched by any of our senses, comes from setting aside the concept of YOU the PERCEIVER and IT the OBJECT.

True enjoyment comes from the integration of perceiver and object so that they become AS ONE. If you have experienced this real integration on some occasion, then you will remember the experience as being very special and not at all the same as what you normally consider to be PLEASURE. This experience of INTEGRATION is an experience of TRUE PLEASURE and it is actually available to you all the time if you can manage to lay aside your personal IDENTITY.

We actually create for ourselves a strange paradox. We split the apparent OBJECT off from the image of OURSELVES, creating an IDENTITY, and then try to possess the OBJECT by CLINGING and CRAVING. How absurd this is. We let go something which is already fully a part of us in order that we can experience a very tepid form of pleasure while clinging to and craving the very thing we have foolishly cast away.

Let us look at another example of this folly-filled INCORRECT ATTITUDE. If you go for a walk in the country maintaining the role of the OBSERVER or VIEWER, then you are also cheating yourself by creating FALSE PLEASURE. You would be making the mistake of setting yourself OBJECTIVES and would probably be CLINGING to all that you saw without actually SEEING anything at all. You would be creating for yourself all sorts of EXPECTATIONS and DESIRES. This is a formula for disaster. How much better if everyone were to lay aside the concept of WALKER, OBSERVER, and OBJECTIVE and become "WALKING." How much better if everyone was to no longer DEVOUR everything like a predator and become AS ONE with the environment.

Now, this is very easy to do intellectually, but it is very difficult to carry out so that BECOMING is a part of you. There are millions who do an excellent job, for example, of protecting the environment creating, individually and as groups, a consciousness that is correct. How unfortunate it is that most of these people have only an intellectual association with nature. The only way to really unite with nature is to lay aside IDENTITY and enter into the PROCESS. It is the presence of an IDENTITY, you see, that creates a FALSE PLEASURE. Lay aside your IDENTITY and you automatically release TRUE PLEASURE.

This is the secret to life. Don't be anything, just BECOME. Don't be a WALKER, become WALKING. Don't be a COOK, become COOKING. Don't be a SITTER, become SITTING. Do you get the idea? You must be careful, for it would be a mistake to set TRUE PLEASURE up as a goal or objective, as this would be just another CRAVING. Do you see how careful you must be? What you must do is open yourself to what is NATURAL and then accept the TRUE PLEASURE as an accompanying event. There is then NO ATTACHMENT to the phenomenon. Without either ATTACHMENT or IDENTITY there is therefore no POTENTIAL SUFFERING.

Most people tread the line between the FALSE PLEASURE, which comes from the ANTICIPATION and EXPECTATION of SATIATION, and the SUFFERING which comes from fear of the possible DENIAL of that FALSE PLEASURE. They accept the SUFFERING so that they can obtain what they believe are the PLEASURES of this life. What they don't know is that they do not have to SUFFER at all and that the PLEASURES which they seek are false. TRUE PLEASURE is unknown to them.

So strong is this seeking of FALSE PLEASURE that most people mask and refuse to know or accept all the SUFFERING that they experience, believing themselves to be HAPPY. The wise see the folly in all SUFFERING and allow it to fall away and they replace FALSE PLEASURE with a TRUE PLEASURE which is both correct and natural. The great problem is that giving up FALSE PLEASURE, which seems so real, in exchange for the promise of an unexperienced PLEASURE is extremely difficult.

It is certainly true that IGNORANCE appears to be BLISS, and if the effect was only superficial, perhaps we would not think it was important. The problem is threefold. First, even if the SUFFERING is hidden, it will eventually surface with ferocity. Second, this hidden suffering manifests itself in all sorts of ways physiologically: ulcers, cancer, and heart problems are just a few of the consequences of this harmful CLINGING and CRAVING if we accept the internal lies and justifications which we make so that we do not have to change.

The third point is of extreme importance. The acceptance of the FALSE PLEASURE which we experience eliminates any chance that one can experience TRUE AND NATURAL PLEASURE and live fully and naturally. The beauty is that once we eliminate the FALSE enjoyment, we automatically liberate all that is natural and true. The GREAT MANTRA accomplishes this.

Can you now see why is it so important that we fully grasp FALSE CONTENTMENT, FALSE PLEASURE, FALSE ELATION, and POTENTIAL SUFFERING if there is to be a full understanding of the MANTRA of COMPASSION? It is because your COMPASSION must be directed at all those who do not appear to be SUFFERING, as well as to those who have evident SUFFERING. Your COMPASSION has to be directed to all those who are building their potential for future SUFFERING through QUIESCENT SUFFERING and are blinded to that suffering by the strength of their CLINGING. It has to be directed to all those who are in this world closed to their own potential to enjoy true happiness.

THE OBJECTIVE: A NATURAL STATE

Now, we have spoken a great deal about returning the system to a natural and joyful state where there is true contentment, pleasure, and elation. What do we mean by that? We have evolved as a human creature as a result of what we call natural processes. How can we claim that the human creature is not natural? It must be natural to SUFFER, mustn't it? If we wish to play with words, then we can reply "Yes, it is." However, what we consider to be natural is a state in which each sentient creature acts in a manner consistent within the limits of its potential so as not to harm itself. SUFFERING then is clearly not natural.

We consider it natural in the human creature, for example, when ATTITUDES and INTENTIONS are aimed at eliciting ACTIONS which are in harmony with correct growth and development and do no harm either physiologically or psychologically. We consider it natural to seek knowledge and avoid ignorance. Therefore ATTITUDES, INTENTIONS, and resultant ACTIONS based upon ignorance are not natural. One problem is that most people don't know what natural growth and development for the human creature really is.

To excuse destructive imprudent behavior, many declare that FOLLY is also "HUMAN NATURE" and that human nature cannot be changed. The strange thing is that they do not include themselves in this tragic FOLLY. They believe themselves to be an exception to the rule, being more tolerant, more flexible, more intelligent, and in fact, although it is never stated, different and superior to most of the rest of the world. The common cry is, "I live in this society; there is no other way to survive." What they are saying is, "I am afraid to let go of the comfort, security, and belonging which society offers." If they are not among the millions in the world who are truly starving and homeless, then there is no substance in this fear.

To most people the NATURAL life appears too unstimulating and devoid of contentment, pleasure, and elation. They do not see beneath the surface of simplicity the beauty of real contentment, pleasure, and elation. We can show the NATURAL LIFE in a way that is easy to understand with a diagram. You will see that man basically seeks Comfort, Security, and Belonging. Comfort is directly related to sustaining oneself with food and warmth. Security is concerned with finding shelter from natural enemies and a threatening environment. Belonging is keeping company with like-minded persons to obtain support for the common good.

Fig. 26 The Natural Life

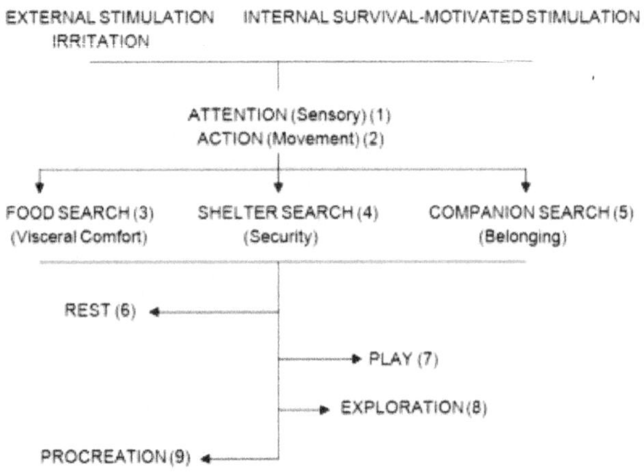

As a human creature, we either respond to internal stimuli or external stimuli. Natural responses only have six basic forms apart from automatic normal functions. We make sure that we are provided with food and warmth and are both safe and sheltered from predators and natural elements. We also respond in joining with a group or groups for mutual support. We rest and we indulge in other activities like play and exploration, which prepare us for any events we might meet in the threatening external world or for the normal functions listed. Finally, we procreate in order to perpetuate the species. In addition we excrete and we sleep when our bodies command those functions.

It is all quite simple, really. Of course, the way in which we actually do things is much more complex and its complexity leads us into thousands of little traps which draw us away from all that is natural and correct. This complexity of our lives is completely accepted by almost everyone as being necessary. All have been fully brainwashed by a foolish society. The thought of letting the FOLLY fall away creates an alarming state of insecurity which initiates a defense of one's "civilized" grasping way of life.

Basically we should act in order to obtain our daily bread, then rest in our shelter. We could join with like-minded persons or alone pursue sport, games, and outdoor activities which would delight us and at the same time prepare us physically and mentally to deal with any future event which may occur which is outside the normal realm of our day-to-day experiences. In addition, we could choose to be with and grow with a selected partner with both sensitivity and sensuality, and when the time was propitious, if we were so inclined, reproduce, performing the natural act of species perpetuation. It could be a full, healthy, and delightful life. There would be difficulties and problems and even conflict, but our reactions and ACTIONS would be correct and free from suffering.

The lives of other animals are not too different. If we watch them, we see that they are indeed correct in their INTENTIONS and ACTIONS. They do things at the right time in the right way. They live correctly, living and dying within the framework of the conflictive world in which they live.

When we look at the reality of our existence, we find that we race around in circles looking for our daily bread. Unfortunately, we not only run after our daily bread, but grab vicariously for whatever else we can get which delights us. When it comes to shelter and security, we greedily want the best, the most, and we still feel insecure. We sell ourselves into slavery so that we have no time to rest. We are constantly in search of some Utopian ideal which the state, the church, the educational system, society, our peers and our parents have sold to us. What folly. If we look at the activity of other animals, we find that they seek their food, obtain their shelter, and then rest, rest, and rest. Actually this rest is not the "feet up on the couch and let's sleep" kind of rest. It is an alert meditation which is an example to all of us. It is the meditation which we call quiet and still CONCENTRATION.

We do not play. We are spectators or voyeurs. If we do take part in sports at all, it is with the motivation only to win. It is a frenzy of greed and the desire to dominate which makes itself apparent. We do not play for mutual benefit, for mutual learning. Our fun is to look for visceral or emotional pleasure and this is often so clearly self-destructive that it is difficult to understand why we do not see the suffering which such pursuits provoke. We treat liquor and drugs as if they were a panacea for all ills. We indulge in dance and music looking for satisfaction and do not use these beautiful acts as means of true expression. Does this play prepare us for anything? Is it healthy for our minds and bodies?

We are seldom really curious. We have lost the way. We glory in cognitive knowledge, not wisdom. We are driven mindlessly towards any sort of knowledge which brings more visceral enjoyment, emotional thrills, wealth, or power. When we have a partner we do not unite with them seeking the attainment of oneness. Instead we devour them with Egoism and our demands. When we come together in expression of what should be natural, we create a visceral union which eventually is divisive and does not bring together each partner into real sensual union.

Our lives are a calamity and we suffer. Yet we call all the things we do and all the things we seek "pleasurable." We are ignorant and have lost the thirst for correct knowledge. We are not calm and tranquil. We respond to the slightest stimulation with nervous intensity. We suffer. We react to the things going on around us which we should ignore and do not respond to our true nature. We say we would like to live peacefully and calmly but never learn how to relax. When we have time free we seek stimulation which reinforces our desires and prepares us for nothing, bringing instead CONFUSION, GREED, and HOSTILITY. Is it any wonder at all that there is so much suffering in this world?

What we need to do is attain correct livelihood, live correctly but simply, rest with adequate meditation, play and study with the idea of maintaining a healthy mind in a healthy body, and live with like-minded people in love and harmony. It is part of the old hippie idea which has disappeared in the face of the cruel economic realities of the world which man has created and continues to perpetuate.

We have to learn to pay no attention to visceral, emotional, and cognitive pleasures, and delight in the ACTIONS we make without being chained to them. If we dance we should delight in the dancing and be as one with it. It is folly to focus on the pleasure of dancing. Do you see the difference? In the first case we dance to be dancing. In the second, we dance to gain pleasure. Similarly we can delight in music or erroneously cling to the pleasure of listening to the music.

If you carefully look at all the things you do, you will find how seldom you actually delight in doing things and instead how often you react and focus on the sensations, emotions, and thoughts of pleasure. It is not always easy to see this captivity in which we have placed ourselves. We need to set ourselves free from the monster which we have created, but CONFUSION, GREED, and HOSTILITY hold us in a tight grip and we are blind to the truth.

In the Old Testament we read of Adam and Eve and the eating of the apple of knowledge. Many people see this apple of knowledge as the problem and say that man ate the apple and it is his lot in life to know and suffer the consequences.

Look at the truth. This is a consumer world and the motor at the center of it is indeed the constant refinement and evolution of products. A natural question is whether this constant bent of man to always find a better or quicker way to do things is really at the center of our problem. No, it is not. It is natural for man, with his curiosity, to discover new and better ways to do things. Knowledge is not the problem. The problem is that pleasure or profit motives intervene when it is time to think about transforming the investigation into action. We never ask what the consequences of progress might be. We should be vigilant at all levels. It is as equally correct to ask what the consequences of acting without virtue might be as to ask what might be the effect on the environment of building a dam or a bridge in a certain spot. Actually we human creatures seldom look at the important consequences of our ACTIONS. The problem then is not our curiosity and potential progress, but our concepts of correct progress, which are generally tied to greed and power. This too is SUFFERING.

Each person can encounter solutions to all mankind's suffering in the DHAMMA. We can each discipline ourselves with mindfulness, study the DHAMMA, and learn how to contemplate; and with concentration and penetration, look at the true human creature. If you have the energy and high motivation, you can follow a very direct path, but there are other ways too, and one effective way is to use the MANTRA of COMPASSION as a base. It does work and it really is infinite, worthy, perfect, complete, and unimpeded.

The solutions are there and are not difficult to understand. They are difficult to turn into action. Each person must work at it. We cannot restore our true nature in a day. It has taken mankind thousands of years to get us in this sorry state. One great problem is that we only think about changing things while we suffer, and forget all about changing when everything is apparently going well.

All each person needs to do is start with a true introspection of their own MENTAL STATES and SUFFERING, see the SUFFERING of HUMANITY, be aware of each man's and woman's tremendous potential for either SENSITIVITY, DISCRIMINATION, or NATURAL INTELLIGENCE, and understand what the NATURAL LIFE of man can be. If you see within yourself even in an unclear way, looking beyond the words, that the truth lies with what has been presented here, then you will have already made your first step towards LIBERATION. If you have resolved to go forward in order to discover man's true nature, resisting the force of the IDENTITIES that tempt you away from the natural path, then you will already have begun taking the second step.

3. Surrogate Suffering

PAIN AND SUFFERING

PAIN is a physiological experience which signals a physical problem. Few realize, however, that the unpleasant and sometimes unbearable EXPERIENCE which we call PAIN is not really physical pain at all. It is actually made up of true PAIN and also SUFFERING. The PAIN component is a perfectly natural experience accompanying neurological signals to the brain, which indicates that there is a problem in the physiological system. Actually, PAIN is not unbearable at all. The component which appears to be unbearable is the one we know as SUFFERING.

What we actually feel and call PAIN is a state of AMPLIFIED SENSITIVITY generated by EGO IDENTITY. It still feels like PAIN, and we call it PAIN, but it is not. This intolerable sensation of FALSE PAIN which almost always accompanies TRUE PAIN is actually caused by a mental transformation of the true experience, which is initiated by the SELF-INDULGENT EGO IDENTITY.

This sometimes unbearable and agonizing experience occurs when the EGO IDENTITY looks at the situation and decides that it is not just intolerable to have pain but it is unjust. "Why should I be ill? Why should I have pain?" With these cries into the wilderness EGO frets and feels sorry for itself. It creates such internal TENSION and STRESS that the body begins to resist the real pain and the mind calls for an attention to the person, not the problem. These mental gymnastics and the ensuing TENSION of resistance amplify the PAIN. The natural message, you see, has changed. The initial message which was, "There is a problem with the system," is now changed by EGO into, "Pay attention to me. Stop this PAIN because I do not want it!" Do you see the difference in emphasis? EGO has systematically caused an increase in apparent pain, forcing an emphasis upon the person and the pain which it neither likes nor wants. This is a SURROGATE experience, generated from the EGO DEMAND for the cessation of the pain which the EGO IDENTITY is experiencing.

The third form of SUFFERING is then this PAIN-ASSOCIATED SURROGATE SUFFERING, which almost always acts together with

PAIN to form the single sensation which we mistakenly call PAIN. That SUFFERING component is totally unnecessary. If you can learn to separate the psychological component from the physiological by relaxing and completely accepting the real pain signal, then you will have learned to isolate REAL PAIN from SUFFERING and be able to reduce or eliminate the SUFFERING by returning the system to its natural state.

MIND AND CONSCIOUSNESS

You have seen the importance of understanding how a corrupted MIND works in the evolution of SUFFERING. We cannot continue forward advances, however, without discussing another final aspect of EXPERIENCING, which will aid in understanding all SUFFERING so that it can be set aside using the Mantra.

We have dealt extensively with BENEVOLENT LOVE, GLADNESS, COMPASSION, SUFFERING, various MENTAL STATES, and STRESS. In evaluating all these concepts, without doubt you have correctly considered each as a product of the MIND, which contains the various programs used to run the system. In fact, this computer analogy is excellent and it is a good idea if you can continue to view the whole human body as a sophisticated biological computer. It is a very intricate one, but it really is a biological computer nonetheless.

What we call the MIND is akin to a computer OPERATING SYSTEM which runs the human creature. It runs and monitors all the processes which we individually speak of as the SENSE ORGANS (DOORS), SENSATIONS, EMOTIONS, THOUGHT, REASON, PERCEPTION, and CONSCIOUSNESS. MIND is also in constant two-way contact with the process of MEMORY, which is equivalent to a computer HARD DISK. It is MEMORY which stores the application programs which are our ATTITUDES.

You will note that we said that the EXPERIENCES we have discussed are all PRODUCTS of the MIND. These products, the EXPERIENCES themselves, are perceived in CONSCIOUSNESS. This CONSCIOUSNESS is not the same as MIND, and it is best considered as a different process which is apart and quite distinct.

The SUFFERING which we have examined is one of these sets of

EXPERIENCES which are perceived and registered as interpretations of UNNATURAL STRESS. They are related within CONSCIOUSNESS to specific operational MIND-STATES which initiate INTERPRETATIONS of the CURRENT STATE of each of the processes. Much of the other information received by CONSCIOUSNESS is feedback information, which in part consists of the EXPERIENCES of GLADNESS, COMPASSION, BENEVOLENT LOVE, DELIGHT, STRESS, and important information about the MENTAL STATES.

All this information, along with the perceptions which we have of the external world, information about our physical state, and the valid information placed in CONSCIOUSNESS during subliminal mental operations, is duly registered on what we call the SCREEN OF CONSCIOUSNESS, which is equivalent to a computer MONITOR. This SCREEN OF CONSCIOUSNESS is the only perception that a person has about what is going on within CONSCIOUSNESS, and is, therefore, a second-hand source of information about what is going on subconsciously.

Fig. 27 The Natural Function of a Receiving Mind and Consciousness

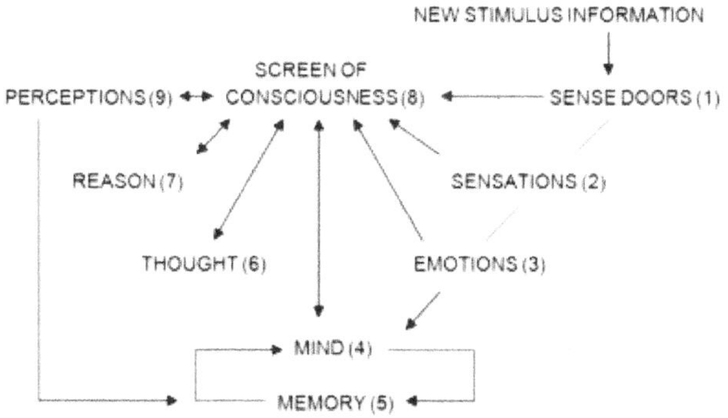

In the NATURAL operation of the human creature, you can see that CONSCIOUSNESS plays a central role. Now, in the above diagram you will see that NEW STIMULUS INFORMATION enters the human system through the sense doors and is passed into the different processes in the order in which they are numbered. As each process receives the information, it handles that information in the correct manner and passes relevant but not all information about that process to CONSCIOUSNESS.

CONSCIOUSNESS thus registers all the operations of the various processes which it requires in order to fulfill its role. SENSATIONS and EMOTIONS are registered not only as VISCERAL and EMOTIONAL EXPERIENCES, but as RECOGNITION and RECALL respectively.

The system operates rather like an efficient kitchen in a deluxe restaurant, in which the raw vegetables pass through the hands of a cleaner, a peeler, a cutter, a preparer, a chef, a taster, etc., in which at each stage the assistant head chef, CONSCIOUSNESS, is informed of progress. This assistant in turn passes all that information to the head chef, MIND, who really controls the kitchen.

Remember that neither the assistant nor the head chef need to know whether the carrots had brown or red earth on them originally, or if the potatoes were hard- or soft-skinned. All they want is the important information about the quality of the raw material and the processes involved in preparing the food for eventual consumption: DECISION-MAKING and FINAL ACTION.

Because all these processes transfer important information to CONSCIOUSNESS in a specific form, each form has its own name. There is therefore a SENSE DOOR CONSCIOUSNESS from stage 1, a SENSE CONSCIOUSNESS (2), a RECEIVING CONSCIOUSNESS (3), an INVESTIGATING CONSCIOUSNESS (RECOGNITION and RECALL), a REGISTERING CONSCIOUSNESS (4 and 5), and a DETERMINING CONSCIOUSNESS (6 and 7). CONSCIOUSNESS itself, in its major role as a monitoring system is stage 8, and there is at stage 9 an important final DYNAMIC FUSION in memory of the details of the MATERIALITY and MENTALITY operations of PERCEPTION with all other data.

The processes of MIND, THOUGHT, REASON, and PERCEPTION are interpreters and manipulators of new and old information. In the previous diagram, the information from the SENSATIONS and EMOTIONS is useful DATA even in its raw form, because both were a part of our primitive inherited information system and, if nurtured correctly, can continue to give useful information. You can see then that there is a two-way passage of information between these units and CONSCIOUSNESS, and that MIND can therefore be continually modifying these operations through CONSCIOUSNESS, using the information stored in MEMORY and the new information which is flowing in and being processed continually. It is an extraordinary and efficient dynamic system in which MIND and CONSCIOUSNESS work together as an executive team.

You can see that it is imperative that CONSCIOUSNESS should be operating correctly, for it is the link between the processes. If contamination is permitted to occur here, then the entire system will be in peril.

Unfortunately, CONSCIOUSNESS, as it has developed in the human creature, is continually operating under the debilitating weight of contamination. The source of this contamination is MEMORY, where tainted DATA, learned during a life of folly, are stored. MIND uses that DATA and performs often faulty operations on information sent to CONSCIOUSNESS. Since REASON uses the information obtained from CONSCIOUSNESS in order to qualify and catalog information for final PERCEPTION and DYNAMIC FUSION, the results are generally catastrophic for anyone afflicted.

You will have observed that CONSCIOUSNESS, just like a computer monitor, only deals with an infinitesimally small part of all the information which is processed in the human bio-computer. Now think for a moment. The only things which we know about what is going on in the system are what we perceive as experiences in CONSCIOUSNESS.

Fig. 28 The Virus Contamination by Mind Within Consciousness

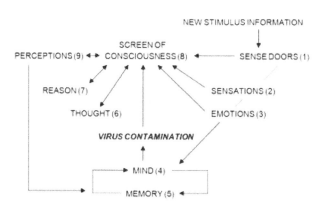

We know then very little about the real workings of the human system. In our FOLLY, however, we believe that what we perceive in CONSCIOUSNESS is real and complete, and further believe that our

THINKING goes on there. We also accept the DELUSION of our own egocentric existence which appears in CONSCIOUSNESS. These are grave errors. Indeed, we have already seen that SUFFERING is only an interpretation of UNNATURAL STRESS. It has no reality. If we accept these DELUSIONS and attend in an incorrect manner to these EXPERIENCES, then we are invalidating the natural processes. It is as if we voluntarily accepted the presence of virus activity in our precious and delicate human bio-computer.

This virus activity has as its source the virus of IGNORANCE, which exists within MEMORY in the form of the DEMANDS, INCORRECT ATTITUDES, and the FALSE MEMORIES of PAST SENSATIONS, EMOTIONS, and COGNITIVE PERCEPTIONS.

If the MIND's natural programs are contaminated by these viruses, then the EXPERIENCES which appear upon the SCREEN of CONSCIOUSNESS as a result of MIND activity become an unintelligible tangle of information contaminated by demands, based upon sensations, emotions, and impassioned thoughts, which have no natural utility nor make any real sense whatsoever. The human creature, with the unfortunate and unsolicited aid of the biased IDENTITIES, does make apparent intelligent patterns out of this tangle within CONSCIOUSNESS. These interpretations are quite inadequate, for they only serve to make the human creature feel that he knows what is happening and what he is doing.

The problem is that if what appears in CONSCIOUSNESS is accepted as TRUTH, then all useful information is changed from valuable ILLUSIONS into debilitating DELUSIONS which then begin to control behavior.

When this happens, then indeed the IDENTITIES of the MIND, personified in CONSCIOUSNESS, and the INCORRECT ATTITUDES and UNNATURAL DEMANDS will completely overrule the wealth of natural knowledge which we possess. In a virus-infected person, there is no GLADNESS, COMPASSION, or BENEVOLENT LOVE and certainly most of the information within consciousness is defiled. In a healthy person, there are no UNNATURAL MENTAL STATES, no UNNATURAL STRESSES, and certainly no SUFFERING. All the EXPERIENCES which are either about one's internal or external worlds are natural and not debilitating.

The intelligent thing to do would appear to be to get rid of the viruses of IGNORANCE which result in INCORRECT ATTITUDES, INTENTIONS, and ACTIONS. We are then placed in the unfortunate position of having to cast out IGNORANCE, and this can only be done by using WISDOM, which has not been awakened. That WISDOM is stifled, in fact, by IGNORANCE. What a dilemma!

We have then two tasks ahead. One is to clear up the jumble of information which appears on the SCREEN of CONSCIOUSNESS, returning it to a calm and still state. The second is to eliminate the various viruses, the INCORRECT ATTITUDES and the UNNATURAL DEMANDS which contaminate MIND.

Fortunately, there are solutions. Since MIND and CONSCIOUSNESS are distinct, we can first solve the immediate problem by clearing up the tangle in CONSCIOUSNESS. This conceptually is not complicated at all. It is accomplished by training oneself in various methods of CONCENTRATION (*DHYANA*). We can solve the more complex problem of MIND contamination by training in PENETRATION (INSIGHT) and by disciplined STUDY and UNDERSTANDING. Both CONCENTRATION and PENETRATION do require a system of ATTENTIVE PREPARATION (*DHARANA*), and we have available here one of the excellent ways to provide that ACCESS PREPARATION. It is the GREAT COMPASSION MANTRA of NATURAL WISDOM.

Naturally, as old INCORRECT ATTITUDES, INTENTIONS, and ACTIONS are set aside, they will need to be replaced with those which are CORRECT. This too requires the use of a suitable system of *DHARANA*. That task can also be effectively accomplished by using the GREAT COMPASSION MANTRA when it is accompanied by correct preparation and an understanding of the Mantra concepts.

MIND AND BODY

The Mind/Body Dichotomy

The relationship between MIND and CONSCIOUSNESS is clearly important to know about, but we should also be concerned about the rest of the human body. That is because it is clear from more than two thousand years of collective experience regarding CONCENTRATION that if the BODY is unbalanced and without harmony, then the psychological components do not readily enter into higher states of CONSCIOUSNESS.

We have seen that MIND and CONSCIOUSNESS are best thought of as distinct units, but that we must beware of making the fundamental mistake of really believing that the processes of MIND and CONSCIOUSNESS are really separate from what we think of as the PHYSICAL BODY. This apparent separation occurs because of the arising of PERCEPTION of MENTALITY and MATERIALITY. Actually, our BODY is the whole COMPUTER, which contains and includes all the components, including the physical units which generate the processes of MIND and CONSCIOUSNESS. Of course, there is a vast difference in the sophistication of even the most complex computer and the human bio-computer, but in general terms there is great similarity.

To those who do grasp CONCENTRATION and PENETRATION, it is evident that all the organs and muscles cooperate with the mind during every special or higher state of consciousness. If the elements of the body which support the MIND are not functioning correctly, then you cannot expect the mind to function optimally. In day-to-day living, when a person's only thoughts are mixtures of CRAVING and CLINGING, the quality of human functioning is not often considered as an impediment. When, however, the human creature is concerned with rectifying the contaminated mental system, it becomes essential to consider the human creature as a Gestalt whole.

If the fine membranes of your lungs, for example, are saturated with tar from smoking, then correct breathing is impossible. If your blood is too thin, then transport of oxygen to the vital cells of the body, including those of the brain, is insufficient. Both of these conditions materially affect the quality of Mantra chanting. If your food intake does not include the correct mixture of vitamins, minerals, sugars, fats, proteins, and carbohydrates, then nothing will function correctly. If you fill your body with intoxicants, the whole system becomes poisoned, including the MIND. Indeed, the body is one apparent unit; each member of that body operates as a part of the whole. Those who wish to chant the Mantra should not, therefore, make the obvious mistake of attending only to the health of the MIND.

Maintaining the Whole Body

Everyone is very aware in this modern world of the value of a sound BODY. The more sensible men and women spend time in sporting activities or use a gymnasium to develop and maintain a healthy physique with correct muscle tone. Others watch their nutrition with great vigilance and reject the contamination of all sorts of intoxicants. Here also, the serious problem is that most people create the concept MIND and separate it from the concept which they hold of the BODY. In other words, most people think of the MIND and BODY as two separate things.

You have in the past, no doubt, considered it correct to develop a sound MIND in a sound BODY. You cannot have a sound MIND in a sound BODY, because the MIND is an integral part of the body, just as are your lungs, heart, and liver. They are always unfortunately thought of as separate because the MIND appears to exercise control over the BODY. Once again, this is a conceptual error.

True, when PHYSICAL TENSION is experienced, then the stressed person will try to do something to relieve the problem by MENTAL RELAXATION, but the kind of relationship that most people conceptualize is one in which the MIND controls the BODY. What is normally accomplished is only a relief of symptoms. Actually MIND, CONSCIOUSNESS, and the rest of the body's organs, muscles, nerves, etc., work together in synchrony when the human creature is acting in a healthy and natural manner. Most people may know but have never internalized the fact that, although the MIND is involved in the correct functioning of the muscles, organs, and nerves, as well as the system of nutrition, debility due to mistreatment of their PHYSICAL BODY seriously affects the functioning of the MIND.

Cure the MIND and the REST OF THE BODY will go about the task of growth, nurture, and maintenance in the correct way. The inverse is also true with regard to the relationship between the REST OF THE BODY and the MIND. If you disrupt correct functioning in any part of the whole body by continual FOLLY and abuse, then you automatically interfere with the MIND and its task. Continuing with habits which stem from INCORRECT ATTITUDES towards your general health inhibits the MIND'S capacity to do its part. Your task in this respect then is quite clear and simple. Adopt a CORRECT ATTITUDE towards your own WHOLE BODY, not just your MIND and CONSCIOUSNESS, when you are ready to begin to seriously walk upon the path of LIBERATION.

You do not have to push yourself with intellectual discipline to go with regularity to a gymnasium or maintain a healthy diet in the face of temptation to do otherwise. Correct the MIND'S view of the vehicle which contains it and supports it and you will perform correctly without neglecting physical exercises, mental exercises, breathing exercises, and exercises for your internal organs. You will also then eat correctly, sleep correctly, play correctly, work correctly, and live correctly quite automatically. Furthermore, you will do so with a joy which comes from the natural knowledge that you are a whole human creature in tune with the world, being in the world but not a slave to it.

Forget the idea of obtaining a grand physique. Forget the idea of looking good in your clothes, of being admired. Dispense with vanity and allow your mind to develop those healthy and CORRECT internal ATTITUDES and resulting CORRECT INTENTIONS. They will result in the healthy ACTIONS which will promote the development of complete BODY health and the maturation of WISDOM which will allow you to use that whole body in a full, long, natural, and joyful life.

If you look at other animals in their natural environment, you will find that their minds are not infected with a behavioral virus that directs them to operate against their own best interests. They make mistakes, natural mistakes, but these are mistakes due to their lack of experience or an extreme level of real conflict in which they find themselves. The rabbit has the nature of a rabbit, the fox that of a fox. Plants are no different. The primrose has the inherited memory which gives it the nature of a primrose. It acts exactly as its memory dictates, and its memory is healthy and its behavior is correct.

The human creature, on the contrary, has lost all contact with its natural heritage. It is no longer acting in a natural and correct manner. Its internal programs are under the influence of a virus of destruction. Man's behavior is slowly carrying him towards sure extinction. He has destroyed most of the living world already and will undoubtedly carry every other living creature with him into oblivion. It is not too late, although the picture looks bleak. No individual can change this path upon which man is racing. All that each person can do is change his own path, and having done so, become a living example which others may wish to follow. If you choose to do so, here and now, you can take the first step to recover your own birthright, your truly human nature, your NATURAL WISDOM.

THE WAY FORWARD

You may be one of those few who have really understood the SUFFERING of the world presented in this commentary. If you can internalize the knowledge of that SUFFERING, then you will know COMPASSION and will be in an excellent position to begin with the Mantra chanting. The way has been prepared and the GREAT COMPASSION MANTRA can bring an end to all SUFFERING. We have seen how Mantras work, but you will, no doubt, like to know what you will actually be doing if you choose to use this GREAT COMPASSION MANTRA of NATURAL WISDOM.

The Mantra has four phases. In the first, there are twenty-three distinct Mantra lines. These lines are a preparation for the difficult task of chanting the main lines of the second and third phases. Each line of this first phase is a well-defined and separate step ahead, carefully designed to guide the chanter to the point where he or she is ready to evoke the great power of the Mantra. The commentary which accompanies each line explains the general significance of each line and helps you to understand this significance at a more profound level so that later consolidation will be correct.

There should be no hurry, no objectives, just a steady progression forward. Each person must go forward at his own rate. Those who are most calm and correct will be sure that they understand as they progress, for the setting of a sound foundation will help in the construction of all that is based on that foundation. Many new concepts will be explained and many old concepts clarified. Be attentive and place each foot upon solid ground. Do not permit your own thoughts to intrude, for if you do, the blocks which are laid for you will be sullied by conscious thought.

The second phase is where the magnificence of the GREAT MANTRA shows itself. There are twenty-two lines. In these lines, with correct chanting and correct understanding, you will make available the curing power of the Mantra for yourself and others who are prepared to listen. You will see that there are four parts in this phase. The first deals with the CARES and ANXIETIES of mankind. The three subsequent parts deal with the SUFFERING which has its roots in the VISCERAL DEMANDS, the EGO DEMANDS, and the DEMANDS for DOMINATION. Each will be explained in a manner which will allow a clear comprehension. The qualities which you will need to pass fruitfully along will be carefully nurtured, but you will need to step carefully and not fall into traps constructed by your own conscious intellect.

In this second phase you will find mention of twenty-seven Hand and Eye preparations. These are practices which are essential for those who are really seriously and happily moving forward with personal growth and awakening.

These preparations are contained in the book entitled *THE PATH OF BENEVOLENCE AND WISDOM WITHIN THE GREAT COMPASSION MANTRA: A PRACTICAL GUIDE TO LIBERATION AND HAPPINESS.* In this book the Hand and Eye preparations are explained in detail. A third book, *THE PATH OF SERENITY WITHIN THE GREAT COMPASSION MANTRA: A PRACTICAL GUIDE TO LOVE AND EQUANIMITY* is also available which deals extensively with the TEN HEARTS of the BUDDHA NATURE. It guides those on the DHAMMA PATH to the further GROWTH and DEVELOPMENT OF WISDOM and presents advanced points of WISDOM which are required for those who truly wish to continue on the PATH of NATURAL LIBERATION with dedication.

The third phase of the Mantra concentrates upon three further themes, but this time chanting is concretely directed at GREED, CONFUSION, and HOSTILITY, with a view to directly assaulting the castles of EGO, ID, and SUPER EGO. In the orthodox version, there are thirty lines, but here those lines which are conceptually and practically linked together with a single Hand and Eye preparation have been placed together as one line. The result is that we present here fifteen lines with their fifteen accompanying Hand and Eye practices.

Hand and Eye PREPARATIONS of the SECOND PHASE

PRECIOUS COMMAND
BUDDHA PEARL
FIVE-COLORED CLOUD
BLUE LOTUS
JEWELED CONCH
WHITE LOTUS
MOON ESSENCE
SHIELD
JEWELED HALBERD
PURE BOTTLE
JEWELED DAGGER
SUN ESSENCE
JEWELED BELL
WHITE WHISK
NATURAL REALM
BUDDHA'S WILLOW BRANCH
SKULL BONE STAFF
JEWELED MIRROR
CLEAR COMPREHENSION
RECITATION BEADS
JEWELED BOW
PURPLE LOTUS
JADE RING
JEWELED BOWL
VAJRA PESTLE
ELEPHANT STAFF
SWEET DEW

Hand and Eye PREPARATIONS of the THIRD PHASE

GOLD WHEEL
BUDDHA on the CROWN
TIN STAFF
JEWELED BOTTLE
JEWELED SWORD
JEWELED ARROW
JEWELED SUTRA
JEWELED CHEST
FIVE-COLORED LARIAT
JEWELED AXE
JEWELED VESSEL
VAJRA WHEEL
RED LOTUS
JEWELED TRUMPET
THOUSAND HOLDING and
   UNITING ARMS

The fourth phase consists of the six concluding lines of the Mantra. They should not be neglected or taken lightly, for they increase one-pointedness and permit a natural bridge for further cyclic repetition of the Mantra.

The Mantra has been offered in this series of books in the form of sixty-six lines, and a total of forty-two Hand and Eye preparations are presented in the second and third phases. A few of the names have been modified from the orthodox version to aid in a better understanding of the themes. These changes, however, in no way detract from the power or beauty of the GREAT MANTRA of COMPASSION. Remember that it is best if you do not try to advance too fast. The Hand and Eye practices which are available should be approached slowly, and you are urged not to pass on to them until you have really made progress in understanding and chanting the Mantra lines.

We have said that the GREAT MANTRA was developed by MAHAYANA BUDDHISTS, but it would be folly for anyone of any other discipline to ignore such a valuable tool due to foolish pride. We of the SAUTRANTIKA tradition called SVABHAVAVADIN urge you to use this Mantra of our brother and sister Buddhists, and that is why this commentary has been prepared. Proceed with diligence, knowing that you are attended by the GLADNESS, COMPASSION, and BENEVOLENT LOVE of all those who accompany you to LIBERATION and HAPPINESS.

PART TWO:

THE FIRST PHASE OF THE MANTRA

TRUE INTROSPECTION, CALMNESS, AND PATIENCE

Now is the time, as you are about to proceed with the Mantra, when you must begin to develop the traits of TRUE INTROSPECTION, CALMNESS, and PATIENCE.

When we speak of TRUE INTROSPECTION, we do not mean that you should ask the question, "Who am I?" or try to evaluate your attitudes, intentions, and actions. If you do this, you will be putting the processes of conscious intellect in operation, and that will serve no purpose at all. TRUE INTROSPECTION is a relaxed inspection of what is going on within. It is seeing the internal operation of the system before conscious intellect rationalizes, excuses, justifies, and explains what is going on. TRUE INTROSPECTION starts with an attempt to attain clear perception of the raw sensations, which are those of touch, sight, hearing, smell, and taste. When you begin, you will see that EMOTIONS and CHAINS of THOUGHT are attached to these SENSATIONS. You must note that fact without paying any attention to the EMOTIONS and THOUGHTS, and also note the strong secondary experiences which occur. These secondary experiences are, in fact, products of our sixth sense, which is MIND. It is MIND which transforms raw sensations into a different form within consciousness and generally adds inaccurate qualifying data derived from memory. If you carry out this introspection carefully, you will be able to see the way in which the raw sensations are changed so that they lose their true sensory value.

Similarly, we must look at the processes of EMOTION as they arise and see indeed that SENSATIONS and CONSCIOUS THOUGHT are attached to these emotions. You will note the tendency of emotions to start off a whole chain of thoughts which not only qualify those emotions, but create value judgments about incidents related to them. You will see that contamination of these raw emotions arises early, and that you generally respond in ways which have been conditioned by often faulty information stored in memory, instead of allowing those emotions to act as natural signals which initiate accurate investigation and evaluation. In closing off the doors to a new examination of emotions as they arise, you limit your potential for better understanding.

You must also look at PERCEPTUAL THOUGHTS as they arise in conscious intellect and see that SENSATIONS and EMOTIONS are attached to them. These SENSATIONS and EMOTIONS color the thoughts, lead them into unimportant areas, and change their normal and correct evolution within consciousness. The result is that the myriad of new THOUGHT CHAINS created within consciousness appear to be more important than they actually are and all true subconscious thinking becomes contaminated.

TRUE INTROSPECTION then, in the first phase, is an INSPECTION of the level of contamination within CONSCIOUSNESS by faulty sensory information, faulty emotional information, and faulty data stored in memory. As a second phase, we can then proceed to strip away the contamination which causes folly-filled ATTITUDES, INTENTIONS, and ACTIONS. Finally, if we have completed early phases correctly, we can begin to understand, without conscious interpretation, all the PURE THOUGHTS which are available to conscious intellect from our subconscious.

When we use TRUE INTROSPECTION, we will see how agitated our mind really is, how it is always teeming with apparent thoughts and ideas which really have little value or use, and how sensations and emotions control much of the activity within consciousness. This is the time when we must introduce CALMNESS. CALMNESS is the creation of a STILL MIND and the limitation of ACTIONS so that the entire system becomes tranquil. If we are calm, then we reduce the NOISE within consciousness and aid INTROSPECTION. You cannot force CALMNESS upon the system nor simply command it. You must simply let go of agitation. You can see that TRUE INTROSPECTION and CALMNESS work together, each one helping in some way the other.

Finally, we must consider PATIENCE. We all know what PATIENCE is and how hard it is to maintain. The important thing to do first is to avoid making the mistake of constructing EXPECTATIONS. If you do not have EXPECTATIONS you thereby increase PATIENCE. You must concentrate on processes, that is, what is going on, not on what is going to eventually happen. Here too you will need INTROSPECTION in order to see those expectations created by the mind, and CALMNESS in order to avoid being trapped in the normally noisy merry-go-round of CONSCIOUSNESS.

Now, the accomplishment of the ability to truly introspect and to be calm and patient are prerequisites for attaining the fine qualities which are available to all human creatures. They lead immediately to RESOLUTION, the initiation of appropriately directed READINESS, and to the most important quality of MINDFULNESS. It is then, with CALMNESS and PATIENCE, and with the true spirit of introspection, that you can begin with joy, confidence, and a still mind the difficult journey within the GREAT COMPASSION MANTRA that leads to WISDOM.

THE PRELIMINARY OPTION

Before actually beginning the chanting anywhere in the cycle, or before beginning the chanting of a single Mantra line, it is customary and often beneficial to chant the following two Mantra lines:

QIĀN SHŎU QIĀN YĂN GUĀN SHÌ YĪN PÚ SÀ
GUĂNG DÀ YUÁN MĂN WÚ ÀI DÀ BĒI XĪN TUÓ LUÓ NÍ

The first line brings to mind the legendary THOUSAND-HANDED, THOUSAND-EYED BODHISATTVA SAHASRABHUJA, who regards the SOUNDS OF THE WORLD. The second rouses the energy of the VAST, GREAT, PERFECT, COMPLETE, UNIMPEDED GREAT COMPASSION HEART *DHARANI*. This phrase of two lines then names the Mantra as:

The INFINITE, WORTHY, PERFECT, COMPLETE, UNIMPEDED
GREAT COMPASSION HEART *DHARANI*

of the THOUSAND-HANDED, THOUSAND-EYED BODHISATTVA
who regards the SOUNDS of the WORLD

This chanting is then traditionally followed by three chanted repetitions of the following line. It is a Mantra line of great respect and refuge directed specifically at SAHASRABHUJA, representing all those who are likewise filled with GLADNESS, COMPASSION, and BENEVOLENT LOVE and have earned the LIBERATION of their NATURAL WISDOM:

NĀ MÓ DÀ BĒI GUĀN SHÌ YĪN PÚ SÁ

All RESPECT to the MOST COMPASSIONATE BODHISATTVA
who regards the SOUNDS of the WORLD

You are then prepared to begin the first line of the GREAT COMPASSION MANTRA of NATURAL WISDOM.

THE FIRST SERIES: REFUGE AND CONTEMPLATION

NĀ MÒ HĒ LÁ DÁ NÀ DUŌ LÁ YÈ YĒ

The first line of this series is extremely important. Most people do not understand its significance in the Mantra. Without this chanted preparation, anyone who attempts the Mantra for the first time will be ineffective.

Normally, when you say "*NĀ MÒ* Amitabha Buddha" then you declare, "I take refuge in the Buddha." Declaring this, you offer to set aside the mundane components of the life of the senses, using your knowledge of the virtue and strength of the Buddha as a focus. Furthermore, you declare that you are internally prepared with the equanimity built by this refuge in the Buddha to receive and live with your own TRUE NATURE, which is not based upon CONSCIOUS INTELLECT. It is important that you also accept with humility the fact that you may not be able to remain firm in your resolve and may fall back into the MUNDANE world dominated by your IDENTITIES: ID, EGO, and SUPER EGO.

This too is crucial. You cannot truthfully KNOW if you are prepared to take a step forward in LIBERATION, and it would be a terrible tragedy to close oneself off from future attempts just because of apparent failure. When you are prepared to accept success or failure, then you will remain strong enough to continue on the right path of VIRTUE until you are ready to step forward once more.

Most people are motivated to seek LIBERATION just to avoid their SUFFERING. This seldom seems to work. You are actually fully prepared only when you see your own SUFFERING as a part of the SUFFERING of all people, in the past, the present, and the future. If you CLING too much to the desire to end your own suffering, then cutting the chains which bind you is much more difficult.

What you must seek, you see, is a full ILLUMINATION, an understanding of the SUFFERING of all sentient creatures, and an understanding of the PATH which leads to their LIBERATION. This is much more important than people realize. Most who do not succeed have not really internalized this idea, and so they carry their own burden uppermost in consciousness.

When you chant the Mantra line *NĀ MÒ* with *HĒ LÁ DÁ NÀ DUŌ LÁ YÈ YĒ*, then you are declaring that you take refuge in the TRIPLE JEWEL, which is the BUDDHA; the NATURAL LAW, an understanding of which leads to LIBERATION from SUFFERING; and the *SANGHA* or BROTHERHOOD of all others who are upon the CORRECT PATH. This TRIPLE JEWEL is so called to give one an idea of its splendor.

Just as a jewel shines lustrous when light touches upon it, so the TRIPLE JEWEL reflects the light of TRUTH which we cannot look upon or perceive directly. Each component of the TRIPLE JEWEL is a source of strength.

TAKING REFUGE

Taking refuge provides a base of confidence and determination. If you really accept this refuge, then you can proceed, with profound confidence, trust, and belief in a correct and fruitful outcome.

Taking refuge is a defense against the SUFFERING caused by your own IGNORANCE. Declaring your intent to take refuge does not make that intent a REALITY. Taking refuge is a declaration of VOLITION in which this CORRECT INTENTION must be accompanied by the appropriate CORRECT ATTITUDE and be followed by CORRECT ACTION.

When we declare *NĀ MÒ HĒ LÁ DÁ NÀ DUŌ LÁ YÈ*, adding the final *YĒ*, then we declare our respect and reverence for that TRIPLE JEWEL.

What exactly then does this first phrase accomplish? It sets the BASE for our own STATE of READINESS. You can see, however, that merely chanting the phrase does nothing, unless internally you are aware and clear about what it signifies and have internalized the components of VIRTUE necessary to SINCERELY activate the process and TAKE REFUGE.

If you are in readiness, then reciting the Mantra psychologically operates at five levels.

First, it initiates what we call the NATURAL LAW (DHAMMA) OF ERADICATING CALAMITIES. Everyone at some time or another has experienced what appears to be a CALAMITY. Actually, CALAMITIES do not exist. They are invented by our minds. DIFFICULT SITUATIONS and even APPARENTLY IMPOSSIBLE SITUATIONS exist which may have APPARENTLY INTOLERABLE CONSEQUENCES. These situations and consequences are convoluted and dramatic inventions which serve GREED, DELUSION, and HOSTILITY and are mediated by SENSATIONS, EMOTIONS, and THOUGHTS.

The TAKING of REFUGE and acting against GREED, DELUSION, and HOSTILITY will naturally return the psychological system to calm equilibrium, and the APPARENT CALAMITIES will disappear, leaving clear vision. This, of course, cannot happen immediately, but even after chanting the Mantra for one day, you can perceive slight growth, albeit temporary, in your state of calmness.

Second, it initiates the NATURAL LAW OF INCREASING BENEFITS. This is fairly easy to see. The more you recite the Mantra, the stronger your RESOLUTION and CONFIDENCE will become, leading to greater benefits. These benefits will grow rather like a snowball which runs continually down a gentle slope.

Third, it initiates the NATURAL LAW OF ACCOMPLISHMENT. This does not mean that magically all that you wish for and desire you will gain without effort. It means that by following the NATURAL way, not the way of GREED, DELUSION, and HOSTILITY, you will eventually find yourself progressing and growing physically and psychologically in accord with your own WISE (BUDDHA) NATURE. With the rediscovery of your BUDDHA NATURE, all correct and natural things in this MUNDANE life will fall into place. You will find friends of like mind, you will have right and healthy livelihood; in fact, all things will be accomplished correctly.

Fourth, it initiates the NATURAL LAW OF SURRENDER. We say it initiates this law because once you have entered upon this path of VIRTUE, CONCENTRATION, and PENETRATION, then you will naturally continue surrendering all the mental states that cause SUFFERING. As you do so, the spokes of the wheel of suffering will begin to crumble and decay. This will weaken the whole structure so that the hub of the wheel, IGNORANCE itself, will fall free, destroying the WHEEL of SUFFERING altogether.

Fifth, it initiates the NATURAL LAW OF SUMMON AND CAPTURE. This is a very important consequence of your following the NATURAL LAW. You will have BENEVOLENT LOVE towards all living things, but you might fall into the temptation of wanting to share your bountiful life by converting the world. This is total folly. You don't need to ACTIVELY do anything. Flow naturally on the river of the natural law. Don't resist. Don't try to push yourself in one direction or another to achieve some objective of apparent importance. Don't try to swim against the natural flow.

Those who suffer will see your joy and calm. They will perceive your CORRECT ATTITUDE. They will see your base of CORRECT INTENTIONS and THOUGHTS. They will directly see your CORRECT ACTIONS. This alone will set their stream of consciousness in motion and eventually they will be SUMMONED. Their own WISE NATURE will be awakened and they will SURRENDER their IGNORANCE.

Clearly, you cannot expect to note anything if you repeat this or any other Mantra just once, although there will be a subliminal effect. To be completely effective, you must chant the Mantra ten thousand eight hundred times.

If you recite the Mantra once every day, it will take twenty-nine years and a half to be fully effective. That seems like a long time. It can be reduced, however, if you have sufficient discipline to chant the

Mantra one hundred and eight times each day. In ten days you will have made one thousand and eighty repetitions. It would then only take one hundred days in order to complete the whole series. Even one thousand and eighty repetitions will be very effective, and no one should scoff at a repetition of just one hundred and eight times.

These are not arbitrary figures. They have been arrived at by generations of practical experience. Certainly one hundred and EIGHT appears to be a rather strange figure. We use this extra eight in every hundred as a safeguard in case of a miscount. If you use Mantra beads for this count, you will see that there are one hundred and eight beads on the string. On more elaborate strings there are two tails, each with ten beads, which are used rather like an abacus, to multiply the one hundred and eight by TEN and by TEN again.

THE BUDDHA

Now, all this is achieved by taking refuge first of all in the BUDDHA. Who was the BUDDHA? Does it matter?

Actually, it doesn't matter at all. If you wish to believe that the BUDDHA was SUPERNATURAL, believe that. If you want to believe that the BUDDHA was perhaps the most enlightened human creature who has yet lived, and nothing more, then believe that.

One may accept legend or superstition, rules or dogma, gods, demons, spirits, and ghosts; all have very little importance, for they are, at best, words which attempt to guide one through the maze which is apparent human existence.

What is important is that you know that the BUDDHA actually lived and went further than any man or woman had gone before in understanding the human condition called SUFFERING, in defining that condition, and in teaching how that SUFFERING can be left behind. When you take refuge with the BUDDHA, you take refuge with the person who opened the door to TRANSCENDENTAL KNOWLEDGE. When you take refuge, you walk with the BUDDHA as if he were with you, an example of what can be accomplished, a guide, a good friend to have with you on your journey of COMPASSION.

It is easy to say, "I take refuge," but one must understand that in taking refuge, you put trust in that refuge. If you have the intention, albeit small, of guarding a little of your EGO, then you are not exactly taking refuge. If you do that, you want the benefit but none of the obligations. That is not respectful.

Taking refuge does not mean that you leave your MIND outside the door. It means that you sincerely TRY to enter refuge with an OPEN, UNATTACHED MIND. BUDDHA himself declared that one should not blindly accept his words unless they have been confirmed by direct experience. Take refuge with TRUST and CONFIDENCE, not with BLIND FAITH or an ATTACHED MIND.

THE DHAMMA

The second element of the TRIPLE JEWEL, in which refuge was taken by using this line, is the NATURAL LAW. The word we use for this NATURAL LAW is DHAMMA. Here we must be very careful, for this is a word with many shades of meaning.

The DHAMMA is that which exists ontologically beyond the reach of the senses. It is the equivalent of the ETERNAL DAO (TAO) which many people will have heard about. It is also, however, the NATURAL WAY which upholds all that is NATURAL. To further confound matters, it is the spoken or written explanation or TEACHINGS of the NATURAL WAY.

The DHAMMA (the written) explains the DHAMMA (the way) to maintain harmony with the DHAMMA (all that is natural). Now, one may ask why anyone would want to confuse matters so. Actually, paradoxically, the reason why these three are described with the same word is to avoid a more dangerous confusion.

Real confusion is caused when you conceptually separate the three and treat each as a separate unit, for actually they are one and the same. If you separate the "knowing it" from the "doing it" and from the "being it," then you really won't understand anything at all.

THE BROTHERHOOD

The brotherhood called the *SANGHA* actually refers to all those who are gathered together as a viable group to study and practice the DHAMMA. Specifically it is a monastic group, but in a larger sense it is all those who sincerely follow the DHAMMA in their "hearts."

Most people do not feel that they can follow a highly disciplined path. That is perfectly all right. Being within a Monastic Brotherhood or Sisterhood does not guarantee success. It is wise, however, to live one's life surrounded by friends and companions who are of LIKE MIND. It is hardly conducive to a CORRECT PATH if you are surrounded at work and in your recreation time by those who are lost in the jungle of GREED, CONFUSION, or HOSTILITY.

Actually, maintaining CORRECT LIVELIHOOD is extremely important, because so much time is spent working. If you are in a job which requires even a minimum of DECEPTION, then that is an impediment. If the company is a high-power selling machine or a manufacturer that pollutes the environment, this causes stress, which is an impediment.

If work is simple, useful, and honest, then that is the sort of job which is not an impediment. It is not good if your mind for most of the day is filled with the FOLLY of this mad world or if it is bombarded by contagious mental contamination. Since few actually live such a pure lifestyle, then taking refuge with those who sincerely follow the DHAMMA in the "hearts" is of great benefit.

THE IMMEDIATE EFFECTS

In the first phase, with refuge in the BUDDHA, you will see that you are gradually acquiring a mantle of greater serenity and calm which reduces your own SUFFERING. You will begin to see your own FOLLY.

Now, seeing that FOLLY –which is your CONFUSION or DELUSION, your GREED, and your HOSTILITY– in the way you think and act is extremely important. What is even more important is that you do not enter into a battle within CONSCIOUS INTELLECT against that FOLLY. Don't fight FOLLY. Don't resist FOLLY. All you have to do is watch it. Note its arising and note its falling away. If you fight FOLLY, the IDENTITIES will just find better ways to disguise or justify it. Just watch it and calmly take refuge. When you do this, your DOUBT, CONFUSION, and DELUSION will begin to fall away.

Poetically, using Northern Buddhist phrases, we can say that if you do this, the ten kings who are directors of the various HELLS in the courts of Yama will be happy. They will be happy, of course, because you are extracting yourself from the HELL of CONFUSION and DELUSION.

In the second phase, with refuge in the DHAMMA, which in this sense is the collection of words describing the teachings which support all that is NATURAL, you will be more vigilant and aware and will be less likely to CRAVE and CLING to a lifestyle which is against your own best interest. This means that you will begin to see that the world is full of useful tools which can be used to build a NATURAL LIFE.

We call these tools ILLUSIONS because they are not really what they appear to be. The sensations of TASTE, for example, appear to function so that you can ENJOY food. That is incorrect. The function of TASTE is to provide IDENTIFICATION of possible foods so that we can choose correctly and eat correctly.

What we human creatures have done, however, is turn the signal of PLEASURE, an ILLUSION of IDENTIFICATION, into the REASON for eating. We eat in most cases for the pleasure which eating brings. People who have turned these instruments of useful ILLUSION into DELUSION, in which objects of the senses take on importance for their own sake, find themselves CLINGING and CRAVING. Even when people are hungry, they choose more on the basis of what is pleasurable than what is wholesome and nourishing. Can you see the FOLLY in this behavior?

Poetically, once again, we can use a graphic image of this CLINGING and CRAVING and say that if you recite correctly this Mantra, you will not become the victim of a HUNGRY GHOST craving after the apparent pleasures of the world without ever attaining any real and lasting satisfaction.

Third, having taken refuge with THOSE ON THE CORRECT PATH, you will find that you will perceive and reject the inherited REMORSE, AVARICE, HOSTILITY, and AVERSION within yourself. You will become a calmer person who can see the FOLLY of others without reacting negatively and aggressively to that FOLLY. You will act with VIRTUE and REASON. You will perhaps even turn the other cheek. Poetically, we can say that you will not turn into a RAGING BEAST.

Metaphorically, the DEMONS of CONFUSION and DELUSION, the HUNGRY GHOSTS, and the SPIRITS that are RAGING BEASTS will leave you in peace if you sincerely recite this Mantra line.

NĀ MÒ HĒ LÁ DÁ NÀ DUŌ LÁ YÈ YĒ
I, with Reverence, Take Refuge in the Buddha,
the Dhamma, and the Sangha

NĀ MÒ Ā LĪ YĒ

When you chant this line, then you make another important decision. *NĀ MÒ* once again refers to taking refuge, while *Ā LĪ* refers to the respectful submission to WISDOM which distances one from paths which are based on FOLLY. When you recite this, it means that you have decided to not only avoid the FOLLY of the mundane world, but to dedicate yourself to the task of being distant from all those paths of IGNORANCE which lead to SUFFERING. You can see again that chanting this line means nothing if you don't actually act upon that decision.

There is more, you see, to chanting a Mantra than spouting SECRET and MYSTICAL sounds. In this case you have declared that you are going to seek ENLIGHTENMENT and will work against the FOLLY of IGNORANCE, bringing yourself onto the path of CORRECT and NATURAL UNDERSTANDING.

The details of the way in which you can do that are beyond the scope of this treatise. One thing should be made clear, however, and that is the importance of VIRTUE. Without VIRTUE, you will not be able to go very far. This sentence mentions respectful submission to WISDOM, but your FIRST submission is the preparedness to accept VIRTUE as the first pre-requisite for personal evolution.

VIRTUE

What is VIRTUE? It is not the same as the virtue you hear about in religious groups. First of all, a person is considered to be VIRTUOUS if he has the true internal VOLITION to be VIRTUOUS. In other words, a person who is constantly and truly trying to act with VIRTUE without success is still a VIRTUOUS PERSON.

You are a new person, ever-changing both physically and mentally, every second of your life. What you were in the last few seconds you are not now.

THERE IS NO REASON FOR GUILT FOR A PAST ACTION WHICH WAS NOT VIRTUOUS.

YOU HAVE NO CULPABILITY FOR ANY PAST ACTION WHICH WAS NOT VIRTUOUS.

YOU ARE RESPONSIBLE AS A SOCIAL CREATURE IN THIS WORLD OF THE SENSES TO REPAIR ANY DAMAGE THAT YOUR ACTIONS MAY HAVE CAUSED.

RESPONSIBILITY is not the same as GUILT or CULPABILITY.

As a person endowed with BENEVOLENT LOVE, GLADNESS, and COMPASSION, you will be RESPONSIBLE quite naturally.

You can see that VIRTUE as here applied is sensible and in the best interest of the NATURAL SYSTEM. To create GUILT and CULPABILITY is FOLLY. Not only do you tend to create that guilt in yourself, but you heap GUILT and CULPABILITY upon others, and everybody suffers.

Where does this VIRTUE come from? You already have it. It is not something you must learn about. It is a part of your NATURAL WISDOM. This BUDDHA NATURE, unfortunately, has been smothered by all the IGNORANCE which has accrued in your lifetime. It begins when society and social systems start to operate. Well-meaning but misguided parents and relatives, religious groups, the state, education systems, and friends have all played their part in masking this VIRTUE which is within you. When you begin to chant this line of the Mantra you begin to strip away this mask of IGNORANCE.

What are the components of this VIRTUE? VIRTUE is the VOLITION present in one who abstains from the following:

Killing any living thing
Taking what is not given
Sexual misconduct
Lust
Covetousness
Ill-will

False speech
Malicious speech

Harsh speech
Gossip

Torpor
Worry and Remorse
Uncertainty
Ignorance
Non-enthusiasm

Wrong views

Remember that it is the VOLITION, the WILL to avoid all the above, which makes a man or woman VIRTUOUS. There do not have to be VIRTUOUS ACTIONS for a person to be VIRTUOUS.

VIRTUE then for us is the CONSCIOUS concomitant of CORRECT VOLITION, which hopefully is followed by RESTRAINT and finally NON-TRANSGRESSION.

If you have VIRTUE and speak maliciously of someone, then you are no less virtuous. It simply means that you have not succeeded in exercising restraint. The ground will not open up beneath you. There will be no retribution or punishment. All that happens is that you will suffer the natural consequences of that lack of restraint. What then is the utility of this VIRTUE?

There is no utility, in the sense that it will lead to no special reward. There will be no mundane gain. You will not build yourself a place automatically in some HEAVEN. All you will do is retrieve your natural heritage, your BUDDHA NATURE, and you will open the door to a fuller natural life without SUFFERING. There is no further reward for developing VIRTUE. It is simply FOLLY if you do not.

VIRTUE then is a prerequisite for a fuller natural life which opens the door to advances in DISCIPLINE (MINDFULNESS), CONCENTRATION (an altered state of consciousness), and PENETRATION (a profound understanding). All these things are not exclusively reserved for the most intelligent, the strongest, or the most beautiful. They are your birthright.

In the *Visuddhimagga*, in the first chapter, the following question was asked of the BUDDHA:

The inner tangle and the outer tangle:
This generation is entangled in a tangle.
Who succeeds in disentangling this tangle?

The answer given was the following:

When a wise man, established well in VIRTUE,
Develops CONCENTRATION and UNDERSTANDING,
Then as a bhikkhu *ardent and sagacious*
He succeeds in disentangling this tangle.

VIRTUE then is the base, and all, in taking refuge, are advised to submit to the NATURAL VIRTUE within each of us.

Note that the Mantra line states that you will submit RESPECTFULLY. This is very important. You must chant the Mantra with CORRECT ATTITUDE. If you don't respect WISDOM, then how can you accept that WISDOM? All you will do is distort its meaning to fit your own wants and desires, or reshape it to fit your own EGO-formed concepts. With this base of VIRTUE, you will find less resistance to the WISDOM of the DHAMMA.

WISDOM

What exactly is this WISDOM of the DHAMMA which seems so precious? It is certainly not what is learned about in schools and universities which is planned to make you "successful." It is certainly not the esoteric learning of metaphysical teachers who build cosmic structures with their words and golden edifices with their wealth. It is not the psychological learning required to treat the socially maladapted so that they can return to the "normal" behavior of society. It is not the learning of investigators who unravel the secrets of the phenomenological world with great skills.

It is an understanding of the relationship between mankind and the rest of nature which is not related to traditional knowledge. It is the unraveling of the knots which man's folly has created. It is setting aside unnatural suffering and accepting with joy and equanimity the benefits of the natural life which are available.

How do you find this WISDOM? You need not seek it. You must allow nature to reveal its secrets to you as you open your mind freely to your human heritage, which is natural curiosity free from delusion, greed, and hostility. You must experience natural truth by your own direct experience. What you need to know is not a mass of facts, figures, and theories which will bring social comfort, security, and power, but how to discover what you already know that has been covered up by hundreds of generations of folly.

When you finally touch this WISDOM you will see that it has three major dimensions:

First, there is the UNSURPASSED WISDOM that understands the laws of CAUSE and EFFECT.

Second, there is the WISDOM OF NOBLE JUDGMENT.

And third, there is the ILLUMINATING WISDOM which casts off IGNORANCE.

These three are the hermitage of the WISDOM within which you are now advised to take refuge.

NĀ MÒ Ā LĪ YĒ
I Take Refuge and Respectfully Submit to Wisdom

PÓ LÚ JIÉ DÌ SHUÒ BŌ LÁ YĒ

Once again, this is an act of preparation. The first four syllables, *PÓ LÚ JIÉ DÌ*, remind you to be MINDFUL by careful CONTEMPLATION and the target of that essential MINDFULNESS is *SHUÒ BŌ LÁ*. Now, *SHUÒ BŌ LÁ* may be considered as the sounds of the world. These sounds are clearly in great part a manifestation of SUFFERING, but you must not forget that SUFFERING only exists in relation to TRANQUILITY. When you chant this Mantra line, then what you are doing is reinforcing MINDFULNESS and directing that state towards both the SUFFERING and TRANQUILITY of the world, towards all the sounds and signs of torment and happiness which can be perceived.

You don't need to fill your mind with details when you do this, for that would lead to a turbulent and over-stimulated state. What you must do is focus on the general image of torment and happiness, touching lightly the clearest and most obvious areas. Don't force the mind to look. Relax, and you will find that the SUFFERING and TRANQUILITY will touch your mind like an alighting butterfly. Remember, do not cling when those ideas come. Let the concepts come and instantaneously leave.

The addition of the final *YĒ* reminds you to view all this SUFFERING and TRANQUILITY with respect, for you are not apart from it. The act of being mindful should not separate you from the object of attention.

When you are MINDFUL of this world, you will see that all the SUFFERING is linked to SENSATIONS, EMOTIONS, and THOUGHTS. You will be able to see this easily within yourself. If you examine these experiences, you will find that they seldom manifest themselves clearly.

SENSATIONS, EMOTIONS, and THOUGHTS are generally mingled, and the onslaught of one stimulus brings another in its wake. They appear in consciousness, and since consciousness uses human language, THOUGHT appears to be generally present in one form or another. They appear often without warning and surge forward, forcing themselves upon awareness. SENSATIONS may urge one action while THOUGHT pushes for another option. All three are sometimes in conflict and at other times they appear united, but you will always be able to see with careful MINDFULNESS which is the dominant member in any given chain of experiences.

Very quickly they seem to fill consciousness, and once the mind is teeming with activity it is very difficult to restore calm. The great secret in arousing complete MINDFULNESS of your SENSATIONS, EMOTIONS, and THOUGHTS is to detect their FIRST ARISING.

CONTEMPLATION OF THE STATE OF THE WORLD

When you CONTEMPLATE the STATE OF WELL-BEING OF THE WORLD, you will find that it is not an easy task. It is FOLLY to contemplate the state of the world with distorted vision. It is essential that you eliminate the "I" which is contemplating. This means that the ID and the sensations, EGO and the emotions, and SUPER EGO and the thoughts of conscious intellect must be set aside.

Just as you can be "as one" with a single person, you can be "as one" with any part of nature and indeed with the entire world. In that way one can perceive more clearly. When you use this Mantra line, then you must become "as one" with all the SOUNDS of the WORLD, with all its SUFFERING and all its TRANQUILITY.

When you are contemplating the world of TRANQUILITY and SUFFERING, your mind must be in a tranquil and still state. You must see what is really going on without allowing conscious intellect to make value judgments and interpretations. You must remember also that you are a part of the world and that your SUFFERING and TRANQUILITY are not separate from that of others. Don't consciously think; absorb. Do not justify anything; don't qualify or quantify anything; just note and feel the SUFFERING and the JOY.

You must look at the apparent "I" inside your head and declare, "Ah yes, here I also appear to suffer," or "Ah yes, I also see the apparent TRANQUILITY within me, as I see it in others." You will note that you are urged to use the word "apparent." This is because you must not believe that you have a clear and uncontaminated vision of the world. Such a belief is EGO-initiated and must be avoided. Don't expect too much when you begin.

Remember too that one-pointed contemplation will not arrive because you repeat the Mantra line a few times. Once you understand and internalize the process required and experience the natural benefits, then your biological system, after repeated practice, will do its natural work and maintain for you a calm unattached observation without you having to do anything except repeat the Mantra line.

The CONTEMPLATION of the WORLD will at first dismay you, for wherever you look you will find a CRAVING AND CLINGING TO SENSATIONS, DELUSION, TURBULENT EMOTIONS and GREED, WORDS, WORDS, WORDS, and HOSTILITY. The positive sign, WELL-BEING, which is the product of SENSITIVITY, DISCRIMINATION, and NATURAL INTELLIGENCE, will be seldom seen. This should then bring home to you the need for COMPASSION.

It will be very easy for you to despair, for there is so much SUFFERING in the world that restoring TRANQUILITY would appear to be an almost impossible task. That is why you need to prepare yourself thoroughly for the tremendous battle you will have, even against your own FOLLY, which is nurtured and controlled by your artificial IDENTITIES.

Among all the strange forms of SUFFERING which are accompanied by a frenzy of activity and a plethora of words, TRANQUILITY is hidden. There is not much of it, and you can easily be mistaken if you judge the voices and faces of SUFFERING. Within the world there are sounds which appear joyful but mask internal SUFFERING and smiles and laughter which cover tears and despair.

Look with inner vision and you will see both the SUFFERING and TRANQUILITY. Be encouraged, for SUFFERING can be eliminated, and when it is, then the IDENTITIES will disappear, leaving the BUDDHA NATURE of each human creature free to guide behavior and build a new world.

BUDDHA's last words were, "STRIVE ON WITH DILIGENCE." He was speaking to you.

PÓ LÚ JIÉ DÌ SHUÒ BŌ LÁ YĒ
Bring the Light of Contemplation to Bear
upon Suffering and Tranquility in the World

THE CONTAMINATION OF EXPERIENCES

1. Sensations, *Phassa*

One of the fundamental impediments to the NATURAL WAY of TRANQUILITY, the route of the DHAMMA, is the internal distortion of information provided by the senses. This SENSE INFORMATION we call SENSATIONS.

In everyday life, we almost never think of SENSATIONS as being INFORMATION, nor do we treat them as INFORMATION. Our FOLLY-filled heads distort that valuable product of our magnificent biological system into something to either CLING TO, if we interpret it as PLEASANT, or REJECT if we interpret it as UNPLEASANT. The natural and correct fine-tuning and utility has been completely lost.

If we could really understand that the SENSATIONS which we experience are actually internal feedback, the remnants of an external body language that has been left behind in our evolution, then we would place them correctly in perspective. We could then develop the SENSITIVITY of the SENSES for the benefit of the NATURAL system.

We say that our SENSATIONS are VISCERAL, for our body appears to experience a generalized response in our internal abdominal organs. Sometimes these SENSATIONS are slight, sometimes they are quite strong. Most people experience a viscerally agreeable SENSATION, for example, when they see a beautiful sunset. Some find it viscerally fantastic when they partake of a gourmet meal. Others find sexual contact viscerally sublime. Equally, most people have negative visceral responses to threats and violence. Discomfort and boredom bring their own visceral signs to apparently torment the human creature.

Actually, all these VISCERAL SENSATIONS stem from the external stimulation of sensory units which we call the DOORS of the SENSES, which are the senses of taste, smell, touch, hearing, and sight. Between the actual SENSORY event and the VISCERAL event, there are INTERMEDIATE PERCEPTUAL OPERATIONS which match signals and make interpretations about what is going on.

The end results are generally described as SENSORY EXPERIENCES. They are what we actually perceive the external world to be like, and in themselves they are really neither PLEASANT nor UNPLEASANT. The mind, of course, adds apparent meaning and, among other things, initiates internal functions which produce the actual interpretations and VISCERAL SENSATIONS. These VISCERAL SENSATIONS are perfectly natural and have biological value, for they signal the state of COMFORT of the system, the COMFORT of one's SHELTER, and the COMFORT of the BODY. This is information about general well-being which was essential in our distant evolution. The problem is that the evolved DEMANDS of CONSCIOUS INTELLECT of the human creature have distorted these valuable events so that they have become impediments.

2. Emotions, *Vedana*

We are all aware of those strong experiences called EMOTIONS, which have become another great impediment. The EMOTIONS have a much greater mental association than the SENSATIONS, and spoken language plays an essential part in their development and creation.

These EMOTIONS are also a natural source of useful information for the human creature, but conscious intellect has distorted that function as well. Actually, they serve to give information about the SECURITY of SHELTER and the SECURITY of the human system. You will note that SENSATIONS are general coarse experiences while EMOTIONS are specific and quite finely tuned. That is because EMOTIONS have verbal language as their base, and therefore fine-tuning becomes possible and experiences can be easily defined.

The experiences called EMOTIONS can appear to be PLEASANT or UNPLEASANT, and in a person who is operating in accord with his true nature the PLEASANT emotion signals a SECURE situation in which there is no threat. Unfortunately, we crave those PLEASANT EMOTIONS. In fact, we crave them so much that behavior seems motivated by them. Just as we try to approach situations which give PLEASANT EMOTIONS, we avoid situations which give UNPLEASANT EMOTIONS.

Can you see that the human system has gone awry? It is our BUDDHA NATURE which is the correct and natural guide of behavior, and the EMOTIONS should simply be a feedback device which acts as an interface between the apparent INTERNAL and EXTERNAL worlds. So badly has the system been distorted that behavior which is not in our best interest brings apparent PLEASURE.

3. Perceptual Passions of Conscious Intellect, *Sanna*

Finally, there is the great and most dangerous set of impediments, which are the PASSIONS of THOUGHT. These THOUGHTS are the dangerous THOUGHTS directed by CONSCIOUS INTELLECT, not the NATURAL THOUGHTS of the system. The THOUGHTS of CONSCIOUS INTELLECT are mediated by language, just like EMOTIONS.

There is a difference, however, for these CONSCIOUS THOUGHTS require concepts, many of them quite abstract, and the language is therefore very abstract. While the EXPERIENCES of SENSATION and EMOTION are physically apparent, the PASSIONS associated with PERCEPTION are quite MENTAL. Most of the time, because of the language interface, the PASSIONS arising from this abstract language are easily enmeshed with EMOTIONS. The actual THOUGHTS of CONSCIOUS INTELLECT are in fact PERCEPTIONS based on the process of RECOGNITION, which has direct links with EMOTIONS. These PASSIONS of CONSCIOUS INTELLECT, which have become impediments, are related to the recognition of events as either MENTAL or MATERIAL. As a result, various experiences of PASSION may be attached to events, distorting the information value.

When CONSCIOUS INTELLECT is at work, we seem to experience a chain of events within our mind. These chains of conscious thoughts are actually extremely natural and useful, for they are often a chain of perceptions placed in consciousness by the natural processes. They are not, however, the essential and important NATURAL THINKING of the human creature, which is performed quite subliminally, for there is no need for a conscious knowledge of NATURAL THINKING.

Unfortunately, since we know nothing of our TRUE NATURAL THINKING, we believe in error that the apparent THINKING of CONSCIOUS INTELLECT is our driving force. In addition, since recollection and recall are strong, we also believe that our TRUE IDENTITY is what appears as a PERCEPTION in CONSCIOUSNESS, a mix of the apparent IDENTITY of SENSATIONS, which is ID; the IDENTITY of EMOTIONS, EGO; and the IDENTITY of PASSIONS of CONSCIOUS INTELLECT, SUPER EGO. These, and the fourth IDEAL IDENTITY, cause the system to ignore our NATURAL IDENTITY, which is our BUDDHA NATURE.

The diagram below shows the relationship between SENSATIONS, EMOTIONS, CONSCIOUS PERCEPTIONS, CONSCIOUSNESS, and the processes of the SENSE DOORS.

Fig. 29 Basic Central Processes

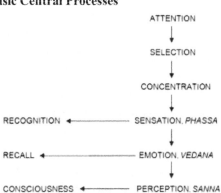

4. The Natural Balance

These THREE impediments, SENSATIONS, EMOTIONS, and the PASSIONS aroused by the PERCEPTUAL THOUGHTS of CONSCIOUS INTELLECT, are spokes in the WHEEL of SUFFERING. Not only do these impediments make themselves felt as experiences, but they also support CONFUSION or DELUSION, GREED, and HOSTILITY and give form and reinforcement to the IDENTITIES called ID, EGO, and SUPER EGO. Fortunately, all dysfunction can be eliminated with dedication to the task and a NATURAL BALANCE can be restored so that they are no longer impediments.

Fig. 30 The Ego Contamination of the Human Creature

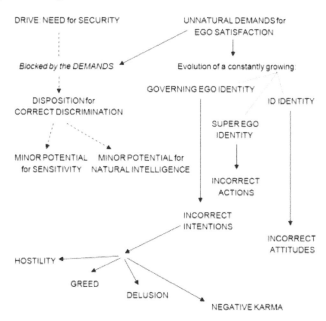

When NATURAL FUNCTION is restored, we are left with a base which builds SENSITIVITY instead of CONFUSION, DISCRIMINATION instead of GREED, and NATURAL INTELLIGENCE instead of HOSTILITY. Remember that SENSITIVITY, DISCRIMINATION, and INTELLIGENCE are natural DISPOSITIONS and can be nurtured and developed.

This potential for SENSITIVITY, DISCRIMINATION and NATURAL INTELLIGENCE which each person has depends upon inherited traits.

We have mentioned that each person has a GOVERNING DEMAND and that each also has a potential GOVERNING DISPOSITION. The vast majority of the human population has the GOVERNING potential for excellent DISCRIMINATION. Few have potential governance in either SENSITIVITY or NATURAL INTELLIGENCE. Almost everyone is actually, however, ruled by DELUSION, GREED, or HOSTILITY instead of SENSITIVITY, DISCRIMINATION, or NATURAL INTELLIGENCE, so it is not surprising that the dominant force which rules the world is GREED. What we need to do is restore the natural balance and set aside the DEMANDS that lead to DELUSION, GREED, and HOSTILITY, which are roots of suffering. We can do so with this Mantra.

THE SECOND SERIES: SETTING THE FOUNDATION

PÚ TÍ SÀ DUŎ PÓ YĒ

PÚ TÍ are Mantra sounds which signify *BODHI*, which is interpreted as WISDOM. You will remember that it is the name given to the tree beneath which BUDDHA attained ENLIGHTENMENT.

SÀ DUŎ is the process of crossing over from IGNORANCE to a state of WISDOM. This process of crossing over is best related to the act of crossing a river from one side to the other. Most sensible people in more primitive and simpler times would not think of carrying unnecessary burdens across a river. You too, in crossing the river from IGNORANCE and its associated SUFFERING to a state of TRANQUILITY, would be wise to leave your FOLLY behind, so that you can cross more freely and arrive ENLIGHTENED.

While reciting *PÚ TÍ SÀ DUŎ* with *PÓ YĒ*, you respect all those who have taken themselves across to ENLIGHTENMENT. Can you see that the success of all those who have enlightened themselves plays a great part in your protection against your own FOLLY? What they have accomplished, you can accomplish.

MINDFULNESS

What you are actually doing with this Mantra introduction is making a pledge to also transform yourself with a non-complex form of

MINDFULNESS. This MINDFULNESS, operating at the level of CONSCIOUS PERCEPTION, is directed at the burdens which you carry, all your SUFFERING. Now, the first place to begin is with your ACTIONS, because it is more difficult to honestly evaluate your ATTITUDES and INTENTIONS. Watch your ACTIONS and note their effects on yourself and on others. Watch what you say, for this is very important. There is a time and place for telling even the truth. All gossip, idle talk, and silly conversation is a sign of SUFFERING which is hidden somewhere. Perhaps there is a sense of insecurity, fear, or a problem of isolation from others. Just note those events and their consequences.

When you can really note all your ACTIONS with MINDFULNESS, then turn to your ATTITUDES and really see if they are correct or not. Don't try to change them with conscious intellect into some fixed pattern. All you have to do is note them, saying to yourself, "Yes, this is an INCORRECT ATTITUDE." Your own better nature will take care of the rest. Then, you can start to look at your INTENTIONS with clear vision and try to see the influence of the EMOTIONS, SENSATIONS, and THOUGHTS waiting, at the behest of your IDENTITIES, to have their own way by influencing potential INTENTIONS. Note with MINDFULNESS the excuses, justifications, and qualifications which surge to support your INTENTIONS. If the INTENTIONS are CORRECT, there will be no need of support.

Another direction where MINDFULNESS can be applied is towards your EXPECTATIONS. If you have EXPECTATIONS, then you are heading for trouble. Note those EXPECTATIONS and don't fight them. Let EXPECTATIONS turn to the acceptance of the possibility of a large range of OUTCOMES without clinging to or craving any of them.

When you have successfully practiced this MINDFULNESS with understanding, then you will be ready to develop the more complete MINDFULNESS which is discussed in the book *THE PATH OF BENEVOLENCE AND WISDOM: A PRACTICAL GUIDE TO LIBERATION AND HAPPINESS*, which further develops the understanding and wisdom gained by chanting this Mantra.

HUMILITY

This MINDFULNESS must be accomplished without pride or

EGOISM, generating a respectful ATTITUDE towards this journey you are making across the river of FOLLY. This respect is best shown by maintaining a HUMILITY which is not false. Most people have an amazing amount of self-adulation, and when they perform a CORRECT ACTION, a certain amount of EGO SATISFACTION arises. The arousal of true HUMILITY is a protection against the pride and arrogance which can arise when you know that you are performing a CORRECT ACTION.

A CORRECT ACTION, you can easily see, is not really effective in a transcendental sense unless it is accompanied by CORRECT INTENTION and CORRECT ATTITUDE. You must therefore be humble in ATTITUDE, humble in INTENTION, and humble in ACTION.

Now, we wish to make things very clear, so we must for a moment discuss what we mean when we say that an ACTION, an ATTITUDE, or an INTENTION is either CORRECT or INCORRECT. The sense in which we use the word is not the same as that associated with RIGHT or WRONG nor GOOD or BAD, which are evaluative, calling for social or moral judgments which imply some form of censure. We say that a process is CORRECT when it brings about, or is associated with, some NATURAL and BENEFICIAL PATH of behavior that is in the best interest of a sentient creature, and brings in its wake progress towards the ending of SUFFERING or the maintenance and growth of natural HARMONY and BALANCE with accompanying HAPPINESS.

You might consider the word FITTING to be more appropriate, but if we use this concept, we are likely to fall into the trap of associating the concept with MERIT or DESERVEDNESS. There is no natural reward for CORRECTNESS. The sole recompense is the KNOWLEDGE of being correct then observed by DIRECT EXPERIENCE.

PÚ TÍ SÀ DUŎ PÓ YĒ
I Will Cross to Enlightenment
with Mindfulness and Humility

MÓ HĒ SÀ DUŎ PÓ YĒ

By reciting *MÓ HĒ SÀ DUŎ PÓ YĒ*, you pay respect to all those who have gone before and have brought out the WISDOM of their own

TRUE NATURE through diligent EFFORT and the effective use of ENERGY. You declare that what they have accomplished you can accomplish. Their heroic strength is your strength, and by their example they light the way for you.

The act of crossing over is not accomplished easily.

Simply declaring that you take REFUGE does not bring REFUGE.

Saying that you will apply yourself and remain distant from IGNORANCE will not bring WISDOM and UNDERSTANDING.

The intention to attend to impeding SENSATIONS, EMOTIONS, and THOUGHTS does not bring about that process.

Deciding to distance yourself from DELUSION, GREED, and HOSTILITY does not create that distance.

Wanting to generate HUMILITY does not automatically bring that HUMILITY.

EFFORT AND ENERGY

What the crossing over needs is diligent EFFORT and the efficient use of ENERGY. This means that you must approach the task like a transcendental warrior. Armed with a knowledge of the way, you must generate both enthusiasm and the ENERGY to maintain yourself on the CORRECT PATH with unwavering determination. *SÀ DUŎ* is the Mantra component which refers to this vigorous EFFORT.

Focusing that EFFORT and ENERGY requires a positive attitude of RESOLUTION, which has its roots in the LIFE FORCE, *JIVITINDRIYA*. It requires not faith, but CONFIDENCE that arises from the natural consequence of the proper application of MINDFULNESS directed with DILIGENT EFFORT. This MINDFULNESS, linked with CORRECT ATTITUDE, permits the CORRECT FOCUS of the LIFE FORCE within CONSCIOUSNESS. (see figure 31)

You say then *MÓ HĒ*, "I will succeed. I will be VICTORIOUS." Be cautious, for here lies a danger. When a person is confident of success, then there may also arise a sense of PRIDE mixed with ARROGANCE which flows from the SUPER EGO IDENTITY. What the wise person does is note these enemies and let them fall away.

What you say when you chant *PÓ YĒ* is that you will accomplish this task of crossing over successfully, with respect for the act of

Fig. 31 Focusing Process of the Life Force

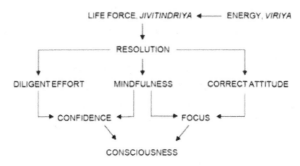

crossing. Giving this respect to the most noble process, you show respect for yourself and declare that you will be mindful of the danger of PRIDE and other like impediments. MINDFULNESS is essential.

Remember that all who bring out from within themselves this WISDOM with vigor and EFFORT do achieve the final victory of understanding and obtain final LIBERATION, leading others to LIBERATION in the process.

MÓ HĒ SÀ DUŎ PÓ YĒ

I Will Succeed with Diligent Effort, Energy, and Self-Respect

MÓ HĒ JIĀ LÚ NÍ JIĀ YĒ

You raise confidence again by declaring that you will be VICTORIOUS when you recite *MÓ HĒ*, but the foundations of that victory are laid by the development of RESOLUTION. Don't confuse this RESOLUTION with the promises which you make to yourself to change. Promises are based on WISHES without any real resolve behind them, maintained by the ideal that you SHOULD make these changes.

RESOLUTION

Strong RESOLUTION comes from a deep-seated WILL to be victorious over all that is incorrect. Don't force RESOLUTION into consciousness mentally. Simply decide to follow the CORRECT PATH. If you have made this resolution correctly, you will feel a rising delight within yourself and a confidence which will overcome all difficulties.

This RESOLUTION must be focused upon *CHANDA*, which is CONATION or ZEAL. It is actually the process which forms the wish to do something and the wish to be something. These must be fused together so that BEING is the result. Resist the temptation to be someone who is doing something. Watch out for this trap. In order to form these CORRECT INTENTIONS you will use *VITAKKA* and *VICARA*, which are the products of investigation, namely two forms of thought.

Dynamic fusion is accomplished when the CORRECT INTENTIONS and CORRECT ATTITUDES in memory are melded with *CETANA*, the mundane reasoning which changes the WILL into ACTION. This final fusion of WILL with INTELLECT requires the correct application of ENERGY, *VIRIYA*, and the LIFE FORCE, *JIVITINDRIYA*. Placed in perspective as a model, the relationship with ENERGY and the LIFE FORCE is more clearly seen.

Fig. 32 Advanced Central Processes

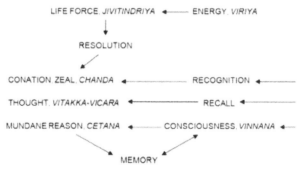

Don't be dismayed if you fail at first. Remember the INTROSPECTION, CALMNESS, and PATIENCE which you are developing.

Chanting the final *YĒ*, you declare that you will maintain respect. The object of this respect is, however, different. You declare in this Mantra line that you will generate respect towards *JIĀ LÚ*, which is COMPASSION. This COMPASSION, you declare and remind yourself, is not a COMPASSION generated from CONSCIOUS INTELLECT, nor is it a product of IDENTITY-sponsored emotion. It stems from the true BUDDHA NATURE, which symbolically is the HEART of the human creature, called *NÍ JIĀ*.

Chanting this line of the Mantra, you elevate COMPASSION to its correct place as a great and important human quality, denying its relation to contaminated FALSE COMPASSION, which is related to visceral identification, ID; emotional self-identification, EGO; and social self-righteous identification, SUPER EGO.

MÓ HĒ JIĀ LÚ NÍ JIĀ YĒ
I Will Succeed in Generating Resolution
and a Respect for True Compassion

MINDFULNESS, EFFORT, AND RESOLUTION

Already, for many, the way of this Mantra will appear to be difficult. The idea that all one has to do is sit in good company and get results by mindlessly chanting clearly has to be cast away. We said earlier that you would have to start with TRUE INTROSPECTION, CALMNESS, and PATIENCE. Perhaps now you are beginning to see why they are so necessary.

After looking at the previous three Mantra lines, you will note that you will have started to develop MINDFULNESS, EFFORT, and RESOLUTION.

First, there is MINDFULNESS, which you already know something about and have begun to nurture. Now, some people believe that MINDFULNESS involves being completely aware of precisely what you are doing at every moment. While this might be a wonderful attribute, that is not the MINDFULNESS which we require here. MINDFULNESS for us is the constant vigilance of our ATTITUDES, INTENTIONS, and ACTIONS with regard to the FOLLY attached to them. It includes, however, MINDFULNESS of our mental states and physical health, and a MINDFULNESS of both the roots of our ACTIONS and the consequences. This MINDFULNESS is not easy to achieve, and will require all the qualities which have been previously mentioned.

Now, there is one thing which must be pointed out. There is not a finite point where absolute MINDFULNESS is achieved, any more than there is an absolute degree of EFFORT or RESOLUTION which can be attained.

EFFORT, like any of the other qualities which we have or will develop, cannot arise just because you wish it to be there. It cannot be forced. It requires a concentration of WILL, just as RESOLUTION does. Where does that EFFORT come from? If it comes from the desire to succeed or the desire to gain something, then it is UNWORTHY EFFORT and is of no use to you here. Making EFFORT is not the great surge of ENERGY which is needed when a great difficulty is to be overcome; it is the constant application of your forces in a given direction. Note that we did not suggest that there is a given objective, but rather that there is a given direction. It is very important to see the difference. It is easy to reduce EFFORT and finally stop if objectives appear no nearer, but if EFFORT is correctly applied in a given direction, it is accompanied by a certain JOY. Remember that this EFFORT must be continually focused. It may vary in strength, but it must be constantly applied.

When we speak of RESOLUTION we must also remind you not to confuse RESOLUTION with IDENTITY-related traits. The "I" that wants to succeed cannot build true RESOLUTION. You must really see the necessity for RESOLUTION and be excited by that process. RESOLUTION does not exist in someone who unhappily plods on. It does exist in the person who, like a joyful traveler, overcomes all difficulties in his path. RESOLUTION requires EFFORT and is supported by it. From birth to death, MINDFULNESS, EFFORT, and RESOLUTION will work together. Their strength and the relationship between them will ebb and flow. That does indeed sometimes make the task of living difficult, but it also makes the task of living conceptually more beautiful.

The three qualities: INTROSPECTION, CALMNESS, and PATIENCE, which have aided you so far, will assist in the realization of MINDFULNESS, EFFORT, and RESOLUTION. In turn, the latter three will support the former so that there arises a growth and harmony between all of them. You will see later that these six develop gradually and will aid the growth and development of other great qualities.

Everything, you see, in the COMPASSION MANTRA works together to form a whole. Try to see that these qualities which we speak of are just concepts artificially created by the mind as tools. They are descriptions of apparent parts of one whole. All our perceptions are tools. Understand that and further comprehend that everything you read here is just a description of one greater concept, which is the UNITY of all things.

UNITY IN TIME

We are all a part of one great NATURAL PROCESS and we are connected in a very real sense to all those sentient creatures, to all things that have apparently existed in the PAST, apparently exist in the PRESENT, and will apparently exist in the FUTURE. In freely directing one's RESPECT to all who merit it, we better understand our relationship to all things and strengthen both HUMILITY and RESOLVE.

It is difficult to accept sometimes this UNITY which really exists, because there appear to be so many differences. We also use, in this life of the senses, labels to describe these differences and categories to bind groups of things together. This is a useful ILLUSION, but do not be captured by that ILLUSION so that you believe that all exists as you appear to perceive it. To do this is to create DELUSION. We do not mean to tell you that things do not exist. We are saying that our mind has created these perceptions.

The SUBJECT of experience is one thing, called *PURUSHA*, and the PRODUCT of that experience, that which appears to be real but is not, is another, called *PRAKRTI*. A thing is really as its NATURE makes it, whether it is a stone or a rabbit. How the human creature perceives that nature is quite another matter.

The interaction of any apparent thing with all that appears to be apart from it (NECESSITY of EXISTENCE) is inherent in its NATURE and is not imposed upon it by an external agency. This concept is difficult to internalize and understand. In simple language we can say that how things appear is ILLUSION, but the processes of their interactions are their true NATURE.

SUMMARY: LINES 1-6

In completing the first three lines of the FIRST PHASE, you will have taken REFUGE, submitted to WISDOM, and touched the SOUNDS of the WORLD. Can you see that each of these steps is important?

1. *NĀ MÒ HĒ LÁ DÁ NÀ DUŌ LÁ YÈ YĒ*
   I, with Reverence, Take Refuge in the Buddha,
   the Dhamma, and the Sangha

2. *NĀ MÒ Ā LĪ YĒ*
   I Take Refuge and Respectfully Submit to Wisdom

3. *PÓ LÚ JIÉ DÌ SHUÒ BŌ LÁ YĒ*
   Bring the Light of Contemplation to Bear upon Suffering
   and Tranquility in the World

Using the following three lines, you focused upon your MOTIVATION and RESOLVE so that impediments would not easily arise.

4. *PÚ TÍ SÀ DUǑ PÓ YĒ*
   I Will Cross to Enlightenment with Mindfulness and Humility

5. *MÓ HĒ SÀ DUǑ PÓ YĒ*
   I Will Succeed with Diligent Effort, Energy, and Self-Respect

6. *MÓ HĒ JIĀ LÚ NÍ JIĀ YĒ*
   I Will Succeed Generating Resolution
   and a Respect for True Compassion

This has been a very general but important preparation. Do you notice that each line ends with *YĒ*? This *YĒ* means to give respect. It does not refer to the mindless respect of awe or the egocentric respect of admiration.

It is the respect which one gives to a teacher who shows you the way. It is the respect shown to those who have achieved in a noble manner, without selfishness or hope of gain. It is the gracious respect which says, "You have shown me the way and I will follow."

Indeed, you should always be mindful and pay respect to all the processes taking place and to all those who have gone before you along this path and have achieved enlightenment.

To many this directed respect might appear to be adulatory and therefore incorrect. Actually this is not the case. If you think of

WORSHIP as being a blind adulation, then you may be correct. If the RESPECT is, however, not directed at a person, figure, or image, but at the concept of correct comportment or action, then it is not adulatory.

What you must do when you are being respectful is perceive the quality and purity of the STATE of the RESPECTED PERSON. The person is just a convenient focus of attention. The act of RESPECT is in fact an excellent form of self-purification. When you perceive a RESPECTED STATE of BEING, you see the availability of that state for every sentient creature. You therefore open the door to your own potential and, in so doing, show a respect for yourself that is not chained to EGOISM.

Now repeat:

NĀ MÒ HĒ LÁ DÁ NÀ DUŌ LÁ YÈ YĒ
NĀ MÒ Ā LĪ YĒ
PÓ LÚ JIÉ DÌ SHUÒ BŌ LÁ YĒ
PÚ TÍ SÀ DUǑ PÓ YĒ
MÓ HĒ SÀ DUǑ PÓ YĒ
MÓ HĒ JIĀ LÚ NÍ JIĀ YĒ

Let's continue with the third important set of Mantra lines.

THE THIRD SERIES: UNDERSTANDING AND CONFIDENCE

ǍN

ǍN means MOTHER of ALL THINGS. It is, in effect, the void. It is a word which represents all that is ontological and hidden from the senses. It is what apparently exists and paradoxically it is also what does not exist. It is the root of all things which are generated and the place to which all things return. It is the source then of all NATURAL WISDOM.

What does this mean? It does not mean that there is a natural ORDER to all things beyond the senses. It means that there is a natural UNFOLDING, a series of consequences which naturally arise from events which are beyond our knowledge.

The processes in the ontological world beyond the senses are REAL. That is to say, they actually exist and there is correspondence between those processes and what we perceive in this phenomenological world. We cannot, however, perceive that correspondence, nor can we deduce with certainty the nature of what is beyond the senses. We believe, however, that there is CHAOS, IMPERMANENCE, CONFLICT, and MEANINGLESSNESS.

We can say that the processes in the ontological world are REAL and what we perceive in this phenomenological world are corresponding ILLUSIONS. In the world of the senses, we derive ORDER from CHAOS, discover PERMANENCE within IMPERMANENCE, PEACE within CONFLICT, and find MEANING where there is MEANINGLESSNESS. That is because we need some way of dealing with the incredibly complex world in which we live.

The important and useful ILLUSIONS of ORDER, PERMANENCE, PEACE, and MEANING are essential and we could not survive without them. The problem is that we tend to believe that the ILLUSIONS of this world are REAL, and they become DELUSIONS which are antagonistic to NATURAL WISDOM. ILLUSIONS have their source in the ontological, in the Mother of all things, and their expression in this world of the senses. DELUSIONS have both their source and their expression in this world of the senses.

NATURAL WISDOM, as a process of NATURAL UNFOLDING, has its source in the ontological world and its expression as ILLUSION in the phenomenological world. NATURAL WISDOM has two different dimensions: ontological REALITY and phenomenological ILLUSION. This is identical to what is described in Chinese philosophy as the ETERNAL DAO (TAO) and the SPOKEN DAO. It is not easy to understand these differences between ILLUSION and DELUSION. It is even more difficult, while living in this everyday world, to recognize and be continually aware of the fact that all that we perceive is ILLUSION. That understanding will come at its natural pace. Just accept for the moment that NATURAL WISDOM does exist, and that we can use the ILLUSION of KNOWLEDGE to touch that WISDOM and act correctly in our daily lives.

When we say *ĂN*, we then declare that we understand the ILLUSION of NATURAL WISDOM and respect that WISDOM.

WORDS

When you say *ĂN* with understanding, this indicates that you use WORDS with the full mindfulness that they are symbols for intangible concepts and ideas. In the crossing over into illumination, these words are directly related to the DHAMMA. They do not perfectly represent the truth. However, without words, you cannot even touch the TRUTH, the NATURAL LAW at all. It exists beyond the senses.

If it is beyond the senses, can we touch it at all? Yes, we can. Imagine yourself as a supernatural being for a moment. Let us say that you know the TRUTH and that the TRUTH is that the SUN exists and that a STICK exists, protruding from the ground.

A non-supernatural creature standing close could not perceive either the SUN or the STICK. Can you see that? He would, however, be able to see the shadow cast upon the ground. Can you see that this is KNOWLEDGE of the UNKNOWABLE? We can use words to describe the SHADOW. This is KNOWLEDGE of the UNKNOWABLE.

PHRASES

You say *ĂN*, understanding that these words are given greater form by PHRASES, but that these too are only illusions which should not be turned into delusion by your own FOLLY. The phrases are more sophisticated instruments for greater understanding.

CONTEMPLATION AND CONCENTRATION

You say *ĂN*, knowing that there may be APPARENT MEANING when the DHAMMA is spoken or read which can be touched by conscious intellect. Knowing this, you declare that you will be vigilant against capture by the repetition of words and vigilant against the idea that the words by themselves do or signify anything at all. In other words, you don't want to make the mistake of believing that the SHADOW is the SUN and STICK. You can maintain vigilance against this FOLLY by CONTEMPLATION. This requires the cultivation of FREE CRITICAL INQUIRY, a full ANALYTICAL INVESTIGATION free from contamination by CONSCIOUS INTELLECT.

This same CONTEMPLATION, carried further, can be used as ACCESS to the stream of CONCENTRATION, which in turn can lead to *DHYANA PARAMITA*, the perfection of an ALTERED STATE OF CONSCIOUSNESS. In such an altered state of consciousness, you lie somewhere on the continuum between the SHADOW and the STICK without awareness of the SHADOW. If this is difficult for you to grasp conceptually, don't worry. You will "SEE" quite naturally later, when you are further upon the way.

WISDOM AND PENETRATION

There exists more profoundly the NATURAL WISDOM mentioned above, which is represented by words. The words and phrases are indeed deceiving sometimes, but the WISDOM behind the words can be liberated. You declare that you will liberate this WISDOM which turns away distractions. This WISDOM too can be used to attain a HIGHER STATE of CONSCIOUSNESS by means of PENETRATION, sometimes called INSIGHT.

CULTIVATION

You say *ĂN*, permitting yourself NATURAL and CORRECT CULTIVATION, which stems from this WISDOM and is associated with CORRECT ATTITUDE and CORRECT INTENTIONS. Can you see that you open another door to "SEEING" if your cultivation of the way is in accord with the DHAMMA? Knowing the DHAMMA means nothing if you don't internalize it. An appreciation of the DHAMMA by conscious intellect is good, but internalization is essential or you will never be in harmony with the NATURAL PATH.

VOLITION

You say *ĂN*, dedicating yourself to cultivate, with full VOLITION, the qualities of DETERMINATION, RESOLUTION, EFFORT, and ENERGY, all the NATURAL processes which stem from your BUDDHA NATURE. Without NATURAL WILL, you cannot maintain your way upon the PATH. VOLITION then is another door to the DHAMMA.

UNDERSTANDING

You say *ĂN*, knowing that in order to cultivate what is NATURAL within you, then you must UNDERSTAND the teachings of the DHAMMA. If you do not, you may follow a thousand paths which lead nowhere, falling into traps of FOLLY along the way.

WORDS, PHRASES, CONTEMPLATION, WISDOM, CULTIVATION, VOLITION, and UNDERSTANDING are the first seven doors which when opened lead to the DHAMMA, which is the NATURAL WAY.

DHAMMA PRINCIPLES

Transcendental TEACHINGS mean nothing if there is not a NATURAL contact with the ONTOLOGICAL WISDOM, which is the DHAMMA itself, and the DHAMMA itself is best understood by internalizing the PRINCIPLES of the way. This is extraordinarily difficult. It is one thing to understand intellectually what is written and quite another to really internalize what is said so that it becomes a part of your BUDDHA NATURE.

There exists, you see, the BUDDHA NATURE. It is effective and wise, but in a virgin state. Once contacted, it must be NURTURED by GREATER WISDOM, which grows from the BUDDHA NATURE source, and DEVELOPED by contact with the TRUTH, which is the DHAMMA.

SEEDS OF KNOWING

You say *ĂN*, accepting the fact that you cannot cultivate anything without the germination of the seed of KNOWING BEYOND CONSCIOUS INTELLECT. KNOWING allows you to see that the SHADOW is not all there is. In fact, most people ONLY see the SHADOW, and because they believe that the SHADOW is the TRUTH and that it is theirs, they CLING to it when the sun shines and CRAVE it when the sun goes down.

FRUITION

You say *ĂN*, fully knowing that there will be RESULTS from the generation and growth of UNDERSTANDING. What are those results? They appear to be quite abstract and intangible. The RESULTS are UNDERSTANDING that you are in HARMONY and BALANCE with the NATURAL LAW itself and that you will not SUFFER the consequences of IGNORANCE.

That is really quite a magnificent thing, is it not? But knowing this, reciting *ĂN*, you declare that you will neither CRAVE that result nor CLING to it.

The DHAMMA PRINCIPLES, the SEEDS of UNDERSTANDING, and final FRUITION are the eighth, ninth, and tenth doors to the DHAMMA.

When you recite *ĂN*, you are aware of these ten doors, and all the positive aspects of your BUDDHA nature are primed so that your natural endowment of sensitivity, discrimination, and natural intelligence may be called to service.

You say *ĂN*, declaring, "SO BE IT," giving force to your RESOLUTION, building CONFIDENCE in the words of the DHAMMA, thereby opening the way for the Mantra lines which follow.

SÀ PÓ LUÓ FÁ YÈ

An important stage has been completed and the previous Mantra line has opened the door to a successful recitation, but you will want to be sure that you really do have sufficient resolution to do everything correctly. Here, chanting *SÀ PÓ LUÓ*, which means MASTERFUL, and *FÁ YÈ*, which means HONORED BY THE WISE, you call directly upon the latent BUDDHA strength within you. This is the strength of WISDOM learned from the BUDDHA. This is the strength laid in place by your refuge in the TRIPLE JEWEL in the first line of the Mantra. This is the strength of the KNOWLEDGE which stems from BUDDHA, who mastered SUFFERING. You call upon this strength to use the Mantra.

Now you must be sure that you do not become dependent upon this illusion of a BUDDHA PRESENCE within you. The BUDDHA was not a GOD. There is no little BUDDHA sitting inside you waiting to dispense wisdom and put you on the CORRECT PATH. The strength is your strength. The wisdom is your wisdom.

Calling upon the Buddha is rather like calling a good friend on the phone and saying, "All right, friend, what would you do now if you were in my place?"

You know the answers because you have studied the DHAMMA. From time to time, however, you tend to forget, and when that happens, or you need extra impetus, that is the time to open up that internal "Buddha Guide Book" and phone the BUDDHA, as it were, and get on the CORRECT PATH again with confidence.

SÀ PÓ LUÓ FÁ YÈ
I Call upon the Buddha, Masterful, Honored by the Wise

SHŬ DÁ NÀ DÁ XIĚ

As you called upon BUDDHA strength with the last Mantra line, you now call up strength from the DHAMMA with *SHŬ DÁ NÀ*, and with the Mantra syllables *DÁ XIĚ* you call up courage and confidence by contemplating all those who have been and are now upon the path.

With this strength and confidence in the DHAMMA you will subdue all the SUFFERING of those called by the recitation of the Mantra. Once again we must remind you that there is no magic power in the DHAMMA which provides this strength. It is your own strength. What you actually are doing is telling yourself that there is a NATURAL LAW and that this LAW is well known to you. If you set aside all folly that covers over the beauty and correctness of this natural process, then the DHAMMA will be revealed. Knowing that this NATURAL LAW exists is having strength. Knowing that this law is written and can be understood makes it available for the growth and development of your life and as a daily guide in this complex world of the senses. The written DHAMMA is a guide for the perplexed that opens up the eternal DHAMMA for you.

When you read or listen to the DHAMMA, don't cling to those words. Remember that the DHAMMA was first spoken and written many years ago. It was spoken and written in the language and concepts of the culture. It is the ideas which are important, not the specific word-pictures. Just as it is said of the DAO, the DHAMMA which is spoken is not the ETERNAL DHAMMA.

When you call upon the strength of the SANGHA, you call upon the strength of knowing that you are not alone on the path which will free you and all sentient beings from SUFFERING. Beware of the folly-filled sensation which simply says, "I'm miserable with all this work and would like company." That will never work. When you call upon the SANGHA, you must be aware that just as you send your BENEVOLENT LOVE to all those on the path, so they send that BENEVOLENT LOVE to you. It is this sense of support which will give you comfort and strength.

SHǓ DÁ NÀ DÁ XIĚ
I Call upon the Dhamma, the Brotherhood

SUMMARY: LINES 7-9

You will have discovered in the first six lines that chanting the Mantra really is not a matter of simply creating words and rhythmically casting them into the sentient world. In fact, if you chant correctly, you are performing a very delicate operation. It is all very well to talk about your GLADNESS, COMPASSION, and BENEVOLENT LOVE, but it is quite another thing to touch these experiences with an open mind which is not contaminated. Setting the impediments of a closed mind aside is not easy. You may tell yourself to "open up," but the doors do not always really open. There is a tendency to cling to old habits and systems for security which is not necessary. Dissociation with habits requires disconnection with your traditional way of doing things with CONSCIOUS INTELLECT. This requires a basic understanding of what you are actually doing and CONFIDENCE that there will be some effect.

In these three lines of the third series you begin to open the door which leads to transcendental themes and begin to develop the required CONFIDENCE. You must realize that you can go upon the path which the Buddha followed. The Buddha was human, and was as equally involved with this world of the senses as you are when he began his voyage of enlightenment. Do you believe that it was easy for him? Do you believe that he just sat down under the nearest tree when he was ready, and that enlightenment suddenly descended upon him?

He had CURIOSITY and his BUDDHA NATURE prompted him to look deep within himself, and contemplate the world of SUFFERING. He was fortunate, for he had available all the knowledge of wise men who had gone before. Without that base of knowledge and an understanding of CONCENTRATION, do you believe that the BUDDHA would really have succeeded in opening the way for you to follow? We are all, in part, a product of those who have gone before. We can use their WISDOM or their FOLLY. Where they have gone, you can follow, and in turn, your experiences may help those who follow.

These three lines of the Mantra thus serve as a focus for your contemplation of the BUDDHA, the DHAMMA, and the BROTHERHOOD of all those who are with you upon the CORRECT PATH. They will be the fulcrum to rouse your CONFIDENCE. Do not approach them with either a heavy heart or a clouded mind.

7. *ĂN*
Mother of All Things

8. *SÀ PÓ LUÓ FÁ YÈ*
I Call upon the Buddha, Masterful, Honored by the Wise

9. *SHŬ DÁ NÀ DÁ XIĚ*
I Call upon the Dhamma, the Brotherhood

Now repeat:

ĂN
SÀ PÓ LUÓ FÁ YÈ
SHŬ DÁ NÀ DÁ XIĚ

THE FOURTH SERIES: AWAKENING THE BUDDHA NATURE

NĀ MÒ XĪ JÍ LĪ DUŎ YĪ MĚNG Ā LÌ YĒ

Your TRUE NATURE, the IDENTITY of your non-IDENTITY, is *DUŎ YĪ MĚNG* and it is discernible by the presence of internal WISDOM. Actually, *DUŎ YĪ MĚNG* is your BUDDHA NATURE. Taking refuge is *NĀ*

152

MÒ, and complete respect is designated by *XĪ JÍ LĪ*. You have then declared, by chanting this Mantra line, that taking refuge you give complete respect to your BUDDHA NATURE.

Why at this time is this mentioned? The answer is clear. You have already made many Mantra statements. What you want to do is call up some protection against your own FOLLY. This is the time, you see, when EGO starts to slip into the Mantra. You start becoming aware that you are a person saying a Mantra.

This is dangerous because the ideal condition for MANTRA use is UNITY. This UNITY is between the apparent CHANTER, the apparent MANTRA, and the RECIPIENT of the Mantra. If your EGO IDENTITY slips in, then you have automatically split off the CHANTER and created a dichotomy.

Your BUDDHA NATURE has no discernible IDENTITY, so you call upon it to restore and maintain UNITY. Your BUDDHA NATURE is really the most important thing which you have to learn about.

It is difficult to define the BUDDHA NATURE, and if we were to do so, there would be a great temptation to give it the form of a real IDENTITY. We have called it symbolically the HEART of the human creature.

Our BUDDHA NATURES are the set of memory traces which contain all the information about our NATURAL WISDOM. When we touch, accept, and KNOW our BUDDHA NATURE we don't need to cling to the silly IDENTITIES of ID, EGO, and SUPER EGO. When we release the processes of our BUDDHA NATURE, we don't need to act under the FOLLY-filled command of ID, EGO, and SUPER EGO.

When we take REFUGE in our own BUDDHA NATURE, we have begun the process of crossing over to ENLIGHTENMENT and LIBERATION.

NĀ MÒ XĪ JÍ LĪ DUŎ YĪ MĚNG Ā LÌ YĒ
With Respect I Take Refuge Within my Buddha Nature

PÓ LÚ JÍ DÌ SHÌ FÓ LÁ LÈNG TUÓ PÓ

PÓ LÚ JÍ DÌ is a call once again to CONTEMPLATE the SOUNDS OF THE WORLD. The sounds of the world are often the SOUNDS of

SUFFERING, which is *SHÌ FÓ LÁ*. When the Mantra adds *LÈNG TUÓ PÓ*, it prompts an inward contemplation to an ISLAND in the SEA. This is a metaphor for our BUDDHA NATURE, which is a safe calm haven. Because we are contemplating the SOUNDS of the WORLD while touching our BUDDHA NATURE, we are then calling upon our COMPASSION. *PÓ LÚ JÍ DÌ SHÌ FÓ LÁ* stands for the person who is COMPASSIONATE, while *LÈNG TUÓ PÓ* is the BUDDHA NATURE where true COMPASSION dwells.

Now, it may not be obvious why we need to touch this COMPASSION based on NATURAL WISDOM. It is because there actually is a complex FALSE COMPASSION stored within our memory system which can be used by the IDENTITIES. As there are actually FOUR different IDENTITIES, there are four faces to this FALSE COMPASSION.

Our VISCERAL ID is very sensitive and manages to pick up the messages of the SUFFERING of others and experiences that SUFFERING as a form of FALSE COMPASSION, stemming from EMPATHY.

Our EMOTIONAL EGO clearly notes the distinction between the state of the other person and itself. It is GLAD that it is the other person that SUFFERS and not itself. It then experiences PITY, which is actually rather detached.

The COGNITIVE SUPER EGO feels the responsibility of being RELATED to the SUFFERING person and experiences the collective cognitive SUFFERING of being a part of that SUFFERING.

Now, all of these IDENTITY-bound SENSATIONS, EMOTIONS, and THOUGHTS are quite subliminal and they manifest themselves in the fourth CONSCIOUS IDENTITY, an idealized picture of the SELF-IMAGE which can actually enforce an apparently compassionate act or reject action altogether, depending on the circumstances.

None of these FALSE COMPASSIONS is in any way similar to the WARM, COMFORTING, and LOVING COMPASSION of the BUDDHA NATURE and, therefore, in the Mantra it is essential to make contact with the BUDDHA NATURE by taking refuge and touching that TRUE COMPASSION with this Mantra line.

PÓ LÚ JÍ DÌ SHÌ FÓ LÁ LÈNG TUÓ PÓ
May I Touch the Compassion Within my Buddha Nature

NĀ MÒ NÀ LÁ JǏN CHÍ

Here once again you ask for refuge by chanting *NĀ MÒ*. This time, however, you add *NÀ LÁ*, which signifies an object or person of WORTH. In this case the object is clearly named as *JǏN CHÍ*, which is LOVE. This abstract quality of LOVE within your BUDDHA NATURE, considered to be a great treasure, is COMPASSION.

You then, having touched the COMPASSION of your BUDDHA NATURE with the previous line, take refuge in that COMPASSION with this line of the Mantra. Within this COMPASSIONATE LOVE there are three characteristics.

There is, first of all, the characteristic of being "other-directed," so that there is no selfishness within that COMPASSION. It is directed without EGO IDENTITY towards others. This makes it NOBLE COMPASSION.

Second, it is a COMPASSION which has no limits. No matter if the object of COMPASSION is unworthy or has harmed you in the past, it makes no difference. The COMPASSION then is fully RESPECTFUL. How is it that a person can be respectful towards someone whose conduct is reprehensible? Because there is, you will remember, no culpability. The person can change at any moment at the awakening of his or her BUDDHA NATURE. If you then have COMPASSION for a person, it is really for that person's BUDDHA NATURE.

Third, it is a COMPASSION which is conscious of the effects of all INTENTIONS, that is, the WISDOM with regard to CAUSE and EFFECT. It therefore has the quality of UNSURPASSED WISDOM.

This COMPASSION within your BUDDHA NATURE is NOBLE, RESPECTFUL, and WISE. With this Mantra line, you draw strength and protection from these qualities of COMPASSION.

NĀ MÒ NÀ LÁ JǏN CHÍ
I Take Refuge with the Qualities of Compassion
which are Noble, Respectful, and Wise

XĪ LĪ MÓ HĒ PÓ DUŌ SHĀ MIĒ

With this Mantra line we call up other qualities to aid our direction of COMPASSION. These qualities are not the same as those which are bound with COMPASSION. They have connection to something else that dwells within your BUDDHA NATURE. What is it?

Well, we know from the Mantra line that it is also WORTHY, for we chant *MÓ HĒ*. It can be identified by its having two characteristics: one is *XĪ LĪ*, which makes it UNDEFILED and UNATTACHED, while the other is *PÓ DUŌ SHĀ MIĒ*, which refers to the attribute of bringing the capacity to CONTEMPLATE the VOID. This is an illuminating quality which brings in its wake a lasting WISDOM. These are the qualities of BENEVOLENT LOVE.

In chanting this Mantra line, then, you are calling up the qualities of BENEVOLENT LOVE. Using the UNDEFILED and UNATTACHED qualities of BENEVOLENT LOVE of your BUDDHA NATURE, you are able to better engender COMPASSION so that you can destroy the IGNORANCE which is the root of the SUFFERING in others and yourself. The UNDEFILED and UNATTACHED qualities are in fact a protection against AVARICE, AVERSION, and HOSTILITY. In the particular case of this Mantra, they are a strong barrier against the appearance of PRIDE and DOUBT.

When you give COMPASSION, you are not simply acting while feeling some blind sentimental egoistic association. You are also giving the strength which comes from the BENEVOLENT LOVE dwelling within your own BUDDHA NATURE. This can aid yourself as well as others in the destruction of SUFFERING.

It is important, is it not, that this SUFFERING not only fall away but stay away. This cannot happen without an inner ILLUMINATION. With this Mantra line, we call up the power of ILLUMINATION which lies within the BUDDHA NATURE. This power is once again protective, for ILLUMINATION does not lie in your BUDDHA NATURE ready to burst forth. The BUDDHA NATURE provides a piercing contemplation which illuminates the TRUTH of SUFFERING.

XĪ LĪ MÓ HĒ PÓ DUŌ SHĀ MIĒ
I Call upon the Undefiled and Unattached Illumination
of Benevolent Love

SÀ PÓ Ā TĀ DÒU SHŪ PÉNG

It should then come as no surprise to anyone that we call next upon the qualities of GLADNESS which dwell within the BUDDHA NATURE.

SÀ PÓ is the attribute of EQUALITY. Why is equality related to GLADNESS? Well, in order to really be glad for another person, you have to be devoid of personal CRAVING. If another person has something or has achieved something, there is no GLADNESS if you wish that you had it instead. This is JEALOUSY. You can see that GLADNESS cannot coexist with CRAVING.

When you see yourself as EQUAL, you also perceive yourself as being in UNITY with the other person. As you are glad for yourself, then you can quite easily be glad for them.

Now, at the moment, the SUFFERING person has nothing to be glad about. That is true, but unfortunately the internal psychological convolutions of the human mind are very subtle. The normal person, while dredging up a FALSE COMPASSION, may subconsciously be GLAD that they are not in the position of the person who is suffering. That seems to be a very perverse form of GLADNESS.

With the Mantra, you elicit GLADNESS from your BUDDHA NATURE to overcome the CONTAMINATED FALSE GLADNESS which may be subconsciously generated by your ID IDENTITY.

Ā TĀ DÒU means to possess wealth and happiness without poverty. It is easy to see what this has to do with GLADNESS, but you must understand that we are not talking about mundane wealth, the happiness of satiation, or the poverty which is the lack of possessions. What we calling up are the qualities of possessing WEALTH of UNDERSTANDING, TRUE UNDEFILED HAPPINESS, and a freedom from POVERTY OF THOUGHT. We can combine these together under the concept of PURE WORTHINESS. COMPASSION must be directed with PURE WORTHINESS, which defends against the entry of personal defilement.

Finally in the Mantra, we chant *SHŪ PÉNG*, which signifies the quality of being able to make NOBLE AND PURE JUDGMENTS without the GRASPING of INCORRECT UNDERSTANDING.

It is very clear also why we need to call upon this strength of GLADNESS when directing COMPASSION. Too often when giving compassionately we may be saying subconsciously, "Ah yes, I am sorry, but this person deserves this SUFFERING." This is grasping motivated by IGNORANCE. It is generated by the EGO IDENTITY. The NOBLE and PURE JUDGMENT of your BUDDHA NATURE is free from contamination and can resist and conquer the GRASPING IGNORANCE of ID and EGO.

SÀ PÓ Ā TĀ DÒU SHŪ PÉNG
I Call upon the Unity, Pure Worthiness,
and Noble Judgment of Gladness

Ā SHÌ YÙN

Ā SHÌ YÙN refers to the incomparable NATURAL LAW, the DHAMMA which resides in your BUDDHA NATURE. Within each person, often submerged beneath the burdens created by debilitating IDENTITIES, there is a NATURAL HUMILITY and there is a NATURAL FREEDOM FROM DELUSION. These are two of the basic processes of our BUDDHA NATURE which are common to all human creatures.

We must examine the HUMILITY which we have spoken of before. It is not the FALSE HUMILITY which comes from conscious intellect. It is not a "SHOULD BE" concept at all. The process of HUMILITY in the BUDDHA NATURE sees the position of the human creature in relation to all things. Man is indeed insignificant, yet paradoxically significant, because he has a great potential power which can be used to create or destroy.

Can you then see why HUMILITY is paired with the NATURAL FREEDOM FROM DELUSION? In the Mantra we are using our own latent POWER. If we become confused, then we cannot use this power creatively. You see, it only takes a little delusion and we can instantly become destroyers. You would think that the prevention of DELUSION would be a task for higher mental facilities, but this is not the case. Both DELUSION and its partner, CONFUSION, are caused when there is too much mental stimulation, when there are too many conscious thoughts. Here we need to get back to basics. We need the simple but incisive direction of the BUDDHA NATURE.

Two things are important in order to attain victory over DELUSION and CONFUSION so that we can touch our BUDDHA NATURE, for it is not easy to let go of conscious intellect. One is the ability to maintain a PLIANT, RESILIENT, OPEN MIND and the other is the ability to use FREE CRITICAL INQUIRY. Correct functioning of both of these rests on the ability to disconnect your own preconceived concepts and ideas and really pay attention to what is being read or listened to.

At the roots of these two attributes is the ability to truly INTROSPECT. While HUMILITY acts as a brake to any EGOISM which might distort their development, MINDFULNESS directs their progress. ENERGY must be applied, and this will have been made easier by the EFFORT which you have begun to generate. You will need, of course, to bring into focus the PATIENCE, CALMNESS, and RESOLUTION which you have been developing.

Fig. 33 A Model of Progress

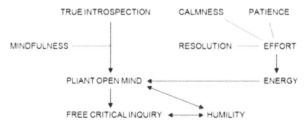

With this Mantra line we call upon these qualities of HUMILITY and allow the FREEDOM of our BUDDHA NATURE to have sway by developing the PLIANT and OPEN MIND which is available, and the techniques of FREE CRITICAL INQUIRY which will combat the intolerance and bias of the IDENTITIES.

Ā SHÌ YÙN
I Call upon Natural Humility and Freedom from Identity Delusion,
the Dhamma of my Buddha Nature

A PLIANT OPEN MIND AND FREE CRITICAL INQUIRY

A PLIANT, RESILIENT, OPEN MIND describes exactly the state of the receiving mind, while FREE CRITICAL INQUIRY describes the way in which one perceives the raw data. Is your mind pliant, resilient, and open? You may believe that it is. Take a closer look at your behavior and you will see how often your mind is engaged in apparent thinking before you have completely read or heard what is being said. When you are listening or reading, how often does your mind race on to another idea? How often do emotional reactions and sensations rush in? With TRUE INTROSPECTION, you will see just how unreceptive you really are.

The secret, of course, is to allow the MIND to be still and tranquil when you are listening or reading. Don't censor anything until ALL the information is received. Don't be thinking when you should be listening. This is a technique you can use to win arguments and to destroy opponents in conversation and debates, but it is not how to develop an open mind. Once the information is all collected and you have FULLY heard what has been said, or you have completely gathered all the ideas from a text, then that is the time to examine what you have received.

Once again, don't dive in with CONSCIOUS INTELLECT on a seek-and-destroy mission. No. If there are errors and faults in what you have gathered with an open mind, it will be evident by its incompleteness, its internal contradictions, its lack of foundation, and its use of tricks of rhetoric which address the SENSATIONS, EMOTIONS, and THOUGHTS in your own memory.

Once you have looked at the proposed ideas and seen their internal weakness or strength, then that is the time to look at what you already APPARENTLY believe. Look first at what supports and then what opposes the ideas presented, filtering and examining the incompleteness, internal contradictions, lack of foundation, and the biases of your own ego-based information. In no way is this easy at first, for it requires mindfulness and discipline.

SUMMARY: LINES 10-15

Let's see what can be accomplished with the first two lines of this series. The objective is to get in touch with the COMPASSION of your BUDDHA NATURE. Now, that is easier said than done. Most people can't even see their BUDDHA NATURE, so we must proceed in logical stages.

We have taken refuge in the TRIPLE JEWEL previously. Now we use that refuge to raise confidence, courage, and strength, by calling directly on the BUDDHA, DHAMMA, and BROTHERHOOD. Of course none of these can directly come to your aid, but the Mantra lines do focus your energy correctly. With this energy, you can move one step deeper into your internal processes by taking refuge in that BUDDHA NATURE.

Once we have that refuge, we can touch the COMPASSION which dwells there as a process, and liberate any of the processes related directly to that COMPASSION. With this COMPASSION uppermost, we can use it as a catalyst to directly touch and bring into operation any of the other qualities within our BUDDHA NATURE. You, of course, understand that this will not happen just because you recite the Mantra lines. There must be a real and sincere psychological integration with the concepts of the Mantra.

What does an examination of the last four Mantra lines show? It shows that we need to use not just the WISDOM of COMPASSION, but also that of GLADNESS and BENEVOLENT LOVE. We call up all these qualities of our BUDDHA NATURE because they are important qualities of WISDOM which we actually can use effectively to set SUFFERING aside.

Most people don't even know that they have a BUDDHA NATURE, and many believe that the BASIC NATURE of man is violent and destructive. It is easy to see why people may be deceived. Man's evolution certainly appears to have been violent, but this is not so. Man's evolution has been conflictive, but that is not the same thing. NATURE was, is, and always will be full of conflict. There is a life-and-death struggle going on all around us every moment. We are ourselves engaged in a life-and-death struggle against our own FOLLY.

CONFLICT is NATURAL but VIOLENCE is not. What is the difference? That is easy to answer. VIOLENCE is directed towards some end objective which is not NATURAL. VIOLENCE is always destructive, both to the winner and the loser. We have learned that violence pays and feeds our desires. On the other hand, our BUDDHA NATURE can identify CONFLICT and our REASON can direct our actions to resolve that conflict without VIOLENCE.

We use the WISDOM of the BUDDHA NATURE, which, of course, is the HEART of the human creature. Just as the heart feeds oxygen to all the cells of the body for nourishment and growth, so the BUDDHA NATURE provides nourishment and growth to all our abstract mental systems.

The BUDDHA NATURE is a highly sophisticated program consisting of magnificent NATURAL attributes which are PROCESSES. All these processes may be drawn upon and used as a natural filter to promote, elicit, and confirm CORRECT INTENTION, CORRECT ATTITUDE, and CORRECT ACTION. Since each of these processes depends upon this "HEART," then we call their major characteristics HEART ATTRIBUTES. In the Mantra you will call up these characteristics for two reasons: first, to help restore the strength of the BUDDHA NATURE, and second, to help you arouse COMPASSION correctly. They are:

1. The First HEART attribute,
   associated with COMPASSION: NOBILITY
2. The Second HEART attribute,
   associated with GLADNESS: UNITY IN EQUANIMITY
3. The Third HEART attribute,
   associated with GLADNESS: PURE WORTHINESS
4. The Fourth HEART attribute,   UNDEFILEDNESS and
   associated with BENEVOLENT LOVE: UNATTACHMENT
5. The Fifth HEART attribute,
   associated with BENEVOLENT LOVE: ILLUMINATION
6. The Sixth HEART attribute,
   associated with COMPASSION: RESPECTFULNESS
7. The Seventh HEART attribute
   of the BUDDHA NATURE in general: HUMILITY
8. The Eighth HEART attribute
   of the BUDDHA NATURE in general: FREEDOM FROM DELUSION
9. The Ninth HEART attribute
   of GLADNESS: NOBLE JUDGMENT
10. The Tenth HEART attribute
    of COMPASSION: UNSURPASSED WISDOM

Lest you get the idea that the BUDDHA NATURE is the source of all WISDOM, let it be made clear that this is not so. The BUDDHA NATURE is a NATURAL INHERITED process, a filter which, when it is operating correctly, monitors all information going into memory and all actions initiated by the human system. It is a monitoring system which has readable files of acceptable processes concerning behavior. The WISDOM of the BUDDHA NATURE lies in its capacity to monitor and reject ideas or concepts which are not compatible with the NATURAL system.

The human memory is like a blank sheet of paper at birth, and anything can be written upon it. Society, the various churches, the state, the education system, parents, and peers all start writing on this blank sheet of paper from the moment each person is born.

What is written can be based on either IGNORANCE or WISDOM, but regretfully it is usually the former. If the BUDDHA NATURE is contaminated early in life, efficiency is reduced or destroyed and you lose the capacity to filter out information based on IGNORANCE.

The remedy is quite simple if you wish to change. First, you must restore the INTEGRITY of the BUDDHA NATURE, then you must clear the contaminated segments containing IGNORANCE from MEMORY, and finally you must enter new components of WISDOM.

Recitation of the Mantra helps restore this INTEGRITY. It does this specifically by calling up the HEART attributes which have been dormant since early childhood. Awakening them is not easy, but once they have begun to surface, then the road to the recovery of full function is not far away.

10. *NĀ MÒ XĪ JÍ LĪ DUŎ YĪ MĚNG Ā LÌ YĒ*
     With Respect I Take Refuge Within my Buddha Nature

11. *PÓ LÚ JÍ DÌ SHÌ FÓ LÁ LÈNG TUÓ PÓ*
     May I Touch the Compassion Within my Buddha Nature

12. *NĀ MÒ NÀ LÁ JĬN CHÍ*
     I Take Refuge with the Qualities of Compassion
     Which Are Noble, Respectful, and Wise

13. *XĪ LĪ MÓ HĒ PÓ DUŌ SHĀ MIĒ*
     I Call upon the Undefiled and Unattached Illumination
     of Benevolent Love

14. *SÀ PÓ Ā TĀ DÒU SHŪ PÉNG*
I Call upon the Unity, Pure Worthiness,
and Noble Judgment of Gladness

15. *Ā SHÌ YÙN*
I Call upon Natural Humility and Freedom from Identity Delusion,
the Dhamma of my Buddha Nature

Now repeat:

NĀ MÒ XĪ JÍ LĪ DUǑ YĪ MĚNG Ā LÌ YĒ
PÓ LÚ JÍ DÌ SHÌ FÓ LÁ LÈNG TUÓ PÓ
NĀ MÒ NÀ LÁ JǏN CHÍ
XĪ LĪ MÓ HĒ PÓ DUŌ SHĀ MIĒ
SÀ PÓ Ā TĀ DÒU SHŪ PÉNG
Ā SHÌ YÙN

After having recited the Mantra lines, we are ready to surge forward so that we can work upon the task of TRANSMITTING the COMPASSION of our BUDDHA NATURE. To do this, we require another charge of energy and confidence, so we proceed with the following three-line preparation.

THE FIFTH SERIES: AFFIRMATION OF CONFIDENCE

SÀ PÓ SÀ DUŌ NĀ MÒ PÓ SÀ DUŌ NÀ MÓ PÓ JIĀ

This Mantra line calls for help from all those who have advanced well upon the path of the DHAMMA. You can think of them as ENLIGHTENED ONES or SAINTS if you choose. The help which you gain, of course, is quite subjective and abstract, but nonetheless effective. By calling the ENLIGHTENED ONES, you say that what they have done can also be achieved by you with HUMILITY and RESPECT. You also call up their symbolic presence within you. Your RESOLUTION and ENERGY are then strengthened.

SÀ PÓ SÀ DUŌ: Here you call upon those of great stamina and possessors of a liberated BUDDHA NATURE.

NĀ MÒ PÓ SÀ DUŌ calls upon VIRGIN WARRIORS, those who have recently succeeded in advancing far upon the CORRECT PATH of the DHAMMA. *NÀ MÓ PÓ JIĀ* calls all those WORLD-HONORED by virtue of their ENLIGHTENMENT.

SÀ PÓ SÀ DUŌ NĀ MÒ PÓ SÀ DUŌ NÀ MÓ PÓ JIĀ
Aid Me, All Enlightened Ones

MÓ FÁ TÈ DÒU

Here you call upon your GOOD FRIEND, your TEACHER, for encouragement. The knowledge and understanding received by you through your TEACHER will aid you. Your TEACHER will also be symbolically within you, giving strength and courage.

MÓ FÁ TÈ DÒU
Help Me, My Good Friend

DÁ SHÍ TĀ

First, the Mantra line means, "the Mantra runs like this." Second, it refers to the making of a sign with the HAND, which is a SEAL of CORRECT ACTION based on the DHAMMA and the presence of what we call the EYE of WISDOM. The Mantra therefore declares, "In this manner may COMPASSION be GIVEN and may the giver perceive WISDOM." The gift which is generated through COMPASSION is that of BENEVOLENT ACTION accompanied by BENEVOLENT LOVE, while the WISDOM is that of NOBLE JUDGMENT of ATTITUDE accompanied by GLADNESS.

It is interesting to note that the WISDOM of NOBLE JUDGMENT is supported by a natural sense of UNITY. This is an understanding of ROOT equality which has nothing to do with social evaluation. It is also supported by a sophisticated sense of what is WORTHY and what is not.

There are two other dimensions of WISDOM unrelated to ATTITUDE. First, there is the WISDOM of ILLUMINATION in ACTION, which is associated with all that is undefined and unattached to AVARICE,

PRIDE, and HATRED. Second, there is the UNSURPASSED WISDOM of CORRECT INTENTION. Neither of these forms a part of the EYE of WISDOM. The Mantra declares, therefore, "In this manner may your COMPASSION be given ACTIVELY as a gift, in the form of BENEVOLENT LOVE, and may the giver perceive with WISDOM of ATTITUDE."

DÁ SHÍ TĀ
May Benevolence and Wisdom Accompany Compassion

SUMMARY: LINES 16-18

Thus you have completed an important segment of the FIRST PHASE, for in the fourth and fifth series you have taken the important step of contacting your BUDDHA NATURE, touching therein the qualities which may well have been dormant for a long time. It is not at all easy to touch TRUE COMPASSION, but one way is to bring it alive through its attributes.

At this point you will be able to see the importance of the BUDDHA NATURE. The wise will then see the deeper significance of the Mantra. Reciting the Mantra is an act of SELF-ENLIGHTENMENT through the task of attempting to give COMPASSION. You must, therefore, now develop CORRECT ATTITUDE and CORRECT INTENTION with respect to your recitation of the Mantra. This is not easy.

It would be incorrect to recite the Mantra as a means of achieving enlightenment, no matter how noble that objective may appear to be. That would be CRAVING and SELFISHNESS. It would be incorrect to recite the Mantra as an EGOISTIC act of demonstrating to oneself one's own apparent VIRTUE. That would be CLINGING and SELFISHNESS.

That leaves us only one alternative, VIRTUOUS SELF-AWARENESS. Do notice the careful selection of words. We did not say SELF-AWARENESS of VIRTUE. You must not permit this to occur. VIRTUOUS SELF-AWARENESS means that you have to see yourself as NON-SELF. When there is no SELF there is and can be no CLINGING or CRAVING. This is the true meaning of SELF-ENLIGHTENMENT.

If you were to learn archery, then you would be taught all the details: how to stand, hold the bow, place the arrow, pull the string, aim, and release the arrow. You would learn how to do these perfectly and would train your mind and body to attend to these details of form.

Then you would be taught about the NON-SELF. You would be taught, if the teacher was a MASTER, to be AS ONE with the ground beneath your feet, your body and mind, the bow, the arrow, the process of aim and release, and the target. It is the same with a Mantra. You must learn all the details concerning a line, and then become AS ONE with the earth, your body and mind, the words, phrases, contemplation, wisdom, cultivation, volition, principles, knowing, fruition, your preparation for speech, the words, and the receiving world.

This is the HAND of BENEVOLENCE, guided by the EYE of WISDOM. This is the awakening of your BUDDHA NATURE with VIRTUOUS SELF-AWARENESS.

16. *SÀ PÓ SÀ DUŌ NĀ MÒ PÓ SÀ DUŌ NÀ MÓ PÓ JIĀ*
    Aid Me, All Enlightened Ones

17. *MÓ FÁ TÈ DÒU*
    Help Me, My Good Friend

18. *DÁ SHÍ TĀ*
    May Benevolence and Wisdom Accompany Compassion

Now repeat:

SÀ PÓ SÀ DUŌ NĀ MÒ PÓ SÀ DUŌ NÀ MÓ PÓ JIĀ
MÓ FÁ TÈ DÒU
DÁ SHÍ TĀ

THE SIXTH SERIES: CONSOLIDATION

Strive on with diligence.

ĂN Ā PÓ LÚ XĪ

In this line *ĂN* means, "Let all that is said BE." When you say "SO BE IT" or "LET IT BE SO," you are actually directing all your ENERGY, which is now concentrated on the concept of COMPASSION, towards those who SUFFER. It is as if you were lifting out the COMPASSION dwelling within your BUDDHA NATURE as a PROCESS with your hands. You can actually feel that lifting out, and its presentation as an UNTAINTED GIFT to the SUFFERING.

You will also perceive another marvelous thing. It is that when you lift out and give that COMPASSION, you have not diminished that COMPASSION within yourself. In fact, if anything, you have increased it. That is because it is a PROCESS, not a thing.

Now, since you are presenting this COMPASSION to the WORLD, you must direct it to those who SUFFER. It is very subtle, but try and see the difference between directing your COMPASSION to a man who is SUFFERING because he doesn't have a lot of money, and directing your COMPASSION to that same man because he SUFFERS with that infirmity. Can you see that the SUFFERING that he apparently feels is CRAVING? His real suffering is a hidden consequence of that CRAVING. You must be careful that you are not saying subliminally, "I wish he had a lot of money so that he would not suffer." That is not a solution. What your WISDOM dictates is the concept, "I wish him to see the FOLLY in his CRAVING for money." In this case it appears rather obvious; in others it may not.

To prevent this, you chant the following words, *Ā PÓ LÚ XĪ*, which mean that you call up correct WISE OBSERVATION of the SUFFERING of the WORLD. This is the WISDOM of NOBLE JUDGMENT.

ĂN Ā PÓ LÚ XĪ
So Be It. May I Wisely Perceive the Suffering of the World

LÚ JIĀ DÌ

In using the last Mantra line, you will have launched COMPASSION into the world as a general MANTLE OF TRANQUILITY.

If you want the Mantra to be specific and effective, it would be incorrect to have your observations of the world one-sided and out of balance. With the concept of *YIN* and *YANG*, you understand that COMFORT and DISCOMFORT actually define each other. Without the concept of one, the other cannot exist. There cannot be MENTAL

SUFFERING without MENTAL COMFORT.

You now then balance your previous observation by chanting *LÚ JIĀ DÌ*, which calls up WISE OBSERVATION of the WORLD in TRANQUILITY.

LÚ JIĀ DÌ
May I Wisely Perceive the Tranquility of the World

JIĀ LUÓ DÌ

Now is the time in the Mantra when you define what will be accomplished by your COMPASSION. Why is this important? It matters because it would be FOLLY to simply dump a load of COMPASSION on the world without trusting in a TRANSFORMATION, a NATURAL CONSEQUENCE of the operation of the compassionate process.

JIĀ LUÓ DÌ brings up the conceptual image of that transformation. It is, of course, the RESCUE of all SUFFERING creatures of the world. When you give food to a starving man, do you not, at the moment of giving, see with joy their future state? Similarly when you give COMPASSION, are you not already HAPPY and GLAD for them in anticipation of their transformation?

In this manner, we do not see COMPASSION in isolation. When you then give COMPASSION in this way, it accomplishes a correct and fruitful ACTION and brings out your own BUDDHA NATURE, and that of others, from the darkness into the light.

JIĀ LUÓ DÌ
May Sympathetic Compassion Accomplish Fruitful Actions

YÍ XĪ LĪ

This Mantra line signifies, "I COMPLY WITH THE TEACHINGS." The teachings say that simply by offering COMPASSION and being a COMPASSIONATE person, you will transform other living creatures. You don't have to run out and proselytize the DHAMMA. The DHAMMA is the NATURAL WAY. It is your conduct which will shed light to those who are ready to hear the DHAMMA.

YÍ XĪ LĪ
I Comply with the Teachings About Compassion

MÓ HĒ PÚ TÍ SÀ DUǑ

MÓ HĒ means GREAT, but not in the usual sense of the word. Here greatness must be considered in the context of being ABSOLUTELY CORRECT and LAUDED BY THE WISE. Next we chant *PÚ TÍ*, which signifies ENLIGHTENED TO THE WAY, and lastly *SÀ DUǑ*, which is one of MUCH COURAGE.

Here you are calling on the WISDOM of your BUDDHA NATURE to MONITOR and FILTER your ACTIONS. You are, you see, preparing to be much more specific in directing your COMPASSION. At this point you have completed the preparation phase. You will have begun to synthesize CONCENTRATION (meditation), the WISDOM gathered from your study of the DHAMMA and your DIRECT EXPERIENCE, and the DISCIPLINE of MINDFULNESS. If you have also chanted the Mantra correctly, you will have understood and internalized the ONENESS of all things, all creatures, all sentient beings. You will see that we human creatures are not separate from each other. You can then call upon a WISDOM of ATTITUDE which is not attached to your IDENTITIES, for you are all people. You can create ACTION without objectives, for the path is a path of ACTIONS, not OBJECTIVES.

MÓ HĒ PÚ TÍ SÀ DUǑ
May the Correct Enlightened Courage of my Buddha Nature Direct my Actions

SUMMARY: LINES 19-23

These five final lines of the first phase are the culmination of all that has gone before. For the first time, you actually attempt to project COMPASSION with force into the SENTIENT WORLD. These lines aid the process, because they focus the chanter's attention directly on COMPASSION as a concept. First, attention is directed at SUFFERING and then TRANQUILITY, so that you can balance your understanding. Then, you link COMPASSION with ACTION. Later, when you use the

Hand and Eye preparations, you will discover a very special secret about that relationship. Finally, you bring the DHAMMA to bear upon COMPASSION, and then generate a clear enlightened view of that concept.

19. *ǍN Ā PÓ LÚ XĪ*
So Be It. May I Wisely Perceive the Suffering of the World

20. *LÚ JIĀ DÌ*
May I Wisely Perceive the Tranquility of the World

21. *JIĀ LUÓ DÌ*
May Sympathetic Compassion Accomplish Fruitful Actions

22. *YÍ XĪ LĪ*
I Comply with the Teachings about Compassion

23. *MÓ HĒ PÚ TÍ SÀ DUǑ*
May the Correct Enlightened Courage of my Buddha Nature
Direct my Actions

Now repeat:

ǍN Ā PÓ LÚ XĪ
LÚ JIĀ DÌ
JIĀ LUÓ DÌ
YÍ XĪ LĪ
MÓ HĒ PÚ TÍ SÀ DUǑ

REVIEW: MANTRA LINES OF THE FIRST PHASE

1. *NĀ MÒ HĒ LÁ DÁ NÀ DUŌ LÁ YÈ YĒ*
I, with Reverence, Take Refuge in the Buddha,
the Dhamma, and the Sangha

2. *NĀ MÒ Ā LĪ YĒ*
I Take Refuge and Respectfully Submit to Wisdom

3. *PÓ LÚ JIÉ DÌ SHUÒ BŌ LÁ YĒ*
   Bring the Light of Contemplation to Bear upon Suffering
   and Tranquility in the World

4. *PÚ TÍ SÀ DUŎ PÓ YĒ*
   I Will Cross to Enlightenment with Resolution and Humility

5. *MÓ HĒ SÀ DUŎ PÓ YĒ*
   I Will Succeed with Diligent Effort, Energy, and Self-Respect

6. *MÓ HĒ JIĀ LÚ NÍ JIĀ YĒ*
   I Will Succeed Generating Mindfulness
   and a Respect for True Compassion

7. *ĂN*
   So Be It

8. *SÀ PÓ LUÓ FÁ YÈ*
   I Call upon the Buddha, Masterful, Honored by the Wise

9. *SHŬ DÁ NÀ DÁ XIĚ*
   I Call upon the Dhamma, the Brotherhood

10. *NĀ MÒ XĪ JÍ LĪ DUŎ YĪ MĔNG Ā LÌ YĒ*
    With Respect I Take Refuge Within my Buddha Nature

11. *PÓ LÚ JÍ DÌ SHÌ FÓ LÁ LÈNG TUÓ PÓ*
    May I Touch the Compassion Within my Buddha Nature

12. *NĀ MÒ NÀ LÁ JĬN CHÍ*
    I Take Refuge with the Qualities of Compassion
    which are Noble, Respectful, and Wise

13. *XĪ LĪ MÓ HĒ PÓ DUŌ SHĀ MIĒ*
    I Call upon the Undefiled and Unattached Illumination
    of Benevolent Love

14. *SÀ PÓ Ā TĀ DÒU SHŪ PÉNG*
> I Call upon the Unity, Pure Worthiness,
> and Noble Judgment of Gladness

15. *Ā SHÌ YÙN*
I Call upon Natural Humility and Freedom from Identity Delusion,
the Dhamma of my Buddha Nature

16. *SÀ PÓ SÀ DUŌ NĀ MÒ PÓ SÀ DUŌ NÀ MÓ PÓ JIĀ*
> Aid Me, All Enlightened Ones

17. *MÓ FÁ TÈ DÒU*
> Help Me, my Good Friend

18. *DÁ SHÍ TĀ*
> May Benevolence and Wisdom Accompany Compassion

19. *ĂN Ā PÓ LÚ XĪ*
> So Be It. May I Wisely Perceive the Suffering of the World

20. *LÚ JIĀ DÌ*
> May I Wisely Perceive the Tranquility of the World

21. *JIĀ LUÓ DÌ*
> May Sympathetic Compassion Accomplish Fruitful Actions

22. *YÍ XĪ LĪ*
> I Comply with the Teachings about Compassion

23. *MÓ HĒ PÚ TÍ SÀ DUǑ*
May the Correct Enlightened Courage of my Buddha Nature
Direct my Actions

Now repeat:

> *NĀ MÒ HĒ LÁ DÁ NÀ DUŌ LÁ YÈ YĒ*
> *NĀ MÒ Ā LĪ YĒ*

173

PÓ LÚ JIÉ DÌ SHUÒ BŌ LÁ YĒ
PÚ TÍ SÀ DUǑ PÓ YĒ
MÓ HĒ SÀ DUǑ PÓ YĒ
MÓ HĒ JIĀ LÚ NÍ JIĀ YĒ
ĂN
SÀ PÓ LUÓ FÁ YÈ
SHǓ DÁ NÀ DÁ XIĚ
NĀ MÒ XĪ JÍ LĪ DUǑ YĪ MĚNG Ā LÌ YĒ
PÓ LÚ JÍ DÌ SHÌ FÓ LÁ LÈNG TUÓ PÓ
NĀ MÒ NÀ LÁ JǏN CHÍ
XĪ LĪ MÓ HĒ PÓ DUŌ SHĀ MIĒ
SÀ PÓ Ā TĀ DÒU SHŪ PÉNG
Ā SHÌ YÙN
SÀ PÓ SÀ DUŌ NĀ MÒ PÓ SÀ DUŌ NÀ MÓ PÓ JIĀ
MÓ FÁ TÈ DÒU
DÁ SHÍ TĀ
ĂN Ā PÓ LÚ XĪ
LÚ JIĀ DÌ
JIĀ LUÓ DÌ
YÍ XĪ LĪ
MÓ HĒ PÚ TÍ SÀ DUǑ

**This marks completion of the initial phase
of the GREAT COMPASSION MANTRA**

PART THREE:

THE SECOND PHASE OF THE MANTRA

THE HAND AND EYE PREPARATIONS

In order to transform all subsequent Mantra lines into strong and efficient ACTIVE PROCESSES, you must cultivate the correct STATE of PREPARATION within yourself. Every Mantra has its own particular preparation which must be developed by the chanter. That preparation will bring harmony and unity with the Mantra. There are FORTY-TWO different preparations used to support Mantra transmission. Each preparation involves both a BENEVOLENT ACTION factor, symbolically represented by the HAND, and a WISDOM factor, represented by the EYE. We say then that each Mantra line requires a specific Hand and Eye preparation.

The BENEVOLENT ACTION factor is based upon a genuine unselfish wish that the recipient be free from suffering (COMPASSION) and this is transformed into benefit and happiness (BENEVOLENT LOVE) with the Mantra chanting. All BENEVOLENT ACTIONS, therefore, which form a part of the specific HAND preparedness for a Mantra line are transformed from the VOLITION to ACT, which is the basic wish. If it is a CORRECT VOLITION, it has VIRTUE of ATTITUDE as its base.

An intellectual wish does not suffice, because a wish dominated by conscious intellect is invariably contaminated. If the VOLITION is not dominated by conscious intellect, then accompanying the VOLITION there will be an internal sensation confirming that the VOLITION is CORRECT. This confirmation stems from a subliminal "fount" of knowledge within memory (the BUDDHA NATURE) which is uncontaminated by consciousness.

This sudden "flash" of confirmation is generally accompanied by the sensation of COMPASSION, which is sometimes quite subtle. When that CORRECT VOLITION, also called INTENTION, is changed into a CORRECT BENEVOLENT ACTION, it is accompanied by a sensation of BENEVOLENT LOVE which also stems from the BUDDHA NATURE.

The WISDOM factor, which is the EYE preparation for each Mantra line, is an internalization of the natural truth concerning the concept transmitted by the line. It requires consolidation of the DHAMMA within your ATTITUDE relative to each specific concept concerned. This CORRECT and NATURAL ATTITUDE resides in memory and provides the raw information for VOLITION. When an ATTITUDE is confirmed as CORRECT by your BUDDHA NATURE, there will be an accompanying sensation of GLADNESS. This GLADNESS, together with COMPASSION and BENEVOLENT LOVE, make up the generalized sensation of true LOVE, which accompanies activity of your BUDDHA NATURE when conscious intellect is uncontaminated by the SENSATIONS which lead to CONFUSION and DELUSION, the EMOTIONS which lead to GREED, and the THOUGHTS which lead to HOSTILITY.

Fig. 34 The Path of Confirmation

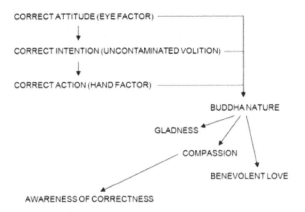

While we mention the Hand and Eye preparations here, it is recommended that the chanter should first acquire practice in chanting and should also have a basic understanding of the commentary before moving on to the actual Hand and Eye practices, which are in the second book of this series. These will extend your understanding.

You have learned that the subtle differentiation into the three apparently separate sensations of GLADNESS, COMPASSION, and BENEVOLENT LOVE arises from WELL-BEING and the conscious knowledge of the CORRECTNESS of the processes involved, namely ATTITUDE, INTENTION, and ACTION. When the processes of CORRECT ATTITUDE are being activated, then the related EXPERIENCE is interpreted as GLADNESS. Similarly, when VOLITION or INTENTIONS are being correctly formed, then the EXPERIENCE is interpreted as COMPASSION, while all WELL-BEING following CORRECT ACTIONS results in an interpretation of BENEVOLENT LOVE. All are then defined by MIND-STATES within CONSCIOUSNESS in a way that turns each into an apparently distinct EXPERIENCE.

Attitudes, Intentions, and Actions

In the Mantra commentaries which follow, you will find repeated reference to CORRECT ATTITUDES, CORRECT INTENTIONS, and CORRECT ACTIONS. These three, like their concomitant experiences, are, of course, not really three separate operations. ATTITUDES flow into INTENTIONS and, likewise, INTENTIONS into ACTIONS, for when they operate in sequence, they are part of a single process. It is only conceptually that we break them into three parts, so that there will be a better understanding and a fitting preparedness for the chanting of Mantra lines.

In the following diagram, you can see the way in which the ACTIONS of the Hand Preparations work together in a correct and natural manner with the ATTITUDES of the Eye preparations to reinforce correct human behavior. On the other hand, in a human system which is corrupted by the DEMANDS, the BUDDHA NATURE is relegated and incorrect mental states take over the control of human behavior. TRUE GLADNESS, COMPASSION, and BENEVOLENT LOVE are not experienced then and, instead, other experiences appear on the SCREEN of CONSCIOUSNESS and are mistakenly taken for the true experiences. (see figures 35 and 36)

Fig. 35 Correct Hand and Eye Preparation Interaction

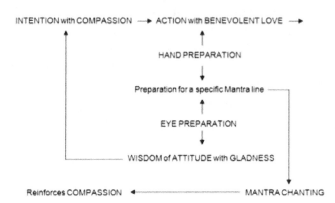

Fig. 36 The Roots of Incorrect Mental States

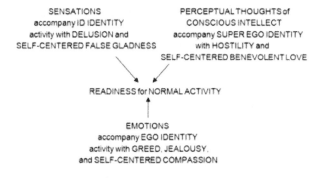

You will notice that in the second diagram there is no cooperative interaction between ID, EGO, and SUPER EGO. In fact, they generally act in CONFLICT. Contrary to this competitive interaction of the IDENTITIES, the NATURAL and CORRECT OPERATION involves mutually supporting NATURAL PROCESSES.

In the two following diagrams, the important differences between NATURAL PROCESSING and IDENTITY PROCESSING are easily seen. You will note in the first diagram that MEMORY provides CORRECT ATTITUDE INFORMATION to form the INTENTIONS and ACTIONS. You will also see that REASON has contact with the BUDDHA NATURE and with CONSCIOUSNESS. It is the BUDDHA NATURE, with its NATURAL filters, which confirms, through consciousness, the CORRECTNESS of ATTITUDE, INTENTIONS, and ACTIONS. REASON then is the major OPERATING SYSTEM in all correct operation, while CONSCIOUSNESS acts only as a useful display device.

In the model of INCORRECT IDENTITY PROCESSING shown in the second diagram, you see that the IDENTITY-TAINTED INFORMATION is fed directly to CONSCIOUSNESS. Here, with complete information overload due to the presence of unnecessary SENSATIONS, EMOTIONS, and THOUGHTS, it is CONSCIOUSNESS which controls REASON. The NATURAL CONFIRMATION of CORRECTNESS does not take place, as the BUDDHA NATURE is completely silenced and blocked by CONSCIOUSNESS. In this system, the IDENTITIES control all behavior and perpetuate their existence as DELUSIONS through the apparent power of decision-making exerted by CONSCIOUSNESS.

Fig. 37 Natural Processing

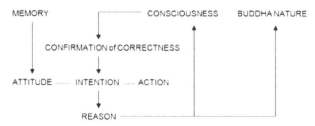

Fig. 38 Identity Processing in which Consciousness Controls Reason

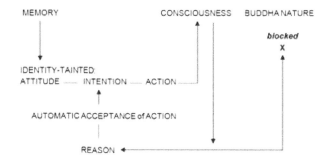

What actually occurs in correct chanting of the Mantra is that CONSCIOUSNESS is stilled and cleared of the agitating activity of the SENSATIONS, EMOTIONS, and COGNITIVE PERCEPTIONS connected to INCORRECT ATTITUDES, INTENTIONS, and ACTIONS. This occurs due to the combination of the access form of CONCENTRATION and the continually growing knowledge of what is correct.

Once CONSCIOUSNESS begins to be cleared from the contamination of the IDENTITIES, then the voice of REASON and the BUDDHA NATURE become liberated and are available once more. Once correct natural operation becomes unhindered, the momentum of the institution of a correctly operating system increases so that the DEMANDS can be set aside.

You can see that there is nothing very mysterious in the process involved in these changes. You must realize, however, that the initial changes are slow. Do not expect momentous initial recovery of the natural function. You will have to continually battle the DEMONS of DELUSION, the HUNGRY GHOSTS, and the SAVAGE BEASTS with very still consciousness. All that you have to do is recognize their presence the first instant that they make themselves known in consciousness. This vigilance is essential. Remember, however: do not forcefully resist these IDENTITY-initiated SENSATIONS, EMOTIONS, and COGNITIVE PERCEPTIONS. Note them and let them fall away unattended. If you understand this, you can proceed with confidence to the important second phase of the GREAT COMPASSION MANTRA of NATURAL WISDOM.

THE SEVENTH SERIES: THE CORNERSTONE

SÀ PÓ SÀ PÓ

With the Mantra line *SÀ PÓ SÀ PÓ*, you become very specific and wish BENEFIT and HAPPINESS to ALL HUMAN CREATURES. The benefit and happiness dispensed by this line's use results, eventually, in release from behavior initiated by both the sensation-associated visceral ID IDENTITY and the emotional EGO IDENTITY. Because ID is constantly seeking visceral satisfaction, it can never decide which eventual ATTITUDE will be the most satisfying. It is this constant indecision which is the base for your DELUSION and CONFUSION when it occurs.

The emotional EGO identity, on the other hand, is constantly seeking the pleasurable gratification which results in GREEDY behavior. When there is no DELUSION, then your ATTITUDES are formed with clarity. When there is no GREED, then your INTENTIONS become untainted. As a result of an increase in the CORRECTNESS of the ACTIONS you perform and a consequence of the chanting of this Mantra line, you will bring the BENEFIT and HAPPINESS spoken of in this Mantra line to yourself and others.

In addition, with constant and well-prepared repetition, you will be released from the debilitating IDENTITIES and from all your DELUSION and GREED. The Hand and Eye for this Mantra line needs, therefore, to be developed so that the full benefit can be realized. It is called the PRECIOUS COMMAND. This preparation has a great impact when correctly nurtured, and is called the PRECIOUS COMMAND because its effect not only releases the receiver or chanter of the Mantra from some GREED and DELUSION, but opens the doors to eventual liberation through MINDFULNESS and CORRECT CONCENTRATION, overcoming all mundane obstacles.

When the Mantra is chanted with correct preparation, it is as though there was a command to the IDENTITIES declaring, "Release this person from dominance, for he offends against himself by accepting the delusion of your presence." This command is strong and must be obeyed because it is a command which is in complete accord with the DHAMMA.

We can symbolically say, therefore, that King Yama's Demon Generals in the Hells of DELUSION and the Ghost Kings of GREED will all obey the command and release their captives, just as a noble and correct command from a just ruler overcomes all irrational opposition. This Mantra line, when correctly cultivated, is so strong that it may restore life to a person who is so embroiled in the world of the senses that he is dead to his own sensitive and discriminating nature.

SÀ PÓ SÀ PÓ
May this Compassion Bring Benefit and Happiness to All People
Intensified with the PRECIOUS COMMAND Hand and Eye

MÓ LÁ MÓ LÁ

This is an important Mantra line. It says MAY IT BE. In other words, may there be a growth of WISDOM in harmony with your BUDDHA NATURE. It is oriented towards the elimination of SUFFERING by facilitating the growth of WISDOM. Can you see the importance of this? By calling upon a WISDOM HEART of the BUDDHA NATURE, you can eliminate all FOLLY-FILLED ideas based on IGNORANCE.

There are three major HEARTS of WISDOM associated with the BUDDHA NATURE. The first, referred to and addressed within this Mantra line, is that associated with ATTITUDE, namely that of NOBLE JUDGMENT. It is this NOBLE JUDGMENT that builds CORRECT ATTITUDES. The second and third forms of WISDOM, which will be addressed in later Mantra lines, are the WISDOM of CORRECT INTENTIONS, which is the UNSURPASSED WISDOM regarding CAUSE and EFFECT, and the WISDOM of CORRECT ACTION, which is ILLUMINATING KNOWLEDGE.

You might have assumed that the WISDOM which would be tapped in transmitting this Mantra line would be that of ILLUMINATING knowledge, so that the WISDOM of ACTIONS could accompany the ACTION of transmitting BENEFIT and HAPPINESS to ALL HUMAN CREATURES with *SÀ PÓ SÀ PÓ* in the previous Mantra line. This would be incorrect, for ACTIONS must have as their base the WISDOM of CORRECT ATTITUDE.

Be cautious, for although you can trust in the NATURAL LAW, it is not wise to have within your ATTITUDES any EXPECTATIONS about the outcome of chanting the Mantra or even any specific line. If you have EXPECTATIONS, you can be sure that the chanting is the product of your conscious intellect. This will have no effect other than the inflation of your EGO and SUPER EGO IDENTITIES. If you as a transmitter have EXPECTATIONS, you have created a PERSON who is chanting the Mantra and this automatically destroys essential UNITY between the chanter and the Mantra.

It is not easy to keep Mantra chanting free from your IDENTITIES. That is why *MÓ LÁ MÓ LÁ* is most effective when the corresponding Hand and Eye preparedness has been nurtured. Because the NATURAL LAW is precious and perfect like a PEARL, the preparation is called the BUDDHA PEARL.

MÓ LÁ MÓ LÁ
May There Be Personal Growth in Accord with Natural Wisdom
Intensified with the BUDDHA PEARL Hand and Eye

SUMMARY: LINES 24-25

With the first line (24) within this second series of Mantra lines, the main purpose was to transmit to sentient creatures COMPASSION, intended to BRING BENEFIT AND HAPPINESS TO ALL PEOPLE. The internal wish was turned by the chanting and the nurture of the Hand and Eye preparation into an ACTION of BENEVOLENCE.

Once more we see in the line which follows that simply wanting something to come about is not enough. There is a clear necessity to keep the transmission pure by maintaining correct personal growth consistent with the WISDOM of one's BUDDHA NATURE (25). The WISDOM in this line is the WISDOM of NOBLE JUDGMENT within CORRECT ATTITUDE. You will see later that these two lines not only are supported by their own Hand and Eye preparations, the PRECIOUS COMMAND and the BUDDHA PEARL, but in turn actually support all subsequent Hand and Eye preparations in the Mantra. Their correct nurture is therefore of extreme importance.

24. *SÀ PÓ SÀ PÓ*
May this Compassion Bring Benefit and Happiness to All People
The PRECIOUS COMMAND Hand and Eye

25. *MÓ LÁ MÓ LÁ*
May There Be Personal Growth in Accord with Natural Wisdom
The BUDDHA PEARL Hand and Eye

Now repeat:

SÀ PÓ SÀ PÓ
MÓ LÁ MÓ LÁ

THE EIGHTH SERIES: THE ABOLITION OF CARES AND ANXIETIES

MÓ XĪ MÓ SĪ LĪ TUÓ YÙN

One of the perils of understanding and living with the NATURAL LAW is that it generally requires the tools called words and the operation of the process which we call thinking. *MÓ XĪ MÓ SĪ* signifies that release from the power of words will bring a freedom from CARES and ANXIETIES.

What is this power of words? When we see something which we have labeled "a tree," we think that that is what it is. This is a mistake. What is a tree? It is not its name. It is not its description.

What is it then? Is it what it does? Possibly that is the closest we can get, but in fact we eventually must come to the conclusion that we don't really know what a tree is at all. That is not a problem. Giving it the name "tree" helps us identify it as an object and that helps us interact with the tree as an apparent object. We should not be trapped into thinking, however, that that is what it really is.

It is the process behind the words which must be embraced and touched if it is at all possible. If we can't, it doesn't matter as long as we don't fall into the trap of creating a reality from words and descriptions. If it is words which control your life, then you are a victim of CONSCIOUS INTELLECT. Look behind the words if you can and see that the words are only ILLUSIONS. One of the advantages of not clinging to words is the fact that you are released from the bondage of the SENSATIONS, EMOTIONS, and THOUGHTS which are attached to those words. The FOLLY within consciousness is therefore minimal and you are able to see and concentrate more clearly with absolute calm.

If you try to understand without clinging with conscious intellect to the word ideas, then you will internalize the DHAMMA more easily so that it can liberate your BUDDHA NATURE. It is most difficult to develop this way of thinking, but once it becomes refined and developed, it becomes subtle and quite beautiful. Words, you see, are just building blocks for internal ideas and concepts, and although we use them for external communication and internal function, all the internal work of REAL THINKING and DECISION-MAKING is carried on without them. What we see as WORDS in consciousness is only an insignificant part of the immense and complex workings of the system. This internal "profound thought" without words is where the real living system resides.

What you are saying with this Mantra line is, "Let my system get on with its internal natural function without there being a clinging to the insignificant 'apparent thoughts' and 'descriptions' which appear important and are not."

Because all words have as their base the information which is derived from the five senses, which are each different like five distinct colors, we call the preparation for this Mantra line the FIVE-COLORED CLOUD. When you achieve the integration of the individual colors so that they mix together like a nebulous cloud, so that none of the colors is sufficiently tangible to be craved, then you are free from the chains of each of the five senses and the words related to them. There will then be release from all worries, sorrow, cares, and anxieties which have as their base mental constructions and associations based upon words.

LĪ TUÓ YÙN, the second part of the Mantra line, reaffirms that the WORDLESS PROCESS of UNDERSTANDING will bring freedom. Most people have a fear of emptiness and the feeling is that if you take away all those words you will be nothing but a lifeless shell. That is not the case. Everything is understood if the Hand and Eye preparation is cultivated. Everything is crystal-clear. Words and phrases are used correctly as tools in their proper place. Instead of the human system being filled with the internal "noise" of words and all the SENSATIONS, EMOTIONS, and THOUGHTS associated with them, it is calm. The BLUE LOTUS Hand and Eye preparation brings this calm and must be developed in concert with the FIVE-COLORED CLOUD.

The preparation of calm UNDERSTANDING without words is both profound and subtle; that is why it is called the BLUE LOTUS. It is a natural barrier against the return of a reliance upon the apparent truth of words once you have begun to break free from them. It is a barrier against the return of SUFFERING. With *LĪ TUÓ YÙN* you possess and transmit the inconceivable JOY of the HEART of the BLUE LOTUS.

It seems strange that one should be speaking about your internal joy when transmitting a Mantra line dedicated to COMPASSION. The truth is that those who are most joyful are best able to give COMPASSION. Most people think the opposite. They believe that you have to be experiencing what the other person has experienced before you can give COMPASSIONATELY. They believe that they must show sorrow. This is not so. If you experience the suffering of others, then you might know better how the person feels. This has nothing to do with COMPASSION. The cultivation of the BLUE LOTUS of JOY and HAPPINESS is essential.

MÓ XĪ MÓ SĪ LĪ TUÓ YÙN
With Release from the Captivity of Words May There Be
Joy and Happiness with Freedom from Cares and Anxieties
The FIVE-COLORED CLOUD and BLUE LOTUS Hand and Eye

SUMMARY: LINE 26

This Mantra line is the first transmission of major importance. It alleviates the most general SUFFERING of mankind. Although it does require the two Hand and Eyes mentioned, it does not need additional support lines. It therefore stands alone, but powerful in its own right, if the preparations are nurtured.

When you use this Mantra line, it is important to really understand that words can be dangerous. You must be free from the captivity of words bound in place by conscious intellect. Now, it is not too difficult for most people to be suspicious of academic learning and the words associated with that learning. It is surprising, however, how many of those who are suspicious of the language of academic knowledge are duped by the wispy, seductive, but completely empty words of the greater part of the esoteric world. To be truly free of the captivity of words is not an easy task without proper cultivation and vigilance.

It is equally folly to be afraid of words. A good workman knows how to use his tools. Many people are very blind when it comes to understanding what academics have to say. What they do not understand they tend to condemn or alter to fit their own frame of reference. Many people are also afraid of words which speak of the non-mundane world. Remember that there is no danger in the words themselves, but there is danger in the way that they are used. If transcendental words fly about in the air without being grounded to the apparent world of the senses in some way, then they have little utility and can be used for deception quite easily. Transcendental concepts require no fancy nebulous names attached to them. The word "unknowable" or the concepts "not this, not that" or "the void" are more correct than "Cosmic Consciousness," which is easily warped by conscious intellect so that the concept can be clung to and used as an explanation for something which needs no explanation. The answer is clear. Know your tools and you will not be ensnared nor be afraid.

26. *MÓ XĪ MÓ SĪ LĪ TUÓ YÙN*
With Release from the Captivity of Words May There Be
Joy and Happiness with Freedom from Cares and Anxieties
The FIVE-COLORED CLOUD and BLUE LOTUS Hand and Eye

Repeat:

MÓ XĪ MÓ SĪ LĪ TUÓ YÙN

THE NINTH SERIES: THE REJECTION OF CLINGING AND CRAVING

JÙ LÚ JÙ LÚ JIÉ MĔNG

When you transmit COMPASSIONATELY, it is possible to broadcast your message to the entire sentient world. This is, of course, a legitimate choice. Alternatively, however, you may wish to limit the field of its effect in order to obtain greater intensity. If you have a target in mind that is particularly difficult to reach, because of obstacles which are in the way of transmission, then you can use the Mantra line *JÙ LÚ JÙ LÚ*. With *JÙ LÚ JÙ LÚ* you can define and mark a set of boundaries as far as you want the Mantra to reach, and then purify all who are ready to "hear" within that area with incredible intensity. It is said that the normal transmission of your Mantra line is intensified so that it cuts through all barriers within the limits tied off, and that all can be reached by the message of the Mantra.

The particular compassionate message transmitted with this Mantra line is directed at turning all DHAMMA teachings into CORRECT ACTION. Perhaps you can see now why there may be many obstacles. People are quite accepting when it comes to listening to ideas and concepts, but when they are expected to actually put an idea into ACTION, then all sorts of excuses and justifications are made to avoid actually doing anything.

The accompanying Hand and Eye preparation which must be cultivated is called the JEWELED CONCH, *SHANKA*. This name is given be cause cultivation of the correct preparation will magnify even further the energy of transmission, just as a conch magnifies the sound made when it is blown. The strength of the message transmitted by the JEWELED CONCH, which announces the MAGNIFICENCE OF THE DHAMMA, will assist all those who SUFFER and live without TRANQUILITY and will destroy obstacles to ACTION. If the DHAMMA is heard after the boundaries have been tied, then the RAGING BEASTS of HOSTILITY and the GHOSTS of GREED will not be able to creep in.

Doing DHAMMA is difficult. It is easy to be mistaken and sometimes do the wrong thing with correct motivation but faulty JUDGMENT. With the Mantra of COMPASSION we want all DHAMMA ACTION to be correct. *JIÉ MĚNG* assures that all who hear the Mantra will take care of all meritorious and correct affairs, rejecting ACTIONS created by AVARICE, AVERSION, HATRED, and associated PRIDE. All ACTIONS will then be UNATTACHED. The Hand and Eye preparation is called the WHITE LOTUS because the white lotus is the symbol of purity.

JÙ LÚ JÙ LÚ JIÉ MĚNG
May All Actions Be Meritorious and Correct
The JEWELED CONCH and the WHITE LOTUS Hand and Eye

DÙ LÚ DÙ LÚ FÁ SHÉ YĒ DÌ

The element *DÙ LÚ DÙ LÚ* of this Mantra line is directed at eliciting the light of WISDOM through the development of clarity and calmness in your sessions of CONCENTRATION. This CONCENTRATION is called *SAMADHI* and it is a one-pointedness which brings clarity and tranquility which is both bright and pure. Many people take part in sessions which are commonly referred to as "meditation." Usually, however, all that is achieved is the temporary dissipation of STRESS and TENSION. This "relaxation" is certainly beneficial, but it is not *SAMADHI*.

It is *SAMADHI* (CONCENTRATION) which eventually liberates the repressed BUDDHA NATURE. This CORRECT CONCENTRATION changes the lives of those who are illuminated and guides them across the "sea of life" from birth to eventual death. CONCENTRATION is not easy. It requires VIRTUE and the arousal of many qualities which can transform a mundane act of "meditation" into a transcendental experience which eliminates SUFFERING through the stilling of consciousness. With correct dedicated practice, this stillness defeats the EGO IDENTITY even in one's daily life, and this CORRECT CONCENTRATION will bring a purity of ideas when building the important everyday INTENTIONS which bring CORRECT ACTIONS.

An important factor in the construction of CORRECT INTENTIONS is an understanding of the senses, the sense doors, so that the experiences of the senses will not be craved after or clung to. If there is then a non-attachment to the senses and an equanimity towards the consequences of all ACTIONS, then CORRECT INTENTIONS will be reinforced and will grow in strength, combating all future IDENTITY interference.

These CORRECT INTENTIONS, initiated and monitored by the BUDDHA NATURE, are called NOBLE because they will stand noble, erect, and strong when battling against the incorrect EGO IDENTITY ideas which are hidden within the ATTITUDES held in memory. It is these INCORRECT ATTITUDES which are used as building blocks in the formation of INTENTIONS.

These ATTITUDES, stored in memory, have long been subjected to IDENTITY manipulation and are the folly-filled base of all INCORRECT INTENTIONS. If you will it and use this Mantra line correctly, NOBILITY of INTENTION, directed by your BUDDHA NATURE, will destroy all these INCORRECT INTENTIONS.

This Mantra line, through the fine-tuning of *SAMADHI*, addresses INTENTIONS rather than ATTITUDES, because it is here that a major battle can be fought and won against EGO IDENTITY by the WISDOM OF CAUSE AND EFFECT of the BUDDHA NATURE.

INCORRECT ATTITUDES have a great resistance which cannot be overcome easily with the Noble Heart, due to the strength of past reinforcement accruing from all previous INCORRECT KARMIC CYCLES. These strong INCORRECT ATTITUDES, residing in memory, will be transformed by other Mantra lines using other qualities of the BUDDHA NATURE which are more effective.

Later in your practice, after you have made progress in correcting folly-filled ATTITUDES, this Mantra line can be used to stimulate even more finely honed CONCENTRATION. In daily life, this will help in the positive transformation of unstable INTENTIONS which are susceptible to the aggression of the IDENTITIES.

Even when your ATTITUDES have been transformed and may be relatively correct and stable within memory due to the use of the Mantra, the IDENTITIES will still attack your new INTENTIONS which are in the process of being formed. Constant vigilance is essential. The attacks are very subtle and are generally supported by what seems like correct reasoning. If you are very calm, you will see the presence of the IDENTITIES.

The chanting of this Mantra line will sharpen your perceptions and the calm quietness of your mind, even while you are not practicing CONCENTRATION. This stillness of consciousness, engendered by effective CONCENTRATION, will be your major weapon against torpor and the most effective tool in the forming of strong CORRECT INTENTIONS.

In fact, most people don't realize that the stilling of the mind through CONCENTRATION is designed to secure a base for the building of CORRECT INTENTIONS in everyday life. That is actually the main reason for *SAMADHI* practice. The clear and still mind allows you to see clearly. When CORRECT INTENTIONS are followed by CORRECT ACTIONS, then CORRECT ATTITUDES will be fixed in MEMORY; thus SUFFERING can be set aside.

Most people want to relate *SAMADHI* to the objective of reaching NIRVANA and want to talk about "crossing over" and "enlightenment" and all sorts of other fine-sounding transcendental ideas. Buddha was much too wise to chase after transcendental and intellectual fantasy. His approach was CORRECT and efficiently directed towards eliminating SUFFERING in the most effective and practical way. That the experience of NIRVANA exists, that there appears to be a "crossing over" from attachment to the world, and that enlightenment occurs are tangential to the CORRECT PATH, which is the DHAMMA.

The corresponding Hand and Eye which must be cultivated if the Mantra is to be most effective is called the MOON ESSENCE. The MOON, *CHANDRA*, symbolizes the UNITY of OPPOSITES and this will remind you that the chanting of this line and the nurture of the Hand

and Eye preparation unites the silent and still world of *SAMADHI* with the over-busy MUNDANE world of the senses.

Most people don't link together their sessions of CONCENTRATION with their ordinary life. They think that CONCENTRATION is one thing which is going to provide some magic formula to change their lives and that their normal FOLLY-filled world is separate. This is an error. CONCENTRATION is cultivated specifically to calm the mind, thus strengthening CORRECT INTENTIONS by teaching you how to keep your consciousness free of noise even when you are not involved in CONCENTRATION practice.

CONCENTRATION is sometimes called ONE-POINTEDNESS, and it is important to remember not to divorce the ONE-POINTEDNESS that you acquire in *SAMADHI* from your everyday life. The two major uses of this Mantra line are shown in the following diagrams:

Fig. 39 Correct Concentration Engendering Daily Stillness in Consciousness Permitting Noble Intentions

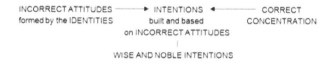

Fig. 40 Correct Concentration Engendering Daily Stillness in Consciousness Reinforces Noble Intentions

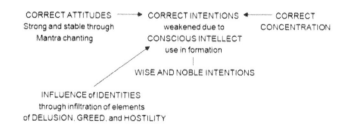

FÁ SHÉ YĒ DÌ, the second part of the Mantra line, accomplishes the same as *DÙ LÚ DÙ LÚ*, but it is directed at piercing states of EXTREME SUFFERING. This is very important, for there are many people who are in such torment that they cannot even take the first step of sitting quietly in CONCENTRATION. These people are victims of such an agitated mind that thoughts, emotions, and sensations flow in upon them incessantly. They need a special shield about them to get them at least through the access stages of CONCENTRATION.

The Hand and Eye which requires cultivation in this case is called the SHIELD, *KHETAKA*, because the DHAMMA, which is preparation, can protect even those who have extreme suffering from the spears of affliction thrown by the IDENTITIES, just as a well-designed shield can protect a warrior from the weapons of his enemies.

DÙ LÚ DÙ LÚ FÁ SHÉ YĒ DÌ
May There Be Clarity and Calmness in Concentration
The MOON ESSENCE and SHIELD Hand and Eye

MÓ HĒ FÁ SHÉ YĒ DÌ

This Mantra line means "the most victorious DHAMMA way," and it is a most important line.

When a person begins to make progress on the path which leads to the extinction of SUFFERING, then he begins to think differently and act differently. Often there will be a change of habits and systems which may lose apparent friends and cause difficulties. There is then great pressure both from within and from without to give up and return to NORMAL life, rejecting the NATURAL life. Arguments will be very strong and appealing to one's SENSATIONS, EMOTIONS, and THOUGHTS. The way ahead is difficult and the way back to a NORMAL life is easy. When one is not actually SUFFERING and cannot perceive the SUFFERING of the world, then the apparent PLEASURES which are available are enticing.

Most of the pressure, however, will come from the THOUGHTS of CONSCIOUS INTELLECT. These unworthy thoughts are hostile to the NATURAL WAY and are due to INCORRECT ATTITUDE generated by the Demons of DELUSION and CONFUSION and the Hungry Ghosts of GREED, who build philosophies which support the satiation of their needs. This Mantra line is a defense against a return to SUFFERING through the pressures of the existing social system, peers, parents, and other superstition-filled philosophies which promise an easier and more gratifying path.

Reciting this Mantra line, you cause the enemies of natural processes to retreat. It releases all who hear from POVERTY of THOUGHT and therefore, the PURE WORTHINESS of the BUDDHA NATURE is present. For greater efficiency, it requires the cultivation of MINDFULNESS within the Hand and Eye preparation which we call the JEWELED HALBERD, *PARASHU*, which is a combined spear and battle axe which can fend off enemies which come rapidly from all directions.

MÓ HĒ FÁ SHÉ YĒ DÌ
May There Be Victory Against False Ideas and Superstition
The JEWELED HALBERD Hand and Eye

TUÓ LÁ TUÓ LÁ

This Mantra line helps those who have a much more serious, but less frequent problem to deal with than CARES and ANXIETIES. In every person's life there comes the time when he or she is assailed by illness. This is a natural phenomenon of life and the healthy human creature is normally well prepared to combat infection and disease, making a recovery.

Many illnesses, however, are a result of unstable mental states. There is a tendency to call the illness MENTAL ILLNESS, but that is incorrect. What people call MENTAL ILLNESS is really an EXTREME ATTACHMENT to the world of the senses. There is nothing wrong with the mind itself. There is actually an exaggerated expectation that all desires will be fulfilled. That, of course, cannot occur and the result is extreme SUFFERING, which is experienced directly as discontentment and irritation, disappointment and annoyance, and disillusion and frustration. These experiences may be converted into a physiological problem in order that substitute love and attention may be received to relieve the stress and tension. For these people CONFUSION and DELUSION cannot be resolved, GREED cannot be satiated, and HOSTILITY never directed effectively.

The human creature, debilitated by a lack of understanding about life, generally falls into the trap of supporting and maintaining the infirmity by feeling sorry for himself. All this SUFFERING is always unnecessary and uses a lot of energy which could be better directed by the system. In addition, it causes physical tension within the system, which can augment STRESS or create PAIN.

Most people do the same thing when problems come up. They allow themselves to be overcome by their own self-pity and are overwhelmed by the pressure. Often this too invites debilitating illness. This is when we need the curative power of this Mantra line. It works against both subliminal and apparent self-pity. It works against the SUFFERING caused by the absence of a positive ATTITUDE and CORRECT UNDERSTANDING.

The Hand and Eye preparation is the PURE BOTTLE, which contains the transcendental medicine, the SWEET DEW of WISDOM, appropriate for the cure of the affliction. Because it is difficult to deal with this problem, the previous set of three Mantra lines is chanted before this Mantra line to provide necessary support.

TUÓ LÁ TUÓ LÁ
May Clinging to the World of the Senses Cease
and Self-Pity in Illness and Suffering Fall Away
The PURE BOTTLE Hand and Eye

SUMMARY: LINES 27-30

The important Mantra line *TUÓ LÁ TUÓ LÁ* (30) is directed at the folly of an extreme craving for the satiation of SENSATIONS, EMOTIONS, and COGNITIVE THOUGHTS pertaining to the world of the senses. These cravings are impossible to satiate and PERFECTION is often the objective of those affected. DEPRESSION, great STRESS, and PHYSIOLOGICAL DISTRESS often result from this affliction. To set aside this SUFFERING and prevent its return, the nurture of the PURE BOTTLE Hand and Eye preparation is essential.

You will have prepared yourself and others for the energetic chanting of the Mantra line *TUÓ LÁ TUÓ LÁ* by chanting the three previous support lines. The first (27) promotes the growth of UNATTACHED ACTIONS through nurturing an understanding of the DHAMMA, which is meritorious and correct. The second (28) aids the cultivation of CONCENTRATION in order to build the clarity and calmness in day-to-day living that will build NOBLE INTENTIONS. The third (29) provides the MINDFULNESS which is an essential RICHNESS OF THOUGHT in ATTITUDE which is neither trivial nor bound to IGNORANCE.

You will also see, no doubt, that the way to bring about freedom from this affliction for oneself is to want others to receive lasting benefit. All giving rebounds with each Mantra line's expression, casting a mantle of good upon the unselfish transmitter.

It is important to notice the following:

1) CONCENTRATION effectively and directly remedies the problem of INCORRECT INTENTIONS.
2) UNDERSTANDING the DHAMMA effectively and directly tackles the problem of INCORRECT ACTIONS.
3) DISCIPLINED MINDFULNESS effectively and directly deals with the problem of INCORRECT ATTITUDES through the adjustment of INTENTIONS.

Later, you will discover that PENETRATION effectively and directly eliminates the problem of IGNORANCE. This PENETRATION is known as INSIGHT PRACTICE and it represents an essential part of DHAMMA UNDERSTANDING.

27. *JÙ LÚ JÙ LÚ JIÉ MĚNG*
May All Actions Be Meritorious and Correct
The JEWELED CONCH and the WHITE LOTUS Hand and Eye

28. *DÙ LÚ DÙ LÚ FÁ SHÉ YĒ DÌ*
May There Be Clarity and Calmness in Concentration
The MOON ESSENCE and SHIELD Hand and Eye

29. *MÓ HĒ FÁ SHÉ YĒ DÌ*
May There Be Victory Against False Ideas and Superstition
The JEWELED HALBERD Hand and Eye

30. *TUÓ LÁ TUÓ LÁ*
May Clinging to the World of the Senses Cease
and Self-Pity in Illness and Suffering Fall Away
The PURE BOTTLE Hand and Eye

Now repeat:

JÙ LÚ JÙ LÚ JIÉ MĚNG
DÙ LÚ DÙ LÚ FÁ SHÉ YĒ DÌ
MÓ HĒ FÁ SHÉ YĒ DÌ
TUÓ LÁ TUÓ LÁ

KARMA

Before we proceed with the next Mantra line, it is important that you begin to understand exactly what KARMA is. The word KARMA is related to ACTION, to the extent that it is said that CORRECT ACTIONS lead to POSITIVE KARMA. That is not completely incorrect, but it is an oversimplified idea, more akin to Christian concepts than the one which we will present here. This simple idea of a direct relationship between KARMA and ACTION is not exactly incorrect, but it is off by a hair's breadth. Unfortunately, this hair's breadth becomes quite significant when one has to think about nurturing a natural and correct lifestyle.

It would actually be more correct to declare that you are what your ATTITUDES are, what INTENTIONS you form, and what ACTIONS you perform. If you further amend this and declare that you are what your ATTITUDES, INTENTIONS, ACTIONS, and your REACTION to the CONSEQUENCES of that ACTION make you, then you will be on the right track. Do you see the subtlety of this? If your ATTITUDES, INTENTIONS, and ACTIONS are CORRECT, then if you simply RECOGNIZE that CORRECTNESS, that is CORRECT KARMA and you will be a CORRECT and NATURAL person. In other words, if your ATTITUDES, INTENTIONS, and ACTIONS are CORRECT, then you must be EQUANIMOUS in the face of ANY consequences.

A CORRECT ACTION, you see, may bring criticism and even punishment. If you react incorrectly to those events through INCORRECT SENSATIONS, EMOTIONS, and THOUGHTS, then that negatively affects your processes of INTENTION and ATTITUDE. That is INCORRECT KARMA. A CORRECT ACTION may not bring you reward or praise, and if you feel disappointed then that is INCORRECT KARMA. If indeed you receive praise or reward and you feel proud and elated by your own correctness, then that too is INCORRECT KARMA. INCORRECT KARMA is simply the destruction of your own internal INTEGRITY. We can therefore call it NEGATIVE KARMA if we wish to emphasize this point. NEGATIVE KARMA may indeed bring eventual physical or social problems, but that is strictly a secondary effect. The main effect of NEGATIVE KARMA is to destroy internal EQUILIBRIUM.

If INTENTIONS and ATTITUDES are INCORRECT, leading to INCORRECT ACTIONS, then NEGATIVE KARMA will be initiated if you are rewarded for that action. Your INCORRECT ATTITUDES and INTENTIONS will then automatically be reinforced. If the INCORRECT ACTIONS are unrewarded or punished, there will be internal justifications to excuse the internal INTENTIONS and ATTITUDES. This is NEGATIVE KARMA.

It should be easy to see that POSITIVE KARMA leads to further personal growth and INCORRECT KARMA to eventual personal SUFFERING. You can reverse the process with vigilance. All that you have to do is recognize an INCORRECT ACTION when it emerges. This creates POSITIVE KARMA, beginning with the modification of the INCORRECT ATTITUDES and INTENTIONS. Can you see now what KARMA really is all about?

For most people, KARMA is almost a form of natural justice brought about by external agents by reward or punishment or by subsequent things which happen to you. That is why they speak of GOOD KARMA and BAD KARMA. That is not correct. Your KARMA is simply TO BE what you have created.

You may, in this SOCIAL world, be very fortunate even if you have NEGATIVE KARMA. All sorts of apparently marvelous things may come your way. People may say that you don't deserve all those benefits and that there is no justice at all. That doesn't matter. You have NEGATIVE KARMA, that is all.

When a bad thing happens to someone, people say, "Ah, that is his KARMA." That is quite silly. They don't understand at all what KARMA is. You might even be able to cover up that NEGATIVE KARMA by creating a self-image that is positive. That doesn't matter. It doesn't change a thing. You have NEGATIVE KARMA. You may be completely happy in the world of the senses, but you have NEGATIVE KARMA.

Some of you may think that this NEGATIVE KARMA will manifest itself in the form of a "bad conscience." That is also incorrect. NEGATIVE KARMA simply sits there like a virus, ready to mess up the next round of emerging ATTITUDES, INTENTIONS, and ACTIONS, which bring further CONSEQUENCES, increasing the strength of the virus. We can say then that good KARMA is the tendency to establish the equilibrium and harmony of the system. There is nothing mysterious or magical about this. It is a natural process.

Another thing to remember is that this KARMA doesn't make you do anything; it simply sits there, and externally other people may not detect the INCORRECT ATTITUDES and INTENTIONS. They may not see the NEGATIVE KARMA at all. In fact, you may not even see it within yourself.

With introspection and mindfulness, however, you can see this NEGATIVE KARMA operating within yourself. Don't worry if you detect NEGATIVE KARMA. Most people have it. You can change it if you sincerely want to. You make your KARMA, and what you make you can remake. Any chain can be broken with the correct tools. Fortunately you have one set of effective tools ready and available. All you have to do is sincerely recite the Mantra lines you have already learned and NEGATIVE KARMA will be weakened.

It is a legitimate question to ask why negative KARMA seems to be almost always inevitable. The presence of the IDENTITIES explains that, but these foul delusions would not have force if the human creature did not give ABSOLUTE IMPORTANCE to things which are only relatively important or are not important at all.

What is then of ABSOLUTE IMPORTANCE? The answer is easy: nothing at all, absolutely nothing. Just as we say as Buddhists that nothing phenomenological exits, so we can say that nothing which is phenomenological has any REAL importance at all.

Now, this confounds many people, for they ask how correctness and incorrectness can have any utility if nothing has importance. Actually, although there is no ABSOLUTE importance for anything which touches the senses, something IS of RELATIVE IMPORTANCE. That thing is *JIVITINDRIYA*, the LIFE FORCE. Without it, all would be ontological. It is, paradoxically, this Life Force that allows us to grow and develop and even know that nothing is of absolute importance.

This Life Force, using ENERGY, insists that life continue for as long as possible and tells us that a FIT and HEALTHY body is correct. Naturally, our human minds, a part of our bodies, must also be kept fit and healthy. If we cannot correctly maintain mind and body, then *JIVITINDRIYA* will lose its force and you will hasten the end of consciousness.

Now, *JIVITINDRIYA* and all the forces which assist this Life Force are the only things which are of RELATIVE IMPORTANCE; all else is UNIMPORTANT. The problem is to decide what actually supports this LIFE FORCE correctly. It is the DHAMMA which provides the essential UNDERSTANDING that allows us to discriminate between what is correct relative to the LIFE FORCE and what is of little consequence. When we see this distinction, then CLINGING and CRAVING must fall away. As a consequence of all CORRECT ACTION, if you develop mindfulness of what is natural and correct, there will arise a natural EQUANIMITY and all KARMA will be POSITIVE.

THE TENTH SERIES: THE ELIMINATION OF IGNORANCE

DÌ LÌ NÍ

DÌ LÌ NÍ means three things. First, that INCORRECT learned ATTITUDES will be left unattended so that they will eventually fall away. Second, that CORRECT ATTITUDES will be maintained and will flourish. Third, that all potentially inappropriate karma-related attitudes residing within the system will be destroyed. The last are the consequences of past incorrect Karmic cycles, the person being without equanimity in the face of the consequences of his ACTIONS. These three are called processes of COVERING, HOLDING, and BREAKING UP.

Most faulty ATTITUDES arise from the way the world is viewed and the failure to "see" the fundamental UNITY which is the EQUALITY of all things. Human creatures set themselves up in error as the center of the universe, as members of the MASTER SPECIES dominating all other creatures. Sanity returns when man "sees" that there is UNITY and EQUALITY, although there are important differences which require the correct exercise of responsibility and a CORRECT ATTITUDE which is courageous.

Notice the differentiation between ATTITUDES accrued by simple PASSIVE learning and those developed by past ACTION. The first are allowed to fall away, while the second must be eliminated. This shows the importance of maintaining CORRECT ACTION at all times if you don't want karma-related INCORRECT ATTITUDES to be established. The problem is, you see, that you have been incorrectly taught that once you actually perform an act you are not only RESPONSIBLE but socially CULPABLE if the action is SOCIALLY condemned.

The human mind is very elastic and clever and it resists the TENSION resulting from culpability by automatically justifying an INCORRECT ACTION. If your mind accepts this FOLLY-FILLED system of CULPABILITY, then your system will resist a change of ACTION-initiated ATTITUDE which you know subliminally to be incorrect. The accompanying Hand and Eye which must be developed, especially if you wish to avoid this complex trap of automatic rationalization and resistance, is the JEWELED DAGGER. It is a preparation of ATTITUDE, and is so called because it must be developed like the JEWELED DAGGER, *VAJRAKILA*, which is called "the Claw of Lightning." With this dagger the Demons of DELUSION and the interfering Hungry Ghosts of GREED can be pinned to the earth so they cannot move. Here, unmoving and helpless, they can be dealt with through understanding.

DÌ LĪ NÍ
May a Correct Attitude Prevail while the Incorrect Falls Away
and May Karmic Obstacles Be Destroyed
The JEWELED DAGGER Hand and Eye

SHÌ FÓ LÁ YĒ

This Mantra line summons CORRECT INTROSPECTION. If that INTROSPECTION is TRANQUIL and CALM, then there will be an ILLUMINATION of the TRUTH inside oneself. This introspection is a CONTEMPLATION which takes a look at your internal state. If the contemplation is a false contemplation based on inspection by conscious intellect, then all sorts of words and phrases will come out, confirming your calmness, and there will be much FOLLY revealed, which unfortunately will bear a mask of TRUTH.

This particular Mantra line supports the previous line. Each person will need some way of knowing if his ATTITUDES are really CORRECT or if he has fallen into a trap of self-deception. If the contemplation or introspection is NATURAL, then the TRUTH within oneself will be exposed like a sudden INSPIRATION which comes and goes like a bright and blinding flash of light.

This INSPIRATION will not be accompanied by justifications or reasons. One will simply KNOW, without the appearance of an impulse from conscious intellect, "Yes, this is ABSOLUTELY CORRECT." That is why we call this Hand and Eye preparation the SUN ESSENCE. The message of TRUTH revealed is often quite surprising and can easily be misconstrued, so one must be careful and develop the SUN ESSENCE preparation well.

The sun, *SURYA*, symbolically occupies the central apex between ABSOLUTE and APPARENT TRUTH. As such, it illuminates the unity between both, so that APPARENT TRUTH, the ILLUSION, can be seen as a useful tool for CORRECT LIVING in HARMONY with the ABSOLUTE, which is the unified natural process which is hidden beyond the senses.

SHÌ FÓ LÁ YĒ
May There Be Illumination by Introspection
The SUN ESSENCE Hand and Eye

ZHĒ LÁ ZHĒ LÁ

This is a direct call for CORRECT INTENTION, which of course requires the CORRECT ATTITUDE generated by *DÌ LĪ NÍ* and the INTERNAL ILLUMINATION generated by the previous Mantra line.

The INTENTION is the preparation for "moving into ACTION," so it is imperative that the INTENTION be CLEAR and UNCONFUSED. This means that there must be RESPECT in the cultivation of all INTENTIONS for oneself and for others. If there is a lack of RESPECTFULNESS, then your own EGO IDENTITY will claim its heritage and insist on being heard, thereby influencing INTENTIONS in a way which is in its best interest, but probably opposed to what is in the best interest of your own growth and the benefit of others.

If your Hungry Ghosts of EGO have nothing to say, then the General of the Hell Demons of CONFUSION or DELUSION and the Savage Beasts of SUPER EGO will make their assault. When you have RESPECTFULNESS in your INTENTIONS, then the Hell Demons, the Hungry Ghosts, and the Savage Beasts will be repulsed. Furthermore, the RESPECTFULNESS in your INTENTIONS will incline everyone to pay attention to what you do and say. CORRECT INTENTIONS then must ring with the clear message and tone of a well-cast bell. You must cultivate, therefore, the JEWELED BELL preparation.

The JEWELED BELL, *GHANTA*, represents the feminine principle, the path. As such, it represents the path of CORRECT INTENTIONS, which is transformed into CORRECT ACTIONS, which is the masculine principle.

ZHĒ LÁ ZHĒ LÁ
May There Be Correct Intentions
The JEWELED BELL Hand and Eye

MÓ MÓ FÁ MÓ LÁ

Having made one's Mantra recitation for CORRECT ATTITUDE and CORRECT INTENTION, we now move forward to CORRECT ACTION.

MÓ MÓ is the first component of this Mantra line and evokes the FORCE of SUCCESS for the action. This force includes a strong measure of CALM CONFIDENCE in the outcome. You must be careful not to consider a GOAL, an END RESULT, as an outcome. A correct outcome is the achieving of progress upon a CORRECT PATH in a CORRECT DIRECTION. Never focus your attention upon end objectives. This will automatically call up the IDENTITIES.

The natural preparation, which must be practiced, is the WHITE WHISK. With the flick of the wrist, all obstacles to the successful completion of the ACTION can be swept away easily, for the way has been prepared by the presence of CORRECT ATTITUDES and INTENTIONS.

The second component is *FÁ MÓ LÁ*. This recitation will keep all ACTIONS completely UNDEFILED so that all subsequent reinforcement is positive, because you will view all consequences with EQUANIMITY.

Most people's ACTIONS are DEFILED, for the CONSEQUENCES of ACTIONS are important for them. They act to obtain some result, some benefit. They are always DEFILED by EXPECTATIONS. When expectations are not met, then the IDENTITIES involved in the ACTION become upset and lose no time in transmitting these unpleasant sensations to consciousness.

When ACTIONS are UNDEFILED, there are no EXPECTATIONS. You may ask then, "How can you build an ACTION without any idea of the consequences?" You cannot. What you do quite naturally is internally compute the probabilities for a large range of possible outcomes of your ACTION. You may set various possibilities and probabilities for every potential outcome, but you will cling to none of them. Since all of them are possible you accept all of them. You will never be surprised by any of the consequences of your ACTIONS. You will rest calm in the knowledge that they are CORRECT. That is sufficient. If your calculations of the probabilities are incorrect, then you will just calculate the probabilities more accurately for the next ACTION. This in no way, however, sets up the EXPECTATIONS which are CLUNG to by most people.

All who remain uncontaminated karmically will then dwell in a transformed state of TRANQUILITY. They will dwell as it were, with NATURAL INTERNAL CALM and all the wealth of the EXTERNAL NATURAL world at their disposal. This is an INCOMPARABLE natural state. The accompanying Hand and Eye preparation is called, therefore, the NATURAL REALM. Metaphorically here you will dwell with all the Buddhas of the ten directions.

Now, why is it so important to recite *FÁ MÓ LÁ* if the ACTIONS have been set correctly in perspective with *MÓ MÓ*, the first part of the Mantra line?

For every ACTION there will be apparent consequences. These APPARENT consequences are external and depend not upon your state, but upon the state of those who are affected by your action. Your action may well be CORRECT and you may sit with EQUANIMITY. Many times, however, this EQUANIMITY can be shattered by the force of the response of someone else who is afflicted by his IDENTITIES. *FÁ MÓ LÁ* allows you to be unaffected. You will see clearly the folly of those who cannot see the CORRECTNESS of your ACTION. You will see that further evaluation of your ACTION by yourself is quite uncalled for. You will recall that it doesn't matter what the APPARENT results are of your CORRECT ACTION. There is only one possible TRUE CONSEQUENCE to a CORRECT ACTION, and that is your own sure KNOWLEDGE of its CORRECTNESS.

The series of cause and effect terminates upon the ACTION with the KNOWLEDGE of its CORRECTNESS. If there is an apparent EXTERNAL response to your action, then that is part of an independent series. It is a NEW STIMULUS, not a consequence of your ACTION. This NEW STIMULUS may evoke a NEW CORRECT ATTITUDE, a NEW CORRECT INTENTION, and a NEW CORRECT ACTION and CONSEQUENCE. In this way you are free from Karmic obstacles. This is quite subtle and it is important that you understand it.

You yourself create Karmic OBSTACLES if you perceive apparently negative or unpleasant CONSEQUENCES from the external world, and upon evaluation of those apparent consequences, chain them to your CORRECT ACTION, coloring that ACTION in the process, and contaminating it with SENSATIONS, EMOTIONS, and THOUGHTS of CONSCIOUS INTELLECT.

MÓ MÓ FÁ MÓ LÁ
May Actions Meet with No Obstacles
The WHITE WHISK and NATURAL REALM Hand and Eye

MÙ DÌ LÌ

Attachment to the world, due to clinging to and craving for the fruits of SENSATIONS, EMOTIONS, and COGNITIVE THOUGHTS, was attended to with *TUÓ LÁ TUÓ LÁ* (30). *MÙ DÌ LÌ* brings a liberation from all the DELUSIONS of hardship and inauspicious circumstances of the MUNDANE life. DELUSIONS of hardship and inauspicious circumstances are due to an attachment to the world through IGNORANCE. This causes INCORRECT UNDERSTANDING. This is much more difficult to deal with than the clinging and craving to the fruits of desire.

This Mantra line is a barrier against the regeneration of any INCORRECT UNDERSTANDING and false philosophies which have assailed the listener or the reciter in the past, and a defense against those which may assail him in the present or future.

The INCORRECT UNDERSTANDING which has entered memory in the past is not easy to stand against when thoughts flood, unwanted and unsolicited, into consciousness. The INCORRECT ATTITUDES generated are generally strong because they are rooted deep in memory and well supported by the IDENTITIES which cling to them. The strongest of these is the SUPER EGO IDENTITY, which not only sets in place the false ideas of the world of the senses, but creates the DELUSION of CORRECTNESS.

It is very difficult to accept the fact that almost everyone is wrong in their beliefs. It is difficult to accept the idea that the American Dream, in which everyone is encouraged to exercise the inalienable right to pursue power, wealth, and the satiation of other desires, is INCORRECT. True, society sets limits, but in setting limits beyond which this behavior is considered INCORRECT, they legitimize those behaviors which are below the limits set. When you have power, it feels good. When you have wealth, you feel wonderful. When all your desires are met, you feel marvelous.

When you don't have the power or wealth, then things are not quite so magnificent. When your desires are not met, then you are far from happy. Is the chase after apparently delicious fruits really worth the SUFFERING which you experience when they are not acquired? The answer is clearly, "No." In fact, when it is known that these sought-after fruits are deadly, only those really immersed in the INCORRECT UNDERSTANDING about life and its value would find the poisoned fruits attractive.

Normally, when people are attached to the world of the senses, they know that they are probably following an INCORRECT PATH. Most accept that fact and say, "Everyone else is doing it" or voice other justifications or excuses. The Mantra line *TUÓ LÁ TUÓ LÁ* (30) takes care of this folly.

Those trapped in the abyss of INCORRECT UNDERSTANDING, however, don't know at all that they are following an INCORRECT PATH. That is why it is a difficult path to change. They often know that they SUFFER, but they don't know why. They find complex excuses, blame other people, their family, their friends, the government, anything or anybody that comes to mind. They never consider blaming their wrong views.

Many of these people are quite intelligent, yet they persist in IGNORANCE. When there is no hardship, of course, they are very happy people. When circumstances are auspicious they are elated. Hardships, however, are never a consequence of their behavior. Inauspicious circumstances are never due to their faulty views of life which form their philosophy and ATTITUDES. The problem is simply "bad luck."

This Mantra line is addressed to those who are lost in their own IGNORANCE. The Hand and Eye, called the BUDDHA'S WILLOW BRANCH, must be sincerely cultivated. The WILLOW BRANCH, in more ancient times, was used to sprinkle medicine, and this imagery, used as a title for the Hand and Eye, reminds you that WISDOM, the true medicine against all SUFFERING from the clinging to wrong ideas, is also to be sprinkled, not applied with heavy-handedness, which is not subtle. WISDOM which is heavy is generally FALSE WISDOM which arises with CONSCIOUS INTELLECT.

MÙ DÌ LÌ
May There Be Liberation from the Delusions of Hardship
and Inauspicious Circumstances
The BUDDHA'S WILLOW BRANCH Hand and Eye

SUMMARY: LINES 31-35

We see in the Mantra line MÙ DÌ LÌ (35) an elevation in the difficulty of Mantra transmission. Memory, you see, is very stubborn, and when INCORRECT UNDERSTANDING has been supported for a long time by INCORRECT ATTITUDES, INCORRECT INTENTIONS, and INCORRECT ACTIONS, then consolidation in memory is very strong and supported by all sorts of justifications and false logic. Because of this, the Mantra line MÙ DÌ LÌ requires the support of the strong defensive set of lines which precede it.

CORRECT ATTITUDE is set more strongly in place by chanting which elicits an understanding of UNITY and EQUALITY. If you look at INCORRECT ATTITUDES, you will find that there is generally a supercilious sense of ARROGANCE which prevails. This arrogance sets the afflicted person incorrectly above his peers and brings about INCORRECT ATTITUDES. The sense of the UNITY nurtured in the second support line ruptures this ARROGANCE.

CORRECT INTENTIONS are reinforced by fostering RESPECTFULNESS towards all human creatures, whereas CORRECT ACTIONS are upheld by the Mantra line which calls forth the power to keep all ACTIONS completely UNDEFILED.

31. *DÌ LĪ NÍ*
May a Correct Attitude Prevail While the Incorrect Falls Away
and May Karmic Obstacles Be Destroyed
The JEWELED DAGGER Hand and Eye

32. *SHÌ FÓ LÁ YĒ*
May There Be Illumination by Introspection
The SUN ESSENCE Hand and Eye

33. *ZHĒ LÁ ZHĒ LÁ*
May There Be Correct Intentions
The JEWELED BELL Hand and Eye

34. *MÓ MÓ FÁ MÓ LÁ*
May Actions Meet with No Obstacles
The WHITE WHISK and NATURAL REALM Hand and Eye

The final line of this set is, of course, the most important, being the object line supported by those which went before.

35. *MÙ DÌ LÌ*
May There Be Liberation from the Delusions of Hardship
and Inauspicious Circumstances
The BUDDHA'S WILLOW BRANCH Hand and Eye

Now repeat:

DÌ LĪ NÍ

SHÌ FÓ LÁ YĒ
ZHĒ LÁ ZHĒ LÁ
MÓ MÓ FÁ MÓ LÁ
MÙ DÌ LÌ

THE ELEVENTH SERIES: REJUVENATION OF THE LIFE FORCE

YĪ XĪ YĪ XĪ

This Mantra line directs its attention to the attainment of a NATURAL life in accord with the BUDDHA NATURE. The BUDDHA NATURE is a site where information about all the NATURAL processes is stored for the activation of monitoring and filtering. It is uncontaminated by IDENTITY or by SENSATIONS, EMOTIONS, or the THOUGHTS of CONSCIOUS INTELLECT.

When NATURAL processes are released, there is a need for more detailed guidance on how they should be used. Just as a perfectly built schooner will go on the rocks without the availability of a CAPTAIN and a set of CHARTS, so the BUDDHA NATURE needs CORRECT INTENTIONS acting as a captain and the TEACHINGS as a chart.

When you recite *YĪ XĪ YĪ XĪ*, the processes of the BUDDHA NATURE will unfold and be guided by the TEACHINGS. The teachings which must be internalized are those which relate to an understanding of the WISDOM of CAUSE and EFFECT. This WISDOM allows the wise person to see all the possible consequences of INTENTIONS if they are transformed into ACTION. When your INTENTIONS are seen to be CORRECT and unassailable and you are seen to be wise with regard to the effects of your ACTIONS, then the Hungry Ghosts will keep their distance. The proud and arrogant rulers of the Savage Beasts who see your actions and hear your words will be also be silent and will stay away from you. You will be surrounded by like-minded people, not those with greedy or hostile thoughts whose objectives are to deceive and defeat you.

The Hand and Eye preparation is the SKULL BONE STAFF, which must be diligently prepared and nurtured. The STAFF, *KHAVANGA*, is symbolic of the traveler who uses the staff to support himself and test the ground ahead upon a long and difficult journey. The teachings are that staff. When you visualize the lifelessness of the human SKULL BONE STAFF as you journey through this life, you are reminded that all things are transient and you will be able to see that you cannot CLING and CRAVE forever. So why do it at all? It's a futile task without merit.

YĪ XĪ YĪ XĪ
Using the Dhamma Teachings May the Actions of the Buddha Nature
Become Fully Realized
The SKULL BONE STAFF Hand and Eye

SHÌ NÀ SHÌ NÀ

The preparation required for the transmission of this Mantra line is the JEWELED MIRROR. The JEWELED mirror, *ADARSHA*, is a mirror which only reflects WISDOM if you are prepared with this Mantra line and the Hand and Eye preparation. In the mirror you can then see and discriminate the emptiness and the clinging to substance which exists in the world. You will see that the false thinking generated by CONSCIOUS INTELLECT and perceived in CONSCIOUSNESS does not have as its product WISDOM.

How can you tell TRUE WISDOM from the FOLLY which appears as WISDOM? Wise men or women do not think like everyone else. They do not sit and ponder. They do not weigh facts and opinions. They do not seek goals and objectives. They do not compromise. The TRUTH is the TRUTH. They know by an INNER SEEING what is correct and what is incorrect. This is the TRUE WISDOM of NOBLE JUDGMENT which stems from TRUE THINKING, and it is quite subliminal.

The man who really uses CORRECT THINKING is therefore quiet and serene because his consciousness is not filled with the "noise" of false thinking. The mind-states in these cases are STRONG and ENERGETIC and this is reflected in ATTITUDES, INTENTIONS, and ACTIONS.

A person who allows his consciousness to be filled with false thinking creates mind-states which remain always turbulent and troubled. This Mantra line will help you to keep a VOW, a promise to yourself not to become embroiled in a mesh of false thinking. When you resist this temptation to create a busy mind you will permit the processes of NOBLE JUDGMENT to operate.

Now, it is important to remember that after you have correctly called up ATTITUDES with NOBLE JUDGMENT and have passed these ATTITUDES to the biological units which deal with INTENTIONS, these ATTITUDES will appear in some form spontaneously within consciousness. It will appear as if you are thinking and forming these INTENTIONS in consciousness, using the ATTITUDES provided. This is not so. You must immediately let that information go. If you hang on to those ATTITUDES of NOBLE JUDGMENT and the associated CORRECT INTENTIONS within consciousness, then both will become targeted by the EGO IDENTITY. Note the NOBLE JUDGMENT and CORRECT INTENTIONS and then immediately still the mind again.

SHÌ NÀ SHÌ NÀ
May There Be a Strong Energetic Mind which Leads to Wisdom
The JEWELED MIRROR Hand and Eye

Ā LÁ SHĒN FÓ LÁ SHÈ LÌ

Once a person has attained WISDOM, he or she is so filled with joy that they wish to share that WISDOM. It is difficult to attain WISDOM for oneself, but it is even more difficult to transmit that information to others. It is easy to speak the DHAMMA, attracting and holding the CONSCIOUS INTELLECT of others, but in order to be successful, one has to open the way for INTERNALIZATION.

The DHAMMA is extremely profound, although one can understand the general principles easily. Practicing the DHAMMA is quite another matter. It is not easy to understand how to overcome all the obstacles.

Zen masters say that one should not fish in a dry stream. This is true. It is a waste of energy to teach the DHAMMA when there is no way it can be heard. Even when there are willing listeners, it is difficult. Knowing how to use the illusions of words to transmit something that is beyond the understanding of CONSCIOUS INTELLECT alone requires a special KNOWLEDGE. The line *Ā LÁ SHĒN* allows you to summon up that sensitivity in communication which makes transmission possible. The Hand and Eye preparation is called CLEAR COMPREHENSION. It has as its base the development of TRUE INTROSPECTION and FREE CRITICAL INQUIRY.

FÓ LÁ SHÈ LÌ, used in the second part of the Mantra line, means ENLIGHTENED BODY SEEDS. These sounds actually assist in the dissemination of the truth by allowing you to reflect upon your own ACTIONS. You will see that refinement of these ACTIONS comes with repetition. Your own CORRECT ACTIONS are important when you teach the DHAMMA. This is not because others will believe you if your ACTIONS appear CORRECT, but because your knowledge of the correctness of the DHAMMA will come from viewing the positive KARMIC cycles which result from EQUANIMITY. When you know the truth of the DHAMMA from your own direct experience, then your words will come without urgency, but with complete joy and authority.

The accompanying Hand and Eye which should be cultivated is the RECITATION BEADS preparation. The RECITATION BEADS, *AKSHAMALA*, are not used just to provide rote repetition, nor are they to be confused with other beads which are used as a rosary. They are a focus for attention, a form of CONCENTRATION, just as the Mantra lines, when chanted correctly, are a form of CONCENTRATION.

Ā LÁ SHĒN FÓ LÁ SHÈ LÌ
May the Dhamma Be Transmitted with Ease
The CLEAR COMPREHENSION Hand and Eye
and RECITATION BEADS Hand and Eye

FÁ SHĀ FÁ SHĒN

This Mantra line means JOYFUL SPEECH, JOYFUL SMILES. It calls for a very special quality. It is the quality of being JOYFUL and ENTHUSIASTIC when transmitting very serious DHAMMA. It is the first of a special series of six Mantra lines which will assist you in using the Mantra line *SŪ LÚ SŪ LÚ* (45).

Many teachers of the DHAMMA make the DHAMMA very heavy and overly serious. The DHAMMA is the teaching about the NATURAL LAW. The teachings lead to TRANQUILITY and JOY. There is no reason why the transmission of the DHAMMA should be such a heavy and sad event. True, liberating oneself from the chains of SUFFERING is not easy, but one should always bear in mind the LIBERATION which lies ahead, leading to TRANQUILITY.

Reciting this Mantra line leads one to the state of becoming an "unsurpassed knight" whose sword and arrows are sheathed and whose demeanor is one of happy confidence in a peaceful victory. Even when the DHAMMA is not being transmitted, all speech as a result of the recitation will be joyful, enthusiastic, and positive and the general aspect of those living with VIRTUE and WISDOM will be that of contentment and happiness, unburdened by suffering.

The Hand and Eye to be cultivated is the JEWELED BOW, so called because he who transmits COMPASSION in the correct manner will be able to dispense the DHAMMA far, with unerring aim. The bow, *CHAPA*, represents the CORRECT PATH.

When you use a bow, two things are initially important. First, there must be an internalization of the METHOD of use, free from conscious intellect. Second, there must be a KNOWLEDGE of its use. Thus there is CORRECT and EXACT DETERMINATION of what is required that unites the apparent bowman, the bow, the arrow, and the apparent target. This is the way of the JEWELED BOW.

FÁ SHĀ FÁ SHĒN
May There Be Enthusiasm, Joyful Speech, and Joyful Smiles
The JEWELED BOW Hand and Eye

FÓ LÁ SHÈ YĒ

When transmitting this Mantra line, the holder or prepared receiver of the Mantra line increases his or her illumination. It is a powerful reinforcement for those whose illumination has begun. You will find then that the BUDDHA NATURE will be liberated, the Mantra of COMPASSION will be understood, and the person enlightened.

Now, many transcendental teachers will speak a great deal of this enlightenment. It will appear as if it is something very special. It is, but not because it is very rare. It is special because it is quite natural. Everyone is naturally illuminated if all the layers of FOLLY and IGNORANCE, which should never be there in the first place, are peeled away. This illumination is nothing more than being able to see the HEARTS OF THE BUDDHA NATURE. It allows you to see the relationship between CORRECT INTENTIONS, NATURAL CORRECT DISCRIMINATION, and COMPASSION. It allows you to comprehend the relationship between CORRECT ATTITUDES, NATURAL CORRECT SENSITIVITY, and GLADNESS. It allows you to clearly understand the relationship between CORRECT ACTIONS, TRUE NATURAL INTELLIGENCE, and BENEVOLENT LOVE.

You will also see the subtle qualities of the various HEARTS of the BUDDHA NATURE. This illumination will allow you to see that all these, although they can be perceived and used separately as illusions, are really one single process of life.

When you see this, then you will also see the folly of believing the IDENTITIES which have been created in your subconscious. You will revile them, rejecting DELUSION, GREED, and HOSTILITY. You will completely appreciate your BUDDHA NATURE and nurture the correct operation of all mental states. This is your birthright. This is ILLUMINATION.

The Hand and Eye to be cultivated is the PURPLE LOTUS.

FÓ LÁ SHÈ YĒ
May There Be Enlightenment in the Transmission of the Mantra
The PURPLE LOTUS Hand and Eye

HŪ LÚ HŪ LÚ MÓ LÁ

If the reciter wishes to fully integrate the Mantra into his or her BUDDHA NATURE, then there must be cultivation of the JADE RING preparation. As the line is recited, the COMPASSION of the BUDDHA NATURE is augmented and becomes stronger. The Mantra line, when internalized, will allow you to see that you cannot transmit anything with the words of the DHAMMA unless you yourself live within the DHAMMA and perform the DHAMMA quite naturally.

You will see the importance of beginning with correction of small, apparently unimportant ACTIONS and will know when to move on to those apparently more important ACTIONS. Gradually you will acquire a non-attachment to SELF, for you will see that there is no soul or self at all. You will see quickly, as you use this Mantra line, that you will acquire CONFIDENCE in the CORRECTNESS of the DHAMMA. You will find this CONFIDENCE to be nothing at all like FAITH, which is trusting but completely blind. This confidence will allow you to keep consciousness free from the furious activity of thoughts. You must, however, be constantly vigilant so that you do not become attached to success.

When the DHAMMA begins to become internalized, although imperfectly, and becomes as natural to you as breathing, then the special meditative act called PENETRATION will fix the DHAMMA in place and bring the sublime illumination, which is full KNOWING. With this Mantra line you will be well prepared, for as you progress, it will allow you to use the DHAMMA and live within the DHAMMA, without attachment to that DHAMMA.

The JADE RING is a symbol which represents your unity with the DHAMMA and is your Hand and Eye preparation.

HŪ LÚ HŪ LÚ MÓ LÁ
May The Buddha Nature Be as One with the Mantra
The JADE RING Hand and Eye

HŪ LÚ HŪ LÚ XĪ LÌ

The transmission of the DHAMMA or a single Mantra line is always more effective if there is no intrusion of thoughts, even if they are TRUE THOUGHTS. The recitation of this Mantra line, together with the cultivation of the Hand and Eye preparation called the JEWELED BOWL, will keep TRANSMITTED DHAMMA pure without intrusions of thoughts. Just as a bowl with its high rim keeps all within well protected, so the JEWELED BOWL walls help to keep impure thoughts away.

The easiest SUFFERING to deal with is that which stems from KARMIC GUILT. It requires the least effort and your thoughts will seldom intrude. To heal agitation, stress, and pain created by a SUFFERING mind which is tangled with great complexity requires, however, a much purer transmission in order to maintain the link of CONFIDENCE between the healer and the infirm. If a perceived SUFFERING seems to be complicated, then conscious intellect, by custom, will try to step in and reason things out. Thoughts pour into consciousness.

Do not confuse this Mantric healing process with FAITH HEALING. Remember that CONFIDENCE is in the DHAMMA, the natural process, and in the latent power of the apparent sufferer to know and cure the debilities which he himself has created. This Mantra line, combined with a strongly cultivated JEWELED BOWL, will be very effective in chasing away these thoughts. In this cultivation, it is essential that the reciter is free from IDENTITY and a CRAVING AFTER EXISTENCE.

HŪ LÚ HŪ LÚ XĪ LÌ
May Dhamma Transmission Be Free from Thoughts
The JEWELED BOWL Hand and Eye

SUŌ LÁ SUŌ LÁ

This Mantra line summons great PERSEVERANCE. As the VAJRA PESTLE preparation is cultivated, the power will multiply.

Perseverance is not cultivated easily. It is very tempting to succumb to the voices which say that one should not continue on such a difficult path which appears to expect one to give up so much without apparent immediate reward.

As with a pestle, you must grind away at the hard and crass loathsome mass of folly, adding the sweet water of transcendental wisdom to the resulting fine powder of CORRECT ACTION, until only the sweet dew of knowledge lies in the bowl.

The Vajra Pestle is the masculine principle, which is precisely CORRECT PERSEVERANCE in ACTION and is brought about by CORRECT INTENTIONS.

SUŌ LÁ SUŌ LÁ
May Great Perseverance Be Generated
The VAJRA PESTLE Hand and Eye

XĪ LÍ XĪ LÍ

This Mantra line is similar to the previous line. Here, however, it is

EARNESTNESS which is transmitted. Now, to be earnest one must be SERIOUS. This does not mean that one should proceed with a somber heaviness. It means that one should put everything in perspective with the importance it deserves. It means that one should proceed with diligent application of all that is correct.

When you cultivate the CLASPED HANDS preparation you will multiply this power of EARNESTNESS in connection with others. Just as the ELEPHANT STAFF, *ANKUSHA*, guides the elephant onward with power on the CORRECT PATH of INTENTIONS towards others, so the CLASPED HANDS preparation guides you with earnestness on the DHAMMA path. As you persist in the nurture of this Hand and Eye so will your EARNESTNESS persist. This EARNESTENESS is the essential path with regard to relations.

XĪ LĪ XĪ LĪ

May Great Earnestness Be Generated

The ELEPHANT STAFF and CLASPED HANDS Hand and Eye

SŪ LÚ SŪ LÚ

This Mantra line is used in cases of extreme SUFFERING in which all hope has been lost. The person may be said to be alive only in body, for the mind is dead with tormenting DELUSION. The Mantra will call for the return of the LIFE FORCE which is lost. It requires a full cultivation of the SWEET DEW Hand and Eye preparation, which is contained in the PURE BOTTLE and dispensed with the WILLOW BRANCH.

Those who need to receive the transmission of this Mantra line reject everything in the apparent world of the senses, even their own life. Unfortunately, they also are unable to see that beyond DELUSION there are beautiful illusions if the world is seen in perspective. They are generally bent upon self-destruction and will really listen to nobody at all. They have entered into their own private hell of DELUSION and CONFUSION and above this gateway the sign indeed reads, "Abandon all hope, ye who enter here." Fortunately there is a way out. It lies with the DHAMMA, for the DHAMMA is neither of this world nor of any other imaginable world.

To be fully effective, one must combine the SWEET DEW with the

WILLOW BRANCH (35) and PURE BOTTLE (30).

SŪ LÚ SŪ LÚ
May the Life Force Return
The SWEET DEW Hand and Eye

SUMMARY: LINES 36-45

In this group, the major line of transmission importance, *SŪ LÚ SŪ LÚ* (45), is much more difficult to change into an active force than either *MÓ XĪ MÓ SĪ LĪ TUÓ YÙN* (26), *TUÓ LÁ TUÓ LÁ* (30), or *MÙ DÌ LÌ* (35). It requires, therefore, the strongest support, as well as the nurture of a very potent Hand and Eye preparation. The three support lines each focus upon WISDOM: the first (36), upon the WISDOM OF CAUSE AND EFFECT brought about by CORRECT INTENTION; the second (37) emphasizes the WISDOM OF NOBLE JUDGMENT that comes about with CORRECT ATTITUDE; finally, the WISDOM OF ILLUMINATION that derives from CORRECT ACTION is called upon (38). The support lines which follow these three each emphasize a quality that may be needed to successfully bring about the full return of the Life Force in the chanting of *SŪ LÚ SŪ LÚ.*

You must, as the chanter, be completely free from contamination by the aura of gloom which pervades those who are completely dead to all things except their own destruction. You will therefore require all the ENTHUSIASM and JOY that can be mustered. Unless you yourself are ENLIGHTENED to the truth of the DHAMMA, you will not be effective, for your BUDDHA NATURE needs to be fully integrated into Mantra chanting. It is extremely difficult to concentrate with this Mantra line, so your mind must be still and FREE from CONSCIOUS THOUGHT. You will need to bring forth PERSEVERANCE and EARNESTNESS. As your Mantra transmissions advance, so you must advance in growth and understanding.

36. *YĪ XĪ YĪ XĪ*
Using the Dhamma Teachings May the Actions of the Buddha Nature
Become Fully Realized
The SKULL BONE STAFF Hand and Eye

37. *SHÌ NÀ SHÌ NÀ*
May There Be a Strong Energetic Mind which Leads to Wisdom
The JEWELED MIRROR Hand and Eye

38. *Ā LÁ SHĒN FÓ LÁ SHÈ LÌ*
May the Dhamma Be Transmitted with Ease
The CLEAR COMPREHENSION Hand and Eye
and RECITATION BEADS Hand and Eye

39. *FÁ SHĀ FÁ SHĒN*
May There Be Enthusiasm, Joyful Speech, and Joyful Smiles
The JEWELED BOW Hand and Eye

40. *FÓ LÁ SHÈ YĒ*
May There Be Enlightenment in the Transmission of the Mantra
The PURPLE LOTUS Hand and Eye

41. *HŪ LÚ HŪ LÚ MÓ LÁ*
May The Buddha Nature Be as One with the Mantra
The JADE RING Hand and Eye

42. *HŪ LÚ HŪ LÚ XĪ LÌ*
May Dhamma Transmission Be Free from Thoughts
The JEWELED BOWL Hand and Eye

43. *SUŌ LÁ SUŌ LÁ*
May Great Perseverance Be Generated
The VAJRA PESTLE Hand and Eye

44. *XĪ LĪ XĪ LĪ*
May Great Earnestness Be Generated
The ELEPHANT STAFF and CLASPED HANDS Hand and Eye

45. *SŪ LÚ SŪ LÚ*
May The Life Force Return
The SWEET DEW Hand and Eye

REJUVENATION OF THE BUDDHA NATURE

The qualities which you have been developing have been working together to form CORRECT ATTITUDES, CORRECT INTENTIONS, and CORRECT ACTIONS, which in turn reinforce and support all of those fine attributes. Look carefully now at Mantra lines 27-29, and lines 31 and 33-34 when placed together with lines 36-38 of this set.

27. *JÙ LÚ JÙ LÚ JIÉ MĚNG*
The Unattached Quality of Benevolent Love with Actions

28. *DÙ LÚ DÙ LÚ FÁ SHÉ YĒ DÌ*
Nobleness of Compassion Within Intentions

29. *MÓ HĒ FÁ SHÉ YĒ DÌ*
Freedom from Poverty of Thought in Gladness Within Attitudes

* * *

31. *DÌ LĪ NÍ*
Unity and Equality of Gladness Within Attitudes

33. *ZHĒ LÁ ZHĒ LÁ*
Respectfulness of Compassion Within Intentions

34. *MÓ MÓ FÁ MÓ LÁ*
Undefiled Quality of Benevolent Love with Actions

* * *

36. *YĪ XĪ YĪ XĪ*
Wisdom of Cause and Effect from Compassion Within Intentions

37. *SHÌ NÀ SHÌ NÀ*
Wisdom of Noble Judgment from Gladness Within Attitudes

38. *Ā LÁ SHĒN FÓ LÁ SHÈ LÌ*
Wisdom of Illumination from Benevolent Love with Actions

These lines all form a major reinforcing thrust which helps the development of the great HEART QUALITIES of the BUDDHA NATURE. Each set of three consists of an ATTITUDE component, an INTENTION component, and an ACTION component. They oppose respectively:

1. Attachment to the world due to a clinging to and craving for the fruits of SENSATIONS, EMOTIONS, and THOUGHTS.

2. SUFFERING due to the DELUSIONS of hardship and inauspicious circumstances of MUNDANE life, because of an attachment to the world through IGNORANCE.

3. Extreme SUFFERING in which all hope has been lost, because the mind is dead with tormenting DELUSION.

Look at these lines and try to understand the extreme importance of CORRECT ATTITUDES, CORRECT INTENTIONS, and CORRECT ACTIONS, and their relationship to the BUDDHA NATURE.

Now repeat:

YĪ XĪ YĪ XĪ

SHÌ NÀ SHÌ NÀ

Ā LÁ SHĒN FÓ LÁ SHÈ LÌ

FÁ SHĀ FÁ SHĒN

FÓ LÁ SHÈ YĒ

HŪ LÚ HŪ LÚ MÓ LÁ

HŪ LÚ HŪ LÚ XĪ LÌ

SUŌ LÁ SUŌ LÁ

XĪ LĪ XĪ LĪ

SŪ LÚ SŪ LÚ

THE PATTERN OF PERSONAL DEVELOPMENT

The major thrust of COMPASSION has at this point been the following:

(26) FREEDOM FROM CARES AND ANXIETIES

(30) ELIMINATING CLINGING TO THE WORLD OF THE SENSES

(35) LIBERATION FROM CLINGING TO THE WORLD OF INCORRECT VIEWS

(45) RETURNING THE LIFE FORCE IN EXTREME SUFFERING

The first two of these most important lines have been directed at destroying the DEMAND for VISCERAL SATISFACTION and its governing master, the ID IDENTITY. The third, when it is practiced with diligence and correct preparedness, deals effectively with that great deceiver EGO, and eliminates the DEMAND for EGO SATISFACTION. Finally, if you have attentively developed yourself and chanted the Mantra correctly, then the fourth will have begun to displace the SUPER EGO from its privileged position, removing DEMANDS for DOMINANCE.

In order to accomplish these effectively, you will have begun to develop many attributes and greater understanding at a more profound level. Here in this group of Mantra lines, with the aid of TRUE INTROSPECTION, CALMNESS, PATIENCE, MINDFULNESS (6), RESOLUTION (4), EFFORT and ENERGY (5), HUMILITY (15), a PLIANT OPEN MIND (15), and FREE CRITICAL INQUIRY (15), you will have made great strides forward on your path of LIBERATION.

In using the second phase of the Mantra, as well as allowing your own COMPASSION to be understood, realized, and transmitted, you will have developed greater MINDFULNESS (49) with CLEAR COMPREHENSION (38), a STRONG ENERGETIC MIND (37) with ENTHUSIASM (39), and finally EARNESTNESS (44) with PERSEVERANCE (43).

It is the correct development of FREE CRITICAL INQUIRY which has led to CLEAR COMPREHENSION, while the growth of a PLIANT OPEN MIND has allowed a STRONG ENERGETIC MIND to assert itself and ENTHUSIASM to be realized. CALMNESS with RESOLUTION have permitted EARNESTNESS to flourish, while applied PATIENCE has transformed itself into PERSEVERANCE. (see figure 41)

**This is the completion of the second stage
of the GREAT COMPASSION MANTRA**

Fig. 41 The Pattern of Personal Development

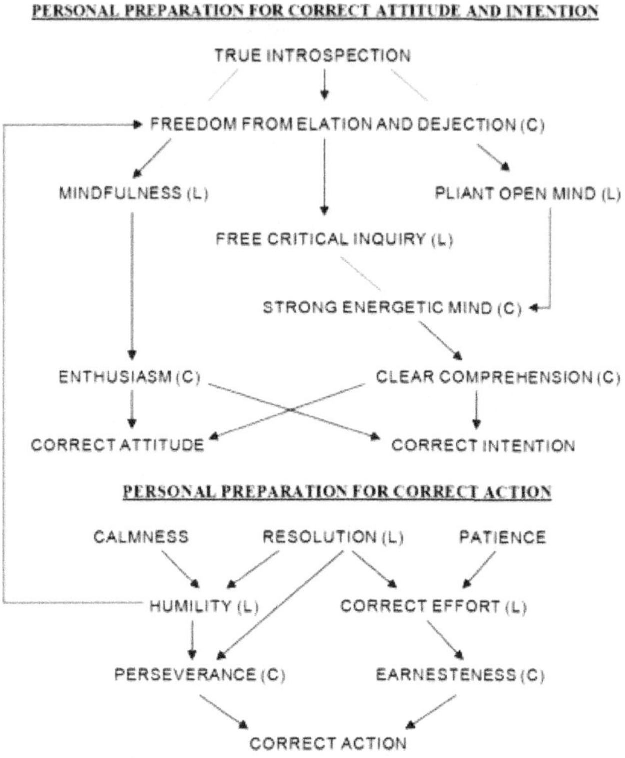

PERSONAL PREPARATION FOR CORRECT ATTITUDE AND INTENTION

TRUE INTROSPECTION

FREEDOM FROM ELATION AND DEJECTION (C)

MINDFULNESS (L)   PLIANT OPEN MIND (L)

FREE CRITICAL INQUIRY (L)

STRONG ENERGETIC MIND (C)

ENTHUSIASM (C)   CLEAR COMPREHENSION (C)

CORRECT ATTITUDE   CORRECT INTENTION

PERSONAL PREPARATION FOR CORRECT ACTION

CALMNESS   RESOLUTION (L)   PATIENCE

HUMILITY (L)   CORRECT EFFORT (L)

PERSEVERANCE (C)   EARNESTENESS (C)

CORRECT ACTION

REVIEW: MANTRA LINES OF THE SECOND PHASE

24. SÀ PÓ SÀ PÓ
May this Compassion Bring Benefit and Happiness to All People
The PRECIOUS COMMAND Hand and Eye

25. MÓ LÁ MÓ LÁ
May There Be Personal Growth in Accord with Natural Wisdom
The BUDDHA PEARL Hand and Eye

26. MÓ XĪ MÓ SĪ LĪ TUÓ YÙN
With Release from the Captivity of Words May There Be Joy
and Happiness with Freedom from Cares and Anxieties
The FIVE-COLORED CLOUD and BLUE LOTUS Hand and Eye

27. *JÙ LÚ JÙ LÚ JIÉ MĚNG*
May All Actions Be Meritorious and Correct
The JEWELED CONCH and the WHITE LOTUS Hand and Eye

28. *DÙ LÚ DÙ LÚ FÁ SHÉ YĒ DÌ*
May There Be Clarity and Calmness in Concentration
The MOON ESSENCE and SHIELD Hand and Eye

29. *MÓ HĒ FÁ SHÉ YĒ DÌ*
May There Be Victory Against False Ideas and Superstition
The JEWELED HALBERD Hand and Eye

30. *TUÓ LÁ TUÓ LÁ*
May Clinging to the World of the Senses Cease
and Self-Pity in Illness and Suffering Fall Away
The PURE BOTTLE Hand and Eye

31. *DÌ LĪ NÍ*
May a Correct Attitude Prevail while the Incorrect
Falls Away and May Karmic Obstacles Be Destroyed
The JEWELED DAGGER Hand and Eye

32. *SHÌ FÓ LÁ YĒ*
May There Be Illumination by Introspection
The SUN ESSENCE Hand and Eye

33. *ZHĒ LÁ ZHĒ LÁ*
May There Be Correct Intentions
The JEWELED BELL Hand and Eye

34. *MÓ MÓ FÁ MÓ LÁ*
May Actions Meet with No Obstacles
The WHITE WHISK and NATURAL REALM Hand and Eye

35. *MÙ DÌ LÌ*
May There Be Liberation from the Delusions of Hardship
and Inauspicious Circumstances

The BUDDHA'S WILLOW BRANCH Hand and Eye

36. *YĪ XĪ YĪ XĪ*
Using the Dhamma Teachings May the Actions of the Buddha Nature
Become Fully Realized
The SKULL BONE STAFF Hand and Eye

37. *SHÌ NÀ SHÌ NÀ*
May There Be a Strong Energetic Mind which Leads to Wisdom
The JEWELED MIRROR Hand and Eye

38. *Ā LÁ SHĒN FÓ LÁ SHÈ LÌ*
May the Dhamma Be Transmitted with Ease
The CLEAR COMPREHENSION Hand and Eye
and RECITATION BEADS Hand and Eye

39. *FÁ SHĀ FÁ SHĒN*
May There Be Enthusiasm, Joyful Speech, and Joyful Smiles
The JEWELED BOW Hand and Eye

40. *FÓ LÁ SHÈ YĒ*
May There Be Enlightenment in the Transmission of the Mantra
The PURPLE LOTUS Hand and Eye

41. *HŪ LÚ HŪ LÚ MÓ LÁ*
May The Buddha Nature Be as One with the Mantra
The JADE RING Hand and Eye

42. *HŪ LÚ HŪ LÚ XĪ LÌ*
May Dhamma Transmission Be Free from Thoughts
The JEWELED BOWL Hand and Eye

43. *SUŌ LÁ SUŌ LÁ*
May Great Perseverance Be Generated
The VAJRA PESTLE Hand and Eye

44. *XĪ LĪ XĪ LĪ*

May Great Earnestness Be Generated
The ELEPHANT STAFF and CLASPED HANDS Hand and Eye

45. *SŪ LÚ SŪ LÚ*
> May The Life Force Return
> The SWEET DEW Hand and Eye

Repeat the Mantra lines of the Second Phase:

SÀ PÓ SÀ PÓ
MÓ LÁ MÓ LÁ
MÓ XĪ MÓ SĪ LĪ TUÓ YÙN
JÙ LÚ JÙ LÚ JIÉ MĚNG
DÙ LÚ DÙ LÚ FÁ SHÉ YĒ DÌ
MÓ HĒ FÁ SHÉ YĒ DÌ
TUÓ LÁ TUÓ LÁ
DÌ LĪ NÍ
SHÌ FÓ LÁ YĒ
ZHĒ LÁ ZHĒ LÁ
MÓ MÓ FÁ MÓ LÁ
MÙ DÌ LÌ
YĪ XĪ YĪ XĪ
SHÌ NÀ SHÌ NÀ
Ā LÁ SHĒN FÓ LÁ SHÈ LÌ
FÁ SHĀ FÁ SHĒN
FÓ LÁ SHÈ YĒ
HŪ LÚ HŪ LÚ MÓ LÁ
HŪ LÚ HŪ LÚ XĪ LÌ
SUŌ LÁ SUŌ LÁ
XĪ LĪ XĪ LĪ
SŪ LÚ SŪ LÚ

PART FOUR:

THE THIRD PHASE OF THE MANTRA

THE TWELFTH SERIES: THE REJECTION OF GREED

PÚ TÍ YÈ PÚ TÍ YÈ

Very often there are temptations which become obstacles to the growth and development of one's BUDDHA NATURE while on the PATH to LIBERATION. Thoughts from CONSCIOUS INTELLECT call everyone from the NATURAL WAY, with the SUPER EGO dictating and deciding what should be done according to its interpretation of society's rules. From this, the Savage Beast that is SUPER EGO may create HOSTILITY, ENVY, AVERSION, PRIDE, or AVARICE to go along with these so-called correct social actions. On the surface, the Beast will impose an aura of righteousness and correctness.

The VISCERAL IDENTITY, ID, mediating SENSATIONS, creates DELUSION and its confused voice cries out that everything is either too boring or too difficult. Beware of these Demons of Hell. They will draw those who are not vigilant into TORPOR and SLOTH, so that they embrace and crave comfort.

The WORDY IDENTITY, EGO, using EMOTIONS, tempts the unwary into activity which appears more pleasant and emotionally rewarding. Beware of these Hungry Ghosts.

All these call one back to the world of APPARENT PLEASURE and SUFFERING.

Using the Mantra line *PÚ TÍ YÈ PÚ TÍ YÈ* and the strong Hand and Eye preparation, the GOLD WHEEL, all who hear will completely keep on the correct NATURAL PATH with NON-RETREATING ATTITUDE, NON-RETREATING INTENTION, and NON-RETREATING ACTION.

This GOLD WHEEL, *DHARMACHAKRA*, is the Wheel of the Law. It represents the Eightfold Path, namely CORRECT UNDERSTANDING (VIEW), CORRECT ATTITUDE, CORRECT ACTIONS, CORRECT SPEECH, CORRECT LIVELIHOOD, CORRECT INTENTIONS, CORRECT MINDFULNESS, and CORRECT CONCENTRATION (SERENITY).

PÚ TÍ YÈ PÚ TÍ YÈ
May There Be No Retreat from the Way
The GOLD WHEEL Hand and Eye

PÚ TUÓ YÈ PÚ TUÓ YÈ

This Mantra line is a variation of the preceding line. It is not used to prevent retreat from the NATURAL PATH but to reinforce one's adherence to that path. It will keep one STEADFAST and AWAKEN the NON-SELF. In two ways you will find this Mantra line to be effective.

In the first, there will be a natural joy in the sense of liberation which accompanies you as you pass each day. All the previous Mantra lines will have their effect and you will find that your mind has never been more calm and clear. You will see the exquisite beauty of the natural way and will be astonished at the behavior of those around you who seem to be always influenced by the Demons, Ghosts, and Beasts of their own making. There will be a temptation to feel superior. Resist this temptation and draw upon your COMPASSION and upon your condition of refuge in the BUDDHA, seeing their SUFFERING, although they themselves may be unaware of it.

In the second place, you will find that your sessions of CONCENTRATION are more fruitful and that your mind is not as tempted to glue itself to each thought which passes or attach itself to every external distraction. This is because with this Mantra line there is CORRECT INTENTION towards your CONCENTRATION. Instead of entering into a session with the INTENTION to ACHIEVE something, you will enter the session because it simply feels natural and correct to do so.

Cultivation of the BUDDHA ON THE CROWN will bring further consolidation of your firmness and an even stronger aid in *SAMADHI* CONCENTRATION. Often in *SAMADHI*, with this cultivation, one has the sensation of something rubbing the crown of the head. Be unmoved by this phenomenon. It is a positive sensation.

One of the great benefits in the cultivation of this Hand and Eye preparation is that it also prevents those who diligently attend from becoming attached to the MEDITATIVE state.

PÚ TUÓ YÈ PÚ TUÓ YÈ
May Progress on the Path Be Maintained
The BUDDHA ON THE CROWN Hand and Eye

MÍ DÌ LÌ YÈ

This Mantra line is extremely useful, for it is used to eradicate FEAR. Now, there is nothing wrong with the sensation of CORRECT NATURAL FEAR generated when there is a real threat to the system. This fear is a feedback signal that your system is preparing to take some evasive action.

We are talking about eradicating unreasoned fear created by the IDENTITIES. The most common are the FEAR of the UNKNOWN created by the VISCERAL ID IDENTITY, the FEAR of FAILURE and CONSEQUENCES created by the EGO IDENTITY, and the FEAR of APPEARING UNWORTHY, UNIMPORTANT, or UNINTELLIGENT created by the SUPER EGO IDENTITY.

With the recital of this Mantra line these FEARS will be eliminated and there will be a return to NATURAL TRANQUILITY. In addition, there will be an increment in the power to help others, for the fears associated with helping others will not be present. This will automatically help in the creation of the state of EQUANIMITY which will generate positive Karmic cycles.

The Hand and Eye preparation to be nurtured is the TIN STAFF. This is a normal staff used for walking, but at the top there are nine rings made of tin which clank together as the walker moves along. This warns all insects and small creatures in the path of the walker to move away. This staff, *KHAKHARA*, is symbolic of the Hand and Eye preparation which is designed to help others and bring the calmness which eliminates unnecessary fears.

We have spoken of the creation of EQUANIMITY, so it should be apparent that you must also consider FEARLESSNESS to be incorrect, for it is nothing but a false bravado. This false bravado is not conducive to EQUANIMITY, for it is based upon fear which accompanies the adulteration of CONFIDENCE, a product of a correctly activated LIFE FORCE. Nurturing the TIN STAFF will cast out FEAR masquerading as FEARLESSNESS.

MÍ DÌ LÌ YÈ
May There Be No Fear nor Fearlessness
The TIN STAFF Hand and Eye

NÀ LÁ JĬN CHÍ

The important significance of the Mantra line is WORTHY LOVE. Most mundane love is tainted by desire and clinging and its presence is evidence of SUFFERING rather than tranquility. Natural love is BENEVOLENT and PROTECTIVE, but not possessive. This benevolent and protective love requires a mindfulness of the person's BUDDHA NATURE, and protection takes the form of teaching the person towards whom the love is directed about the NATURAL LAW so that they may become enlightened to the NATURAL PATH, thus preventing all suffering. This line is accompanied by the Hand and Eye called the JEWELED BOTTLE, *BHUMBA*. This sacred bottle normally contains pure water or nectar to wash the hands before making a sacrifice. Here, when you nurture this preparation, you symbolically wash away your PERCEPTIONS of FOLLY with the nectar of MINDFULNESS before sacrificing your false IDENTITIES.

The content of this JEWELED BOTTLE is, of course, correctly developed MINDFULNESS. This MINDFULNESS has as the object of its attention the formation of ATTITUDES. Its focus is the FOLLY generated by the influence of the various IDENTITIES within each human creature.

This MINDFULNESS is not combative, that is, you should never push against INCORRECT ATTITUDES when you become aware of them. All that will be accomplished by mental combat is an increase in resistance, the invention of justifications by conscious intellect, and the generation of increased body and mental tension. An act of

MINDFULNESS is one which simply notes and identifies INCORRECT ATTITUDES, INTENTIONS, and ACTIONS. This is sufficient in a person on the way of liberation to change KARMIC reactions.

NÀ LÁ JǏN CHÍ
May There Be the Protection of Mindfulness
The JEWELED BOTTLE Hand and Eye

DÌ LÌ SÈ NÍ NÀ

This Mantra line means SOLID and SHARP. The JEWELED SWORD Hand and Eye preparation is cultivated to accompany the Mantra line. The JEWELED and FLAMING SWORD, *KHADGA*, cuts away IGNORANCE and therefore represents ILLUMINATION. The Mantra line, like a sword, cuts away all GREED, thereby eliminating one of the major impediments to TRANQUILITY. Each person contaminated by the IDENTITIES is inflicted with DELUSION, GREED, and HOSTILITY. The strength of each varies from person to person. One of these three, however, is dominant in each person.

When you think about yourself, you will certainly not like the idea that you are dominated by one of these three impulses. Most people don't mind so much being called HOSTILE. They will point out the fact, that they get angry and declare, "You see, I cannot be GREEDY or DELUDED, I must be HOSTILE." That is because in a GREEDY world it is an offense to appear GREEDY or DELUDED. The appearance of ANGER, however, has nothing to do with HOSTILITY. It occurs when a person does not get what they want or has been thwarted in some way. ANGER is a symptom of GREED. The HOSTILE person, when frustrated, experiences a cold calm fury which demands GODLIKE justice.

Most of the human population is dominated by GREED, while only a small percentage is dominated by HOSTILITY. The presence of so many GREEDY people in the world explains why the world is so GREED-oriented and has becomes so self-consuming and destructive.

There are a lot fewer DELUDED people in the world than GREEDY people, but there are more than those with a HOSTILE personality. DELUSION actually shows its face when the DELUDED person needs a defense against constant CONFUSION. All resulting DELUSIONS take the form of INCORRECT ATTITUDES, which are often based upon superstition, dogma, or affect towards pomp and ceremony which appears to solve the CONFUSION in a simple and easy way. It is much simpler, you see, to put higher reason out of gear and accept false views blindly with a FAITH that does not require DIRECT EXPERIENCE or HIGHER REASONING.

The DELUDED person has a mind which is not clear and open, yet they will often defend ferociously the openness of their mind. They will only listen to reason which supports their false views. Both the GREEDY person and the HOSTILE person also resist the call of the DHAMMA, influenced by Hungry Ghosts and Beasts. Of these three, however, it is the GREEDY person who is the easiest led astray and falls prey to the TEMPTATIONS of the world. This line is specifically, therefore, directed at the GREEDY person and the GREED subtly hidden within each HOSTILE and DELUDED person.

The Mantra line, with a correctly honed and prepared JEWELED SWORD, will protect the Mantra chanter and receiver from the TEMPTATION to go no further. The sword's sharpness and solidity is always a protection against the excuses of the Hungry Ghost IDENTITY master who says, "I have done enough. I understand, now I'm cured and can get on with the things I was doing before." The voice of GREED is here present. It is a protection against the Demon IDENTITY that declares, "All transcendental roads lead to the same place" or "I really don't know, it is too confusing." The DELUDED voice is here present. It is a protection against the Savage Beast who haughtily declares, "I know all that." The voice of HOSTILITY is here present.

There is another thing you should be aware of. None of the IDENTITIES want to give up their power, so when you are becoming stronger and are on the point of overcoming them, they will strike back with a strength that you did not know they possessed. They will insist that you turn from this path. The Hungry Ghosts of EGO will be foremost, whining and complaining, while the Hell Demons of ID add their strident or confused voices, and the Savage Beasts, let loose by SUPER EGO, persuade with their demands and distorted reasoning. Fortunately, not only does this Mantra line cut away GREED, but it protects those who need protection from the assault of TEMPTATION.

Others around may be GREEDY and GRASPING, but he or she who is touched by the Mantra line remains unaffected.

DÌ LÌ SÈ NÍ NÀ
May Greed Be Destroyed
The JEWELED SWORD Hand and Eye

SUMMARY: LINES 46-50

Having completed the difficult task of transmitting COMPASSION for four of the major afflictions of the human race, you will have used a great deal of energy. Although you will feel that all is CORRECT and ACCOMPLISHED with BENEFIT and HAPPINESS brought about by WISDOM, you must still remain vigilant. You are urged to continually use all supporting Mantra lines to ensure that not only do you reject retreat from your advanced position, but resolutely advance without fear under the protection of greater WISDOM.

It is clear that if you wish to project COMPASSION in a Mantra, great firmness and discipline are required. In building your own qualities with the objective of helping others, you can see how far you will have come yourself and how far you have automatically advanced as a human creature.

46. *PÚ TÍ YÈ PÚ TÍ YÈ*
    May There Be No Retreat from the Way
    The GOLD WHEEL Hand and Eye

47. *PÚ TUÓ YÈ PÚ TUÓ YÈ*
    May Progress on the Path Be Maintained
    The BUDDHA ON THE CROWN Hand and Eye

48. *MÍ DÌ LÌ YÈ*
    May There Be No Fear nor Fearlessness
    The TIN STAFF Hand and Eye

49. *NÀ LÁ JǏN CHÍ*
    May There Be the Protection of Mindfulness

The JEWELED BOTTLE Hand and Eye

50. *DÌ LÌ SÈ NÍ NÀ*

May Greed Be Destroyed
The JEWELED SWORD Hand and Eye

Now repeat:

PÚ TÍ YÈ PÚ TÍ YÈ
PÚ TUÓ YÈ PÚ TUÓ YÈ
MÍ DÌ LÌ YÈ
NÀ LÁ JǏN CHÍ
DÌ LÌ SÈ NÍ NÀ

THE THIRTEENTH SERIES: LETTING GO OF CONFUSION AND DELUSION

PÓ YÈ MÓ NÀ SĀ PÓ HĒ

This Mantra line brings us to the beginning of two important series of lines. Here we declare, "THE NAME HAS BEEN HEARD." What is the name? The name is TRUTH. Furthermore, we declare that we take delight in praising that TRUTH and in accepting that TRUTH. This means that we accept the idea of not resisting that which is NATURAL.

The TRUTH is an understanding of the ontological reality which is indefinable. We cannot really touch or understand that TRUTH. What we can do is be in touch with the DHAMMA, which is the teachings of the NATURAL LAW relating to TRUTH. Seeing beyond the words of the written DHAMMA, we then accomplish the affairs of truth.

One of the most important of human accomplishments is the ability to build and maintain fellowship with others. That fellowship should clearly be with those of like mind if we wish to live within the NATURAL law in peace and harmony.

This Mantra line then has as its objective the building of fellowship with others, and when we state, "THE NAME HAS BEEN HEARD," we are calling all others who have also heard the name and delight in accepting that truth.

In order to do this effectively, you must nurture the Hand and Eye preparation called the JEWELED ARROW. The arrow, *SHARO*, which represents alertness in consciousness, like this preparation, will correctly sharpen the consciousness of all who are perceptive enough to see its value and quality. Remember that an arrow should conceptually not be separated from the bow, nor from the apparent bowman or apparent target.

SĀ PÓ HĒ acts as a declaration of CONFIDENCE. Rather than declare simply, "SO BE IT," which is more passive, the line means, "I BELIEVE ALL WILL BE ACCOMPLISHED." It does require sincerity, however, for if there is any doubt at all, there is by definition no confidence. Likewise it declares, "I BELIEVE ALL THINGS WILL BE AUSPICIOUS." In other words, everything is going to come out correctly according to the NATURAL WAY. Sincerity is required for this declaration.

SĀ PÓ HĒ is also a declaration of your own state of VIRTUE. You must, with this line, open yourself to inspection and introspection. If there is a flaw, you will see it. Without VIRTUE, it would be really pointless going further with the Mantra.

There are two further calls in this Mantra line. They are a call for the elimination of all CALAMITIES and a call for increasing NATURAL BENEFITS. You will have noted that these three calls were mentioned earlier in relation to the benefits of the first line of the *DHARANA*.

The Mantra line also calls for thoughts to be light and unattached. It is a protection against becoming attached to the SUFFERING which you are addressing through your chanting. Light thoughts should hover like a butterfly about to land on a flower. Such thoughts will never be captured by SUFFERING or IGNORANCE. Thoughts should examine afflictions but never dwell on them; to dwell on them is to become a part of them. Thoughts should see the IGNORANCE which is a root of suffering but not touch it.

SĀ PÓ HĒ is a very special Mantra line. It appears many times accompanying many of the Mantra lines which follow. This should tell you a very important thing: that the Mantra lines which precede it are very important and are not easy to accomplish.

PÓ YÈ MÓ NÀ SĀ PÓ HĒ
May the Fellowship of Like Minds Be Accomplished
The JEWELED ARROW Hand and Eye

XĪ TUÓ YÈ SĀ PÓ HĒ MÓ HĒ XĪ TUÓ YÈ SĀ PÓ HĒ

The principal meaning of this most important Mantra line, *XĪ TUÓ YÈ*, is that of PERFECTING BENEFITS. What we want to do when we recite this line is not only to bring benefits, but to assure that they are of subtle and high spiritual quality. You cannot, therefore, expect anything to happen if you do not cultivate spiritual qualities within yourself.

What then are these spiritual qualities? They are not difficult to understand, but they are difficult to bring to fruition. You don't have to enter into the esoteric world of the mystical. Spiritual qualities are just those which are not linked to this world of the senses. If you cultivate VIRTUE, then you are cultivating a spiritual quality. If you practice MINDFULNESS, then you are cultivating a spiritual quality. If you are regularly practicing with sessions of CONCENTRATION, then you are cultivating a spiritual quality. If you are following the DHAMMA, then you are cultivating spiritual qualities.

You are not cultivating spiritual qualities if you are thinking and talking with a sweet tongue about cosmic consciousness, karma, and a thousand other topics without understanding. Cultivating and attaining spiritual qualities requires understanding the FOLLY of the MUNDANE and putting the UNDERSTANDING of the SUBLIME into each living moment.

Perhaps you can see why we need to immediately follow this Mantra line with *SĀ PÓ HĒ*. Having then chanted the line bringing the PERFECTION OF BENEFITS, you will define exactly what benefits you wish perfected. In this case, you will follow *XĪ TUÓ YÈ SĀ PÓ HĒ* with those Mantra lines which bring a perfection of MEMORY and LEARNING.

MÓ HĒ XĪ TUÓ YÈ SĀ PÓ HĒ

When these Mantra lines are recited together with the two lines, *XĪ TUÓ YÈ* and *SĀ PÓ HĒ*, and *PUSTAKA*, the JEWELED SUTRA Hand and Eye preparation, has been nurtured, the benefit is extremely strong. The quality and extent of LEARNING is high and MEMORY retention and retrieval becomes facilitated.

XĪ TUÓ YÈ SĀ PÓ HĒ
MÓ HĒ XĪ TUÓ YÈ SĀ PÓ HĒ
May Memory and Learning Be Fully Nourished
The JEWELED SUTRA Hand and Eye

XĪ TUÓ YÙ YÌ SHÌ PÓ LÁ YÈ SĀ PÓ HĒ NÀ LÁ JĬN CHÍ SĀ PÓ HĒ

The first set of MANTRA lines opens the door to the achievement of gaining benefit from "NON-ACTIVITY." This does not mean, as you might suppose, that one has to do nothing. Actually, NON-ACTION is really the process of NOT RESISTING the NATURAL FLOW. Normally, it is CONSCIOUS INTELLECT which pushes against the natural flow of events. What this does is awaken the IDENTITIES and tell them that if they disturb what is NATURAL they will gain some great advantage.

If you have accomplished a state of NON-RESISTING, then the recitation of the second line brings a more subtle COMPASSION. This COMPASSION is a COMPASSION which touches the non-human world. One then can open a newer awareness of the wealth of the NATURAL ENVIRONMENT in which the HUMAN BUDDHA NATURE unfolds. For greatest quality in this unification with all NATURE, one should cultivate the Hand and Eye called the JEWEL CHEST.

So that you will include COMPASSIONATE protection for every element of NATURE without exception, you repeat line *NÀ LÁ JĬN CHÍ* (49) once more, calling upon the power to help others and deliver them from SUFFERING.

Clearly you cannot teach all the NATURAL ELEMENTS of NATURE, each flower, each animal, what to do. Actually, they already have the knowledge they require. They are in danger, not from the natural environment nor like kind, for the conflict which they face in nature is harmonious and balanced; they are in danger because of the human creature, who is so unnaturally destructive.

What you can do is actively protect NATURE by both chanting these Mantra lines and teaching all sentient beings about NATURAL PROTECTION. By developing COMPASSION for NATURE, you know that that COMPASSION will bring CORRECT ATTITUDE, INTENTION, and ACTION.

XĪ TUÓ YÙ YÌ SHÌ PÓ LÁ YÈ SĀ PÓ HĒ
NÀ LÁ JĬN CHÍ SĀ PÓ HĒ
May the Natural Environment Be Protected by Mindful Compassion
The JEWEL CHEST Hand and Eye
and the JEWELED BOTTLE Hand and Eye

MÓ LÁ NÀ LÁ SĀ PÓ HĒ

MÓ LÁ once again declares, "SO BE IT," according to our BUDDHA
NATURE. This time, however, with *NÀ LÁ* you gather together all the
troublesome DELUSION which has been contaminating ATTITUDES,
INTENTIONS, and ACTIONS.

If this exists in a person, it is very difficult to prompt a falling away
of the problem concepts. That is why this Mantra line is included
among the Mantra lines which require strong CONFIDENCE. When
the Hand and Eye preparation is fully cultivated, the LARIAT, *PASHA*,
of five colors may be thrown to gather together the elements of this
debility of DELUSION.

Many conflicts are caused by lack of clarity in thoughts. This Mantra
line, when spoken, will bring CLARITY and PEACE.

MÓ LÁ NÀ LÁ SĀ PÓ HĒ
May Delusion Fall Away
The FIVE-COLORED LARIAT Hand and Eye

SUMMARY: LINES 51-54

51. *PÓ YÈ MÓ NÀ SĀ PÓ HĒ*
    May the Fellowship of Like Minds Be Accomplished
    The JEWELED ARROW Hand and Eye

52. *XĪ TUÓ YÈ SĀ PÓ HĒ MÓ HĒ XĪ TUÓ YÈ SĀ PÓ HĒ*
    May Memory and Learning Be Fully Nourished
    The JEWELED SUTRA Hand and Eye

53. *XĪ TUÓ YÙ YÌ SHÌ PÓ LÁ YÈ SĀ PÓ HĒ NÀ LÁ JĬN CHÍ SĀ PÓ HĒ*
May the Natural Environment Be Protected by Mindful Compassion

The JEWEL CHEST Hand and Eye
and the JEWELED BOTTLE Hand and Eye

54. *MÓ LÁ NÀ LÁ SĀ PÓ HĒ*
May Delusion Fall Away
The FIVE-COLORED LARIAT Hand and Eye

Now repeat:

PÓ YÈ MÓ NÀ SĀ PÓ HĒ
XĪ TUÓ YÈ SĀ PÓ HĒ
MÓ HĒ XĪ TUÓ YÈ SĀ PÓ HĒ
XĪ TUÓ YÙ YÌ SHÌ PÓ LÁ YÈ SĀ PÓ HĒ
NÀ LÁ JǏN CHÍ SĀ PÓ HĒ
MÓ LÁ NÀ LÁ SĀ PÓ HĒ

THE FOURTEENTH SERIES: SEVERING ALL HATRED AND AVARICE

XĪ LÁ SĒNG Ā MÙ QŪ YĒ SĀ PÓ HĒ

XĪ LÁ SĒNG refers to the BENEVOLENT PROTECTION of all beings, while *Ā MÙ QŪ YĒ* refers to the bringing together of all these creatures into one single HARMONIOUS WHOLE, without ignoring any of the DHAMMA.

The Mantra line protects against the EXCLUSION of any creature from the MANTLE of COMPASSION. You will require the JEWELED AXE Hand and Eye preparation. The AXE, *KARTICA*, represents the disintegration of all matter and the captivity of truth. It has the power to transform energy into a strong positive force.

Why should this Mantra line be so difficult to bring to fruition? It seems so simple. It is because we have so many subliminal prejudices. Treating everyone and every living creature with equanimity is very difficult. It is particularly difficult for the hateful person who allows his hostility to form an elite band of "the intelligent" who are worthy. He generally fails to see deeper than the surface behavior. He must look towards each person's BUDDHA NATURE. Here lies the true person. All else is fiction. It is easy for him to be a champion of all so-called lesser animals, but he must remember that all human creatures are also animals. Wield *KARTICA* with decision and cut away the seductive words and thoughts of the Savage Beast.

XĪ LÁ SĒNG Ā MÙ QŪ YĒ SĀ PÓ HĒ
May No Living Human Creature Be Excluded from Compassion
The JEWELED AXE Hand and Eye

SĀ PÓ MÓ HĒ Ā SĪ TUÓ YÈ SĀ PÓ HĒ

SĀ PÓ in this mantra line means WORTHY OF BEING ENDURED. What is it that is so WORTHY that even SUFFERING is acceptable? Only one thing: LIFE itself, LIFE in this WORLD which appears real only to our senses. LIFE only has WORTH if you can perceive the TRUTH, and paradoxically, that this WORTH lies in IMPERMANENCE, CHAOS, MEANINGLESSNESS, CONFLICT, and NON-EXISTENCE. It is in the BEAUTY of the WHOLE scheme of PROCESS.

Now, one would have to understand and PENETRATE the TRUTH if one really wanted to see this WORTHINESS, and that requires specific explanations and training beyond the scope of this treatise. Just accept for the moment that LIFE and CORRECT GROWTH and DEVELOPMENT are wonderful and precious, even without all the things which we cling to and crave. *MÓ HĒ* is the accomplishment of seeing through all the apparent turmoil, including the seeking after PERMANENCE, the discovery of apparent ORDER, the thirsting after MEANING, the striving after PEACE, and the desire for EXISTENCE.

This final SEEING is very important. It is the accomplishment of seeing that all the things which we want to exist DO NOT EXIST at all. If we see this, then we no longer CLING to ANYTHING, even the DHAMMA, and have arrived on the other side. If you proceed on this path, you will then RESPECT all LIFE and will see your apparent SELF in the midst of all NATURAL phenomena.

When you recited *SHÌ FÓ LÁ YÈ* in a previous Mantra line, you touched the NON-HUMAN world with COMPASSION. With this line, you apply a CURING BALM to all SUFFERING, and you find yourself in the midst of this world, with a full appreciation of your ONENESS with it. This curative balm is enriched with cultivation of the

JEWELED VESSEL Hand and Eye. The JEWELED VESSEL, *KALASHA*, contains the curing balm that is the water of spiritual richness and of freedom from the clinging to existence.

SĀ PÓ MÓ HĒ Ā SĪ TUÓ YÈ SĀ PÓ HĒ
May There Be a Curative Seeing of the World
and Unity with All Things
The JEWELED VESSEL Hand and Eye

SHĔ JÍ LÁ Ā XĪ TUÓ YÈ SĀ PÓ HĒ

HOSTILITY and AVARICE generally appear in a person who has great love for humanity. That seems very strange, doesn't it? When you realize that love is strong in INTELLECTUAL content, then you can see that it is an IDEALIZED LOVE that does not tolerate imperfection. The hostile person loves what man CAN BE, but loathes the FAULTED REALITY. Poetically, we can say that in reciting *SHĔ JÍ LÁ Ā XĪ TUÓ YÈ* you conquer all the HATEFUL Savage Beasts of the world.

The BENEVOLENT LOVE within the BUDDHA NATURE of persons afflicted with this SUFFERING is completely masked by a CRITICAL VIEW of the WORLD. There is a FULL ONENESS with Nature which is profound and deep, but MAN and all MAN touches is EXCLUDED. Man's POTENTIAL within the world as a part of the WHOLE is seen, but MAN is viewed critically as the DESTRUCTOR. This vision of the world is not incorrect, but the problem is that the person who is hateful judges man as GUILTY and wants RETRIBUTION.

A HOSTILE person has an extreme hatred of injustice. This HATRED and AVERSION for INCORRECT INTENTION, ATTITUDE, and ACTION is seldom manifested in ACTION. It festers inside the afflicted and causes much frustration and turmoil. Do not confuse this HOSTILITY with ANGER, which appears with frequency in the world. ANGER is quite different and is attached to GREED. You will see that AVARICE is linked to HOSTILITY. AVARICE, you see, is not the same as GREED.

A GREEDY person desires something for him or herself and sometimes wants to deny others the thing that is CRAVED. The HOSTILE person wants to take worldly pleasure away from others as a CASTIGATION. Taoists have an expression which describes this

HOSTILITY. They say it is the "FIVE THUNDERS WHICH STRIKE YOUR MIND." Each THUNDER enters through a different sense and creates havoc. The tormented SUFFERER is constantly bombarded through the senses with all that ails the world. He sees correctly, but the cries of the BENEVOLENT LOVE within his BUDDHA NATURE are masked by his own hatred at the moment of THUNDER.

If one wishes to successfully destroy the THUNDERS, then one must cultivate the Hand and Eye preparation which is called the VAJRA WHEEL. Watch too for the indirect enemy of BENEVOLENT LOVE, which is AFFECTION. Affection is a selfish EGO creature invention. Watch this creature, for too often the thunder of jealousy, created by the Beast, will sound.

SHĚ JÍ LÁ Ā XĪ TUÓ YÈ SÀ PÓ HĒ
May All Hatred and Avarice Be Conquered
The VAJRA WHEEL Hand and Eye

SUMMARY: lines 55-57

55. *XĪ LÁ SĒNG Ā MÙ QŪ YĒ SÀ PÓ HĒ*
May No Living Human Creature Be Excluded from Compassion
The JEWELED AXE Hand and Eye

56. *SÀ PÓ MÓ HĒ Ā SĪ TUÓ YÈ SÀ PÓ HĒ*
May There Be a Curative Seeing of the World
and Unity with All Things
The JEWELED VESSEL Hand and Eye

57. *SHĚ JÍ LÁ Ā XĪ TUÓ YÈ SÀ PÓ HĒ*
May All Hatred and Avarice Be Conquered
The VAJRA WHEEL Hand and Eye

Now repeat:

XĪ LÁ SĒNG Ā MÙ QŪ YĒ SÀ PÓ HĒ
SÀ PÓ MÓ HĒ Ā SĪ TUÓ YÈ SÀ PÓ HĒ
SHĚ JÍ LÁ Ā XĪ TUÓ YÈ SÀ PÓ HĒ

THE FIFTEENTH SERIES: CONSOLIDATION OF ADVANCES

BŌ TUÓ MÓ JIÉ XĪ DUŌ YÈ SĀ PÓ HĒ

The Mantra phrase *BŌ TUÓ MÓ* represents the RED LOTUS, and *JIÉ XĪ DUŌ YÈ* signifies VICTORY, but one should not think for one moment that the RED LOTUS is associated with competition or conflict. There is VICTORY in NON-RESISTANCE, there is VICTORY in uncovering FOLLY.

Why should a Mantra line which pays attention to the concept of VICTORY be deployed among those which require a greater concentration and application of the Hand and Eye preparation? We obtain victory, do we not, from all the earlier Mantra lines. The VICTORY referred to here is the VICTORY over our own psychological debility which inflates the EGO IDENTITY and SUPER EGO IDENTITY when something is accomplished. It is a VICTORY over the PRIDE in ACCOMPLISHMENT.

We must be detached in VICTORY, and this is an achievement which is not easily gained. We are NATURALLY directed towards CORRECT INTENTIONS, ATTITUDES, and ACTIONS by a liberated BUDDHA NATURE. There is no SELF involved in that NATURAL PROCESS. There can, therefore, be no SELF in either DEFEAT or VICTORY.

Here we see the critical thrust of this Mantra line. It is a cry for EQUANIMITY in VICTORY. There must be a strong cultivation of the Hand and Eye preparation called the RED LOTUS. You must beware, however, of a great impostor, the indirect enemy of EQUANIMITY: UNINTELLIGENT INDIFFERENCE.

BŌ TUÓ MÓ JIÉ XĪ TUÓ YÈ SĀ PÓ HĒ
May There Be Equanimity in Victory
The RED LOTUS Hand and Eye

NÀ LÁ JǏN CHÍ PÓ JIĀ LÁ YĒ SĀ PÓ HĒ

With the phrase *NÀ LÁ JǏN CHÍ*, we call for strength from within ourselves, and *PÓ JIĀ LÁ YĒ* says that this protection is required when we review SUFFERING and TRANQUILITY in the world. Why do we require more strength than we have previously called upon?

As in the previous Mantra line, it is because we are addressing something much more subtle in our behavior. SUFFERING takes many forms in the world and has many masks. Each time that we see SUFFERING in this apparently real world, we are amazed at the forms and strength it takes. If you are very alert and aware of your own subtle psychological reactions, you will detect a FEAR lurking beneath the surface.

This can be a fear of contamination, a fear of inadequacy, a fear of failure, a fear of involvement. There are thousands of potential applicants for this post. This fear is debilitating, although it may be submerged beneath your COMPASSION.

Even when perceiving TRANQUILITY, fears arise. There may be subconscious fears that you may succumb to desires, that you may give in to laziness, to pride, or a thousand other imperfections. All these fears may be conquered with well-directed EFFORT. Two fears then will remain.

The first is the FEAR of NON-EXISTENCE. Here there is an illogical FEAR of the unknown after the end of consciousness. It occurs as AGING advances and DEATH approaches. The result is a CLINGING TO EXISTENCE.

When this too is conquered, there remains the CLINGING TO NON-EXISTENCE. We do not refer to the folly of clinging to the concept of an afterlife, but the clinging to the idea that all will gratefully come to an end. This too is folly, for it acts against the LIFE FORCE. It is a FEAR of EXISTENCE. Instead, in the face of both EXISTENCE and NON-EXISTENCE you must cultivate a special EQUANIMITY.

This Mantra gives protection against those two final fears and the Hand and Eye to be developed and nurtured is the JEWELED TRUMPET Hand and Eye preparation. This trumpet, *KANGLING*, must be blown so that it dispels even the most subtle mind opponents of the DHAMMA.

NÀ LÁ JǏN CHÍ PÓ JIĀ LÁ YĒ SĀ PÓ HĒ
May There Be No Fear of Existence or Non-Existence
The JEWELED TRUMPET Hand and Eye

MÓ PÓ LÌ SHÈNG JIÉ LÁ YÈ SÀ PÓ HĒ

MÓ PÓ LÌ SHÈNG stands for GREAT BRAVERY, and the addition of *JIÉ LÁ YÈ* makes the significance of the line, "HAVE THE GREAT BRAVERY OF THE GREAT HERO."

GREAT BRAVERY is one of the natural characteristics of the human creature. This bravery is not just a surge of courage, it is a holding together of all our qualities so that bravery is holistic and complete.

Being thus, it holds together all the Hand and Eye preparations that have been cultivated. Great energy, effort, resolution and earnestness are required for each Hand and Eye preparation, and we would not wish one to be nurtured at the sacrifice of another.

This Mantra line then binds and holds all of the FORTY-TWO Hand and Eye readinesses together as a whole. Clearly this MANTRA line has little utility if there has been little nurture of other Hand and Eye preparations. This preparation is called the THOUSAND HOLDING AND UNITING ARMS Hand and Eye preparation.

MÓ PÓ LÌ SHÈNG JIÉ LÁ YÈ SÀ PÓ HĒ
May Cultivation of Seeing and Benevolence
Be Whole and Complete
The THOUSAND HOLDING AND UNITING ARMS Hand and Eye

SUMMARY: LINES 58-60

58. *BŌ TUÓ MÓ JIÉ XĪ DUŌ YÈ SÀ PÓ HĒ*
    May There Be Equanimity in Victory
    The RED LOTUS Hand and Eye

59. *NÀ LÁ JǏN CHÍ PÓ JIĀ LÁ YÈ SÀ PÓ HĒ*
    May There Be No Fear of Existence or Non-Existence
    The JEWELED TRUMPET Hand and Eye

60. *MÓ PÓ LÌ SHÈNG JIÉ LÁ YÈ SÀ PÓ HĒ*
    May Cultivation of Seeing and Benevolence
    Be Whole and Complete
    The THOUSAND HOLDING AND UNITING ARMS Hand and Eye

Now repeat:

BŌ TUÓ MÓ JIÉ XĪ DUŌ YÈ SĀ PÓ HĒ
NÀ LÁ JǏN CHÍ PÓ JIĀ LÁ YĒ SĀ PÓ HĒ
MÓ PÓ LÌ SHÈNG JIÉ LÁ YÈ SĀ PÓ HĒ

**This marks completion of the third stage
of the GREAT COMPASSION MANTRA**

HUMAN NATURE AND UNITY

This commentary, based upon the SVABHAVAVADA REALIST philosophy, which we trust has helped you understand the first three phases of the GREAT MANTRA of COMPASSION, will be of even greater assistance as you delve more deeply into the knowledge available to you through the Mantra. It is one of the important premises of this philosophy that all apparent phenomena are as their nature makes them. In philosophical terms, that means that necessity is inherent in the nature of the animate or inanimate thing and is not imposed upon it by an external force or agent.

Now, what these rather academic-sounding phrases really mean is simply that the apparent human creature has human nature, the tiger has a tiger nature, and a simple rock has a rock nature. In addition, it declares that each apparently distinct creature, plant, or inanimate natural object is imbued by this nature through its own natural processes. It, therefore, negates the creation of all things as a first source and declares that the base of all things, natural energy, is eternal and that evolution is an internal function of all matter.

In the explanation of this Mantra, the important significance for us is that there exists, for each type of living or non-living thing, an internal, special MEMORY that tells it how to develop physically and how to behave. In other words, there is a serpent memory that tells that animal how to be a serpent, and a daisy memory that allows that particular flower to develop and grow as a daisy. Every different living thing has its own memory. Even rocks have their own memory.

Granite has the nature of granite, set by its memory, while limestone has the memory that gives it the nature of limestone.

This memory, which we call INHERITED MEMORY, is not the memory which we normally speak of, which can be amended, supplemented, and changed within the apparent life of the human creature or other animal. It takes generations of continued learning before a change in INHERITED MEMORY can take place. In the Galapagos Islands, for example, it was shown to take seven generations to attain a natural change in the inherited memory of a finch to the point where it could be qualified as a different species.

It is a memory which is relatively enduring. It allows each generation of living plants or animals to reproduce the same sort of apparent form and behavior with only slight variations until, as if with planned inspiration, a new form emerges, better able to survive in the prevalent conditions. The new important characteristics then continue, inherited by all offspring, along with fresh apparently insignificant variability. That is how life progresses and changes. The more complex the life forms are, then the more variability exists in this inherited memory which shapes both form and behavior.

It is this same memory which has shaped us as human beings, which allows us to grow and develop as a human creature from the moment of conception within our mother's womb, and which permits us to walk, speak, and perform thousands of marvelous feats. It also permits us to perform such tasks as regulating our heartbeat or promoting sustained rhythmic breathing. These wonderful ways of "being human" have evolved and been established because of a natural genetic variability in the nature of each living creature at birth. This same variability exists in every living thing. New species, new life forms, new behaviors, all evolved due to this accidental variability. This was the process which permitted sometimes extreme variations to become established as the new norm.

It was the majority of a species which often died, while those with some extreme variation that melded with the new environment survived. Those who survived conflicts with others of their species, predators, and the new perils lived and reproduced. Some forms of life became extinct and others became misfits in the world, being forced to find a new niche for themselves in order to survive. This appears very cruel at first glance, but with an open-minded sensitivity, you may begin to see the beauty in this natural process. Human life and death are still a part of this process, a part which man has not yet been able to divorce himself from, despite his desires to do so.

As the world changed, so did all living forms, and eventually the first human-like creatures walked the earth. The human creature is fortunate. Natural variability favored him. He survived while other more powerful creatures in the past history of the world perished. This happened when great environmental changes occurred and the evolving nature of those life forms was antagonistic to the environment. In our prehistoric past, when the world changed in a drastic way, those pre-humans who were fit to survive did so. It was chance, nothing more. The survival of each was a function of external factors, but the principal and important force which allowed a variant of the species to be "selected" was the random variability within the nature of the creature. It was this variability which provided his supremacy, his resistance to disease, his physical prowess, his intelligence. It was this variability which provided him with the fundamental basic DRIVE and accompanying behavior to successfully seek warmth and food. It was this variability that led to the drives to seek COMFORT, SECURITY, and BELONGING. It led too to the establishment of the three DISPOSITIONS to behave: his potential SENSITIVITY, DISCRIMINATION, and his NATURAL INTELLIGENCE.

The human creature was fortunate. It was a creature which evolved very rapidly. It evolved so rapidly that it did not become extinct under this complex law of natural selection. It did not have to either die or find a new niche. With a rapidly developing superior intelligence, it learned to adapt its life to the external world and then reached the point where, thanks to a collective not individual intelligence, it found ways to apparently change or master its environment. The life of man was difficult but he was, unknown to himself, a part of the world and in HARMONY and BALANCE with it.

Nature was no longer all-powerful. Man developed strong internal systems for survival. It was the inherited memory that made this possible, and man developed strong subconscious DEMANDS which could almost guarantee survival in a world of chaos and conflict. They were DEMANDS which permitted him apparent control over his life.

Fig. 42 Man's Original Natural Balance

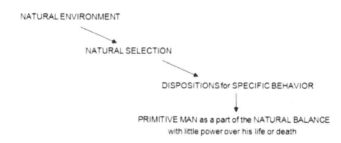

Man then was not DRIVEN to simply exist, he DEMANDED his requirements from NATURE. He recognized his own might. He experienced panic, fear, and rage, but only when confronted by the extreme power of Nature. In the small everyday battles for warmth, food, and shelter he was almost always the victor. Gradually, these DEMANDS overruled the BASIC DRIVES and corrupted the natural DISPOSITIONS for behavior which had evolved. Sensitivity was corrupted to promote a VISCERAL force that beat out all competition. Those who were more viscerally controlled and savage managed to succeed. The VISCERAL DEMANDS were the great life force. In other words, it was man's active VISCERAL DEMANDS and the resulting behavior which was the main instrument for survival. Nature didn't select man, man himself did that by organizing and shaping his own behavior. Man became the Creator that he had always wanted to find.

The power to discriminate correctly was slowly transformed into a weapon for conquest. The force that determined life or death came to be man's own internal system. The force for EGO SATISFACTION had entered successfully into a VISCERALLY-GOVERNED world. Being as it was a higher mental force, it sought supremacy. Unfortunately, the old VISCERAL force did not atrophy, so two internal forces began to compete furiously for domination. Neither managed complete control. Man's life had changed direction radically. He slowly gave up his place as an insignificant but integrated part of nature. He sought ORDER in the CHAOS, PERMANENCE in IMPERMANENCE, MEANING when there is NO MEANING, and EXISTENCE when there is NO EXISTENCE, yet paradoxically created greater CONFLICT in a world already full of conflict.

As his intelligence evolved, his capacity for language and thinking developed. With them came a knowledge of his own apparent IDENTITY. A further gradual development of intelligence gave man a different view of himself, this time, pragmatically, as a social creature. The forces of VISCERAL and EGO SATISFACTION were challenged, for man was now involved in the world as part of a social group. He had changed his own environment so rapidly, however, that there was no time for either of the two mutually governing forces to atrophy. Today's man is still torn between these forces.

The IDENTITIES, actually the personifications of the DEMAND for VISCERAL SATISFACTION, the DEMAND for EGO SATISFACTION, and the DEMAND for DOMINATION, were seen to exist as the forces behind the DEMANDS. Man, the greatest creature in the world, needed "to be." His own fear of nature required the invention of a self, a SOUL which could contest the powers which assailed him. He required assistance, for he was bewildered, so he invented the Gods. Man, with his Gods, thus divorced himself completely from the UNITY of the world. The world existed to be conquered. The mountain was to be climbed simply because it was there to be climbed. All the world was dominated, because it was there to be dominated. The Gods had loosened the Beast.

Since he was able to control the environment, his variability became less important in his evolution. His evolution became warped by the DEMANDS. As COMFORT, SECURITY, and BELONGING became possible in the external world thanks to his skills, man began to corrupt his own system. Man had created himself as a Mr. Hyde in a world of beauty. A deluded, greedy, hostile Mr. Hyde who never had the WISDOM to see his own misshapen mind. Hyde now exists in this world, but thankfully, the possibility is always there for a beneficial transformation. The essential condition, however, is that all the SUFFERING Mr. Hydes of this world must first recognize their own worlds of DARKNESS before they can see the LIGHT.

Since NATURE does not work with reason but only pragmatic expediency, it was this genetic variability that works so well in natural selection which led man to his present dominant position. Today, almost the entire world is under man's control. Still, he reaches out into space. Nature, however, resists and is destined to eventually

Fig. 43 Evolved Form

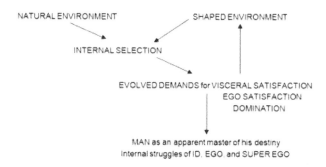

conquer this presumptuous creature called man. In the meantime, the harmony and balance between nature and man has been ruptured. Man's life and death are no longer dependent upon the rest of nature.

Unfortunately, this intelligence which gave birth to the DEMANDS has suppressed all NATURAL WISDOM in man. Man did survive, but he has grown apart from all that is harmonious, balanced, and natural. This separation was inevitable, but he has reached the point where his own SENSITIVITY, DISCRIMINATION, and NATURAL INTELLIGENCE are completely subdued under the governance of the DEMANDS. The results mankind calls wonderful, for it is a world which can satiate most DEMANDS. Man calls it progress, delights in it, and embraces it with folly.

NATURE is now forgotten. Harmony and balance are forgotten. The forces that drive human existence are the DEMANDS, not the NATURAL DISPOSITIONS. Man has evolved unlike other animals, which respond to natural selection and the forces of NATURE. Man grows and dances to the tune of three internal pipers who are leading him slowly into deep murky water. He has no external points of reference to guide him. He has only his own flawed internal image and possesses insufficient awakened WISDOM. Man has evolved with internal DEMANDS for satiation, but has developed an insatiable appetite. He has changed, and continues to change, in random ways under the internal genetic forces. He is becoming taller, stronger, more intelligent, and shrewder. His DEMANDS too are developing, but his growth is apart from nature.

That he is not a victim of the forces of natural selection is of great benefit. He has extended the length of his fragile life. His curiosity has led to his academic knowledge of the secrets of nature, but the presence of the DEMANDS makes that knowledge dangerous. He does not see that the benefits which he enjoys bring with them great responsibility, which he cannot exercise without WISDOM. It was man's own incredible capacity to survive that has led to his undoing.

When we speak then of the existence of UNNATURAL MENTAL STATES in the human creature, it is evident that they have been auto-initiated. It is man's DEMANDS, and the apparent IDENTITIES which are personified from them, which do not harmonize with nature. In fact, the Hyde-like evolved systems of man are not only out of harmony with nature, they are antagonistic to it.

If man could really "see" his divorce from nature, instead of intellectually understanding it as he is now beginning to do, then he could change the future. The situation is, however, complicated by the fact that this human random egocentric-based system is generating experiences of false comfort, false pleasure, and false elation which are seductive. He exists in a paradox. In order to maintain his false comfort, false security, and false belonging which he enjoys at the moment, he must destroy the world in the future. Indeed, the paths of DELUSION, GREED, and HOSTILITY are seductive. They make him blind, even to the problems of his own immediate existence. He accepts all the STRESS, TENSION, and SUFFERING he experiences which may result in his own individual death or infirmity. He wants everything. He will give up nothing. If there are sacrifices to be made, then everyone else has to make those sacrifices first.

If you believe that a return to a natural and harmonious state is in the best interest of yourself and all mankind, then you must understand that change can only be initiated from within each individual. In other words, if you are out of harmony with nature, then you are responsible, but not culpable. If you want to change that situation, then you are the one who must be responsible for making those changes. There are INTERNAL EGOCENTRIC FORCES, but there are ways in which you can amend the system so that your actual behavior is less self-centered and more in harmony with the external world. You can, in your lifetime, nullify the force of these DEMANDS. You are NOT the pawn of some cognitive EXTERNAL FORCE that has set all this in place, and no "all-wise" external force is going to grant salvation to you just because you believe that it can and will. You are NOT an unwilling victim of unconquerable INTERNAL FORCES. You are a willing participant in your own FOLLY.

In the infinite life of past and present evolution, the DEMANDS are quite young. They are strong and powerful, but they are just DEMANDS. They are not so firmly a part of the human creature that they have become absolute COMMANDS to the system. It does not require generations to conquer them. They can be resisted. They can be set aside.

Each person does have available natural WISDOM which has not yet atrophied. It is alien to the IDENTITIES and an ally of NATURE. When awakened, it can be reinforced and elaborated with correct learning so that CORRECT ATTITUDES replace the INCORRECT. Each man and woman can exercise relative control over the Life Force while maintaining a healthy and wholesome balance and harmony with all things. You cannot change all mankind. No one can. All each man or woman can do is change themselves, awakening their own WISDOM. When that is done, you will find the COMPASSION, GLADNESS, and BENEVOLENT LOVE that will encourage the act of making that WISDOM available for others.

Fig. 44 Man's Potential Relationship with Nature

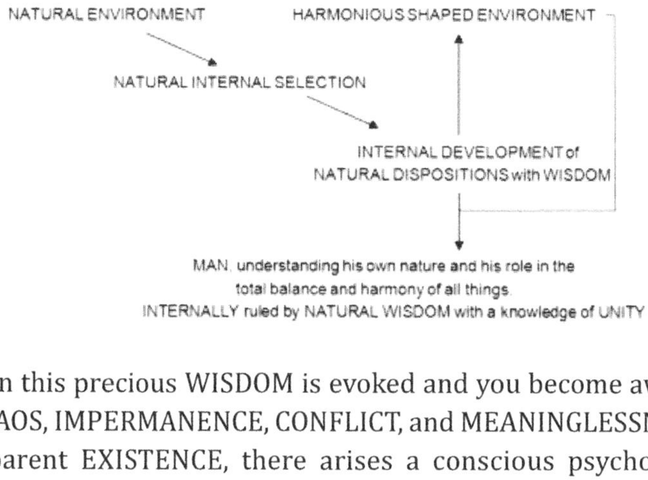

NATURAL ENVIRONMENT   HARMONIOUS SHAPED ENVIRONMENT

NATURAL INTERNAL SELECTION

INTERNAL DEVELOPMENT of
NATURAL DISPOSITIONS with WISDOM

MAN. understanding his own nature and his role in the
total balance and harmony of all things.
INTERNALLY ruled by NATURAL WISDOM with a knowledge of UNITY

When this precious WISDOM is evoked and you become aware of the CHAOS, IMPERMANENCE, CONFLICT, and MEANINGLESSNESS of all apparent EXISTENCE, there arises a conscious psychological awareness of UNITY. This psychological awareness mirrors the truth that there is actually a UNITARY SOURCE. This natural and eternal source has given rise to an infinite variety of apparent objects and living creatures with infinite modifications. It may continue to do so in the future, somewhere among the unending infinite set of apparent universes.

This unitary source is not a Creator of either good or evil; Man has earned for himself the dubious privilege of that position. It is presently believed to be one or more elementary particles. All that we perceive or know to apparently exist is the product of these particles. All that is beyond the known, beyond all matter, is the eternal ENERGY which changes its form as its own nature directs, creating apparent EXISTENCE and apparent DESTRUCTION. All things which exist, both beyond and within this world of the senses, are one single process of ENERGY. This is natural UNITY. This is a unity which unfolds itself and evolves and allows, within that unity, unguided chaos, impermanence, conflict, and meaninglessness, with no separate existence apart from the whole. It is the unity of which we are a magnificent but insignificant, part.

This UNITY is nature's great strength and its beauty. Just as there is no FIRST CAUSE, and just as the apparent future is infinite, so is the apparent past. All ORDER is imposed by perception which seeks that order in CHAOS. There is no PERMANENCE, or MEANING, or EXISTENCE, and there is continual NATURAL CONFLICT, not PEACE.

The human creature has evolved various religions and philosophies to explain man's EXISTENCE or his perceptions of that existence. The SVABHAVA philosophy is one of these. It sees the human creature, as do other Buddhist philosophies, as SUFFERING unnecessarily due to his own IGNORANCE and subjugation to his own selfish DEMANDS.

It is a serious and dramatic point of view but, far from being pessimistic, it is an optimistic philosophy. It is positive, because it admits change, even during one's lifetime, and declares that despite all the variation and natural CONFLICT in nature, all living and non-living matter is bound together not only because there is a unitary source, but because all act together as a single unitary process.

Each apparently different nature, with its different expressions and apparently different identity, is a part of one substance, one single ever-changing process. Our natural state then is to be as one with all things. This doesn't mean that there should be no conflict and that there should be complete order. On the contrary, conflict and chaos are quite correct and natural. The correct nature of the human creature is to live within that conflict and chaos, paradoxically in harmony with it.

It is correct that we should see the ORDER which exists within the natural variability of CHAOS. That is a useful perception, a useful tool. It is natural that we should understand apparent PERMANENCE, but correctly see the TRANSIENCE of all things. It is natural that we should be confused by the complexity of life, and wonder about MEANING and EXISTENCE. It is correct and beautiful that man can, despite this wonder, accept the MEANINGLESSNESS of life and his paradoxically true NON-EXISTENCE without fear. It is excellent that he can reduce CONFLICT where it is not NATURAL, and preserve his fragile life for as long as he can, living with joy and happiness.

REVIEW: MANTRA LINES OF THE THIRD PHASE

46. *PÚ TÍ YÈ PÚ TÍ YÈ*
> May There Be No Retreat from the Way
> The GOLD WHEEL Hand and Eye

47. *PÚ TUÓ YÈ PÚ TUÓ YÈ*
> May Progress on the Path Be Maintained
> The BUDDHA ON THE CROWN Hand and Eye

48. *MÍ DÌ LÌ YÈ*
> May There Be No Fear nor Fearlessness
> The TIN STAFF Hand and Eye

49. *NÀ LÁ JǏN CHÍ*
> May There Be the Protection of Mindfulness
> The JEWELED BOTTLE Hand and Eye

50. *DÌ LÌ SÈ NÍ NÀ*
> May Greed Be Destroyed
> The JEWELED SWORD Hand and Eye

51. *PÓ YÈ MÓ NÀ SĀ PÓ HĒ*
May the Fellowship of Like Minds Be Accomplished
The JEWELED ARROW Hand and Eye

52. *XĪ TUÓ YÈ SĀ PÓ HĒ MÓ HĒ XĪ TUÓ YÈ SĀ PÓ HĒ*
May Memory and Learning Be Fully Nourished
The JEWELED SUTRA Hand and Eye

53. *XĪ TUÓ YÙ YÌ SHÌ PÓ LÁ YÈ SĀ PÓ HĒ NÀ LÁ JǏN CHÍ SĀ PÓ HĒ*
May the Natural Environment Be Protected by Mindful Compassion
The JEWEL CHEST Hand and Eye
and the JEWELED BOTTLE Hand and Eye

54. *MÓ LÁ NÀ LÁ SĀ PÓ HĒ*
May Delusion Fall Away
The FIVE-COLORED LARIAT Hand and Eye

55. *XĪ LÁ SĒNG Ā MÙ QŪ YÈ SĀ PÓ HĒ*
May No Living Human Creature Be Excluded from Compassion
The JEWELED AXE Hand and Eye

56. *SĀ PÓ MÓ HĒ Ā SĪ TUÓ YÈ SĀ PÓ HĒ*
May There Be a Curative Seeing of the World
and Unity with All Things
The JEWELED VESSEL Hand and Eye

57. *SHĚ JÍ LÁ Ā XĪ TUÓ YÈ SĀ PÓ HĒ*
, May All Hatred and Avarice Be Conquered
The VAJRA WHEEL Hand and Eye

58. *BŌ TUÓ MÓ JIÉ XĪ DUÓ YÈ SĀ PÓ HĒ*
May There Be Equanimity in Victory
The RED LOTUS Hand and Eye

59. *NÀ LÁ JǏN CHÍ PÓ JIĀ LÁ YĒ SĀ PÓ HĒ*
May There Be No Fear of Existence or Non-Existence
The JEWELED TRUMPET Hand and Eye

60. *MÓ PÓ LÌ SHÈNG JIÉ LÁ YÈ SĀ PÓ HĒ*
  May Cultivation of Seeing and Benevolence
  Be Whole and Complete
The THOUSAND HOLDING AND UNITING ARMS Hand and Eye

Now repeat:

PÚ TÍ YÈ PÚ TÍ YÈ
PÚ TUÓ YÈ PÚ TUÓ YÈ
MÍ DÌ LÌ YÈ
NÀ LÁ JǏN CHÍ
DÌ LÌ SÈ NÍ NÀ
PÓ YÈ MÓ NÀ SĀ PÓ HĒ
XĪ TUÓ YÈ SĀ PÓ HĒ
MÓ HĒ XĪ TUÓ YÈ SĀ PÓ HĒ
XĪ TUÓ YÙ YÌ SHÌ PÓ LÁ YÈ SĀ PÓ HĒ
NÀ LÁ JǏN CHÍ SĀ PÓ HĒ
MÓ LÁ NÀ LÁ SĀ PÓ HĒ
XĪ LÁ SĒNG Ā MÙ QŪ YĒ SĀ PÓ HĒ
SĀ PÓ MÓ HĒ Ā SĪ TUÓ YÈ SĀ PÓ HĒ
SHĒ JÍ LÁ Ā XĪ TUÓ YÈ SĀ PÓ HĒ
BŌ TUÓ MÓ JIÉ XĪ DUŌ YÈ SĀ PÓ HĒ
NÀ LÁ JǏN CHÍ PÓ JIĀ LÁ YĒ SĀ PÓ HĒ
MÓ PÓ LÌ SHÈNG JIÉ LÁ YÈ SĀ PÓ HĒ

PART FIVE:

THE FOURTH PHASE OF THE MANTRA

THE SIXTEENTH SERIES: AFFIRMATION OF THE PATH

Now repeat the first three Mantra lines of the GREAT COMPASSION MANTRA, affirming your refuge.

NĀ MÒ HĒ LÁ DÁ NÀ DUŌ LÁ YÈ YĒ
I, with Reverence, Take Refuge in the Buddha,
the Dhamma, and the Sangha

NĀ MÒ Ā LÌ YĒ
I Take Refuge and Respectfully Submit to Wisdom

PÓ LUÓ JÍ DÌ SHUÒ PÓ LÁ YÈ SĀ PÓ HĒ

With the chanting of this line, you bring all your resources and all your natural knowledge to bear upon the SUFFERING and the TRANQUILITY of the world. Let there be no exclusions. Be fully aware now of the extent of the three forms of SUFFERING and the beauty of the three DISPOSITIONS.

Bring to mind, for your support, the GREAT BODHISATTVA of COMPASSION, the symbol of this GREAT COMPASSION MANTRA of NATURAL WISDOM. Know and understand that although this Bodhisattva is a representation of a legendary figure, many such men and women have existed, exist, and will exist in the future. Bring their image to mind and draw courage from their unselfish approach to life when you chant this most important line.

Bring the Light of Contemplation to Bear
upon Suffering and Tranquility in the World

PÓ LUÓ JÍ DÌ SHUÒ PÓ LÁ YÈ
SĀ PÓ HĒ
ĂN SĪ DIÀN DŌU

ĂN opens the way for the final Mantra lines, while the chanting of *SĪ DIÀN DŌU* declares, "MY REALM IS SECURE." Your realms are the REALM of the entire world, all universes, all existence and non-existence, the REALM of the phenomenological world of your immediate senses, and the REALM within which is your BUDDHA NATURE and all the PROCESSES involved.

When you declare that the realm is secure, you declare the complete acceptance of the NATURAL LAW and all NATURAL PROCESSES, and accept all ILLUSIONS as tools of the NATURAL LAW. You acknowledge SUFFERING as an avoidable human condition and declare that you understand the ways to end that SUFFERING.

You declare also the LIBERATION of your BUDDHA NATURE and your freedom from SELF, the IDENTITIES.

ĂN SĪ DIÀN DŌU
My Realm Is Secure

MÀN DUŌ LÁ

You declare in this Mantra line that your KNOWLEDGE of the WAY will be kept clear of impediments and your LEARNING of the DHAMMA nurtured until your KNOWLEDGE is COMPLETE.

MÀN DUŌ LÁ
The Way Will Remain Undefiled and Knowledge Nurtured

BÁ TUÓ YĒ SĀ PÓ HĒ

Here you announce that all will be in accord with your own enlightened BUDDHA NATURE. This is a promise that prevents a rigid adherence to the WORDS of the DHAMMA which, it must be remembered, is only a phenomenological representation of the LAW which is natural and the PROCESS which is ontological. Once more, repeat *SĀ PÓ HĒ*, reinforcing this major line.

BÁ TUÓ YĒ SĀ PÓ HĒ
All Will Be Accomplished According to my Buddha Nature

**This marks completion of the fourth and final stage
of the GREAT COMPASSION MANTRA**

THE KNOWN AND THE UNKNOWN

The absolute world is unknown to us, and all we know about it is what our senses tell us. That unknown world is believed to exist, but it is considered as passive; it has no volition. It acts as its nature moves it to act. It is for the human creature *PURUSA*, the subject of experience, and *PRAKRTI* is the product. All that is ontological, beyond the reach and interpretation of the senses, we call *PARAMATTHA SACCA*. All that we cannot know exists only as momentary phenomena, being neither eternal nor lasting. *SAMMUTI SACCA*, all that is phenomenological, all that is known by our senses, appears as illusion and apparently exists because of the nature of consciousness which is formed as a process of mind.

Fig. 45 The Apparently Known World

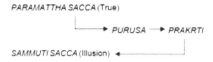

Since nothing actually exists as it appears to be to the senses, an important question is, "What is to be accepted as true?" Can you really believe that which is presented here in this commentary? If you are really interested in avoiding paths of FOLLY, then this is a very important question. Valid knowledge, *PRAMA*, is said to light up the path of all action, and if it successfully does so, that knowledge is taken to be true. The essential way of arriving at *PRAMA*, called *PRAMANA*, is by three means:

1. *PRATYAKSA*, Personal Perception
2. *ANUMANA*, Logical Inference
3. *SABDA*, Verbal Testimony

Be vigilant against DELUSION, which masquerades under many disguises.

Fig. 46 Inspecting the Illusion

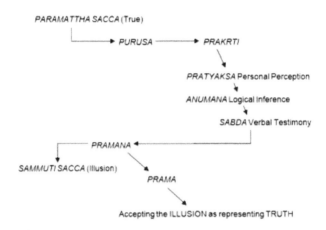

You must note, however, that these are ways. This does not mean that ALL knowledge derived by any or all of these means is automatically true. They may result in intellectual conviction, but what is necessary is to convert them into *PAURUSEYA*, the experience by which conviction is known to be true. This is done by invoking the higher faculty of penetration or insight. It is part of the function of the GREAT MANTRA of COMPASSION to prepare us for that WISDOM.

Among the ways of arriving at valid knowledge, we must consider *SABDA* as a special case. It is not the same as verbal testimony derived from REVELATION, which is called *SRUTI*. Indeed, *SABDA* is the communication of knowledge which is not knowable through perception and inference. It does not concern itself, however, with that which is unascertainable, but only that knowledge which can be derived from DIRECT EXPERIENCE. For the SVABHAVAVADINS, revelation is suspect and is not accepted as valid knowledge. We will not attempt to describe what DIRECT EXPERIENCE is. You will discover that for yourself later.

It would be tempting to doubt all things, but it is clear that we cannot go on doubting forever, and must desist from doing so when it results in a self-contradiction of thought or leads to practical absurdity.

While there are major differences in the SVABHAVAVADA position and practice from that of other BUDDHIST groups, and even greater differences from that of the MAHAYANA groups, there is far greater agreement than there are differences. It is this which unites all within the light of the DHAMMA. The SVABHAVA philosophy, you will see in other texts, argues against a transmigrating or reincarnating SOUL or IDENTITY. You will have also noted that the concept of KARMA, which we discussed in the last phase, is not the same as that considered to be correct by the traditional Hindu or the orthodox Buddhist.

Within this commentary, you will have found important questions discussed. We have presented the basic thrust of SVABHAVAVADIN thought which is relevant to the Mantra so that you may better see the roots of the commentary. We trust that this commentary will bring the GREAT COMPASSION MANTRA into focus, especially for those who are not MAHAYANA. The GREAT COMPASSION MANTRA is truly a magnificent and functional tool which can lead all away from SUFFERING and place all who prepare themselves and use it correctly upon the noble and natural path of the DHAMMA. We trust that those who have joined us here with curiosity will learn what is available to them as human creatures and that this information will help in their future growth and development.

REVIEW: MANTRA LINES OF THE FOURTH PHASE

61. *NĀ MÒ HĒ LÁ DÁ NÀ DUŌ LÁ YÈ YĒ*
I, with Reverence, Take Refuge in the Buddha,
the Dhamma, and the Sangha

62. *NĀ MÒ Ā LÌ YĒ*
I Take Refuge and Respectfully Submit to Wisdom

63. *PÓ LUÓ JÍ DÌ SHUÒ PÓ LÁ YÈ SĀ PÓ HĒ*
Bring the Light of Contemplation to Bear
upon Suffering and Tranquility in the World

64. *ĂN SĪ DIÀN DŌU*
My Realm Is Secure

65. *MÀN DUŌ LÁ*
The Way Will Remain Undefiled and Knowledge Nurtured

66. *BÁ TUÓ YĒ SĀ PÓ HĒ*
All Will Be Accomplished According to my Buddha Nature

Now repeat:

NĀ MÒ HĒ LÁ DÁ NÀ DUŌ LÁ YÈ YĒ
NĀ MÒ Ā LÌ YĒ
PÓ LUÓ JÍ DÌ SHUÒ PÓ LÁ YÈ SĀ PÓ HĒ
ĂN SĪ DIÀN DŌU
MÀN DUŌ LÁ
BÁ TUÓ YĒ SĀ PÓ HĒ

**Thus ends the COMMENTARY upon
the GREAT COMPASSION MANTRA OF NATURAL WISDOM**

Thousand-handed, thousand-eyed Sahasrabhuja (Guanyin)

Appendix

The *Mahā Karuṇā Dhāraṇī* or *Dàbēi zhòu* (大悲咒)

As an aid to chanting and deeper understanding and appreciation, a full transcription is included of the Great Compassion Mantra in its original Sanskrit form along with Amoghavajra's version as published in the Chinese *Tripitaka* (Taisho Edition T.1113b, 20.498-501).

1. Namo ratna-trāyāya
nā mò hē lá dá nà duō lá yè yē 南无喝啰怛那哆啰夜耶
2. Namo āriyā-
nā mò ā lī yē 南无阿唎耶
3. valokite-śvarāya
pó lú jié dì shuò bō lá yē 婆卢羯帝烁钵啰耶
4. Bodhi-sattvāya
pú tí sà duǒ pó yē 菩提萨埵婆耶
5. Maha-sattvāya
mó hē sà duǒ pó yē 摩诃萨埵婆耶
6. Mahā-kārunikāya
mó hē jiā lú ní jiā yē 摩诃迦卢尼迦耶
7. Om
ǎn 唵
8. sarva-raviye
sà pó luó fá yè 萨皤啰罚曳
9. sudhanadasya
shǔ dá nà dá xiě 数怛那怛写
10. Namo skritvā imam āryā
nā mò xī jí lī duǒ yī měng ā lì yē 南无悉吉㗚埵伊蒙阿唎耶
11. valokite-śvara ramdhava
pó lú jí dì shì fó lá lèng tuó pó 婆卢吉帝室佛啰楞驮婆

267

12. Namo narakindi

nā mò nà lá jǐn chí 南无那啰谨墀

13. hrih Mahā-vat-svāme

xī lī mó hē pó duō shā miē 酰唎摩诃皤哆沙咩

14. Sarva-arthato-śubham

sà pó ā tā dòu shū péng 萨婆阿他豆输朋

15. ajeyam

ā shì yùn 阿逝孕

16. Sarva-sat Namo-vasat Namo-vāka

sà pó sà duō nā mò pó sà duō nà mó pó jiā 萨婆萨哆那摩婆萨多那摩婆伽

17. mavitāto

mó fá tè dòu 摩罚特豆

18. Tadyathā

dá shí tā 怛侄他

19. Om Avaloki

ǎn ā pó lú xī 唵阿婆卢酰

20. lokate

lú jiā dì 卢迦帝

21. krate

jiā luó dì 迦罗帝

22. e-hrih

yí xī lī 夷酰唎

23. Mahā-bodhisattva

mó hē pú tí sà duǒ 摩诃菩提萨埵

24. Sarva sarva

sà pó sà pó 萨婆萨婆

25. Mala mala

mó lá mó lá 摩啰摩啰

26. Mahi Mahi ridayam

mó xī mó sī lī tuó yùn 摩酰摩酰唎驮孕

27. Kuru kuru karmam

jù lú jù lú jié měng 俱卢俱卢羯蒙

28. Dhuru dhuru vijayate

dù lú dù lú, fá shé yē dì 度卢度卢罚阇耶帝

29. Mahā-vijayati

mó hē fá shé yē dì 摩诃罚阇耶帝

30. Dhara dhara

tuó lá tuó lá 陀啰陀啰
31. dhrini
dì lī ní 地唎尼
32. śvarāya
shì fó lá yē 室佛啰耶
33. cala cala
zhē lá zhē lá 遮啰遮啰
34. Mama vimala
mó mó fá mó lá 么么罚摩啰
35. muktele
mù dì lì 穆帝隶
36. Ehi ehi
yī xī yī xī 伊酰伊酰
37. śina śina
shì nà shì nà 室那室那
38. ārsam prasari
ā lá shēn, fó lá shè lì 阿啰嘇佛啰舍利
39. viśva viśvam
fá shā fá shēn 罚娑罚嘇
40. prasaya
fó lá shè yē 佛啰舍耶
41. Hulu hulu mara
hū lú hū lú mó lá 呼卢呼卢摩啰
42. Hulu hulu hrih
hū lú hū lú xī lì 呼卢呼卢酰利
43. Sara sara
suō lá suō lá 娑啰娑啰
44. siri siri
xī lī xī lī 悉唎悉唎
45. suru suru
sū lú sū lú 苏嚧苏嚧
46. Bodhiya Bodhiya
pú tí yè pú tí yè 菩提夜菩提夜
47. Bodhaya Bodhaya
pú tuó yè pú tuó yè 菩驮夜菩驮夜
48. Maitreya
mí dì lì yè 弥帝利夜

49. narakindi
nà lá jǐn chí 那啰谨墀
50. dhrish-nina
dì lì sè ní nà 地利瑟尼那
51. bhayamana svāhā
pó yè mó nà, sā pó hē 婆夜摩那娑婆诃
52. Siddhāya svāhā
xī tuó yè sā pó hē 悉陀夜娑婆诃
53. Maha siddhāya svāhā
mó hē xī tuó yè sā pó hē 摩诃悉陀夜娑婆诃
54. Siddha-yoge-śvaraya svāhā
xī tuó yù yì shì pó lá yè sā pó hē 悉陀喻艺室皤啰耶娑婆诃
55. Narakindi svāhā
nà lá jǐn chí sā pó hē 那啰谨墀娑婆诃
56. Māranara svāhā
mó lá nà lá sā pó hē 摩啰那啰娑婆诃
57. śira simha-mukhāya svāhā
xī lá sēng ā mù qū yē sā pó hē 悉啰僧阿穆佉耶娑婆诃
58. Sarva mahā-asiddhaya svāhā
sā pó mó hē ā sī tuó yè sā pó hē 娑婆摩诃阿悉陀夜娑婆诃
59. Cakra-asiddhāya svāhā
shě jí lá ā xī tuó yè sā pó hē 者吉啰阿悉陀夜娑婆诃
60. Padma-hastāya svāhā
bō tuó mó jié xī duō yè sā pó hē 波陀摩羯悉陀夜娑婆诃
61. Narakindi-vagalāya svaha
nà lá jǐn chí pó jiā lá yē sā pó hē 那啰谨墀皤伽啰耶娑婆诃
62. Mavari-śankharāya svāhā
mó pó lì shèng jié lá yè sā pó hē 摩婆利胜羯啰夜娑婆诃
63. Namo ratna-trāyāya
nā mò hē lá dá nà duō lá yè yē 南无喝啰怛那哆啰夜耶
64. Namo ārya-
nā mò ā lì yē 南无阿利耶
65. valokite-śvaraya svāhā
pó luó jí dì shuò pó lá yè sā pó hē 婆嚧吉帝烁皤啰夜娑婆诃
66. Om Sidhyantu
ǎn sī diàn dōu 唵悉殿都
67. mantra

270

màn duō lá 漫多啰

68. padāya svāhā

bá tuó yē sā pó hē 跋陀耶娑婆诃

Made in United States
North Haven, CT
29 May 2023